Competing with Information

Executive Development from IMD

Marchand, D.A.   Competing with Information — A Manager's Guide to Creating Business Value with Information Content

Forthcoming titles from IMD:

Strebel, P.   Focused Energy — Mastering Bottom-Up Organization
ISBN 0-471-89971-2

Competing with Information

A Manager's Guide to Creating Business Value with Information Content

Edited by

Donald A. Marchand
IMD, Lausanne

JOHN WILEY & SONS, LTD
Chichester • New York • Weinheim • Brisbane • Singapore • Toronto

Other Wiley Editorial Offices

John Wiley & Sons Inc., 111 River Street, Hoboken, NJ 07030, USA

Jossey-Bass, 989 Market Street, San Francisco, CA 94103-1741, USA

Wiley-VCH Verlag GmbH, Boschstr. 12, D-69469 Weinheim, Germany

John Wiley & Sons Australia Ltd, 33 Park Road, Milton, Queensland 4064, Australia

John Wiley & Sons (Asia) Pte Ltd, 2 Clementi Loop #02-01, Jin Xing Distripark, Singapore 129809

John Wiley & Sons (Canada) Ltd, 22 Worcester Road, Etobicoke, Ontario M9W 1L1

Wiley also publishes its books in a variety of electronic formats. Some content that
appears in print may not be available in electronic books.

British Library Cataloguing in Publication Data

A catalogue record for this book is available from the British Library

ISBN-10: 0-471-89969-0 (hbk)
ISBN-13: 978-0-471-89969-3 (hbk)

Typeset in 10/12pt Garamond by Best-set Typesetter Ltd, Hong Kong
Printed and bound in Great Britain by Biddles Ltd, King's Lynn, Norfolk
This book is printed aon acid-free paper responsibly manufactured from sustainable forestry, in which at
least two trees are planted for each one used for paper production.

Contents

Foreword

To succeed in the global marketplace, companies must reposition themselves to tap the sources of sustainable growth and to exploit the vast opportunities for e-business and the so-called new economy. Managers must develop a new mindset that leverages three key assets in a business.

Firstly, companies must be prepared to make full use of the intellectual assets residing in their people. We must manage our companies so that our people can contribute their knowledge fully in our businesses.

Secondly, companies must create business value through using information on products, customers and services more effectively than their competitors. We must have one face to the customer and the customer must see one face from us.

And thirdly, companies must deploy information technology and e-business capabilities to support global and local processes, to act in a boundaryless manner toward their customers, and to enable relevant information to move wherever in the company it is needed.

Competing with Information discusses the mindset and the tools required for managers to define how information and knowledge can create business value for a company to achieve sustainable growth. It also examines how to develop the right mix of business strategies and information capabilities for the e-business economy. General managers may not be expected to be information and IT specialists in their business. But they are expected to create the conditions in their business for effective information sharing and use improve with the aim business performance. This book by Professor Don Marchand and his colleagues at IMD provides practical insights on how business managers can further develop the ways they manage information, people and IT capabilities to achieve superior business performance and e-business success.

As customer-focused companies like ABB increasingly take a knowledge-and-service-centric view of their businesses, our managers must develop the mindsets and frameworks to lead our company to effectively compete with information, people and IT in the new e-economy. *Competing with Information* addresses a central issue and will provide essential input into our own discussions on the best way forward in the new era.

Göran Lindahl   Jim Barrington
Chief Executive Officer   Chief Information Officer

ABB
Zurich, Switzerland

Preface

For more than fifty years, IMD has focused on one thing — state-of-the-art executive development.

Each year, more than 7,000 managers, from all continents and in all industries, visit our Lausanne campus to be educated, challenged, and inspired. They receive practical guidance on current issues, not abstract theories. They work with a team of outstanding faculty, who bring conceptual rigor and real-world experience into the classroom.

The approach we take in the classroom also characterizes the books in *Executive Development from IMD*. Each book brings together in a coherent whole the latest thinking from IMD's world class faculty. The books are clearly written, efficiently presented, and focus on the most important issues for managers.

We are delighted to be working in partnership with John Wiley & Sons to create *Executive Development from IMD*. We are confident you will find the books in this series to be informative, relevant, challenging and, as importantly, enjoyable.

Peter Lorange
IMD President and Nestlé Professor

Acknowledgements

This book is very much a product of IMD's business and faculty culture. A faculty member, like myself, steps forward with a key business idea for the project born of his/her experiences in executive development programs, research interests and many consulting assignments. A group of faculty volunteers to participate in making the idea a reality. From the moment that the faculty team accepts the idea – the project moves forward until it is successfully completed. Individual colleagues do what they can and must to make the overall project a success with little fanfare and hesitance. The project ends and the members of the team move on to the next key idea that needs implementing at IMD.

The key idea behind this book is that information – its content and use in a business – can create significant business value. This idea takes on special significance in the 'e-Economy' where information capabilities are at the center of new business opportunities and models. But, it is also central to running any service or manufacturing company today. Surprisingly, however, there are few books written for general managers, as compared to IT and information specialists, about how to systematically leverage information content in a business.

My colleagues and I believe that using information today is too important to be left solely to IT and information specialists. General and senior managers have a critical role in leading and managing the company to use information to create business value. This book is directed at filling this gap in managerial thinking and action. We think companies that succeed in the new era will seek out, process and use business information faster, smarter and better than their competitors in pursuing their strategies and building business capabilities.

As editor and leader of this project, my first thanks go to the IMD faculty team that developed with me the original content for this book: professors Andy Boynton, Jean-Philippe Deschamps, Xavier Gilbert, Stewart Hamilton, Jacques Horovitz, Bob Howell, Sean Meehan, Piero Morisini, Bart Victor and John Walsh. The international character of the book as well as the specific knowledge of business information use and general management came from this experienced faculty team.

In addition, our Wiley editors, Claire Plimmer and John Moseley, were enthusiastic about this book from the beginning and steered the project to successful completion. In particular, a special thank you goes to a very talented editor, Jeremy Kourdi, who demonstrated remarkable flair and interest in this project and provided superior editorial support to me as editor and all my colleagues.

At IMD, special thanks goes to Professor Philip Rosenzweig who, as Director of

R&D, provided unfailing encouragement and support for whatever had to be done to make this initial book of the new *Executive Development from IMD* happen. Also, to Professor Peter Lorange, the President of IMD, whose boundless enthusiasm for 'making good better' and energetic support for generating innovative intellectual capital of practical relevance to international managers, inspires the can-do spirit that is IMD International.

Finally, to Joyce, my wife, and Lauren, my daughter, thank you for being editors, critics and coaches for another of Dad's projects. Since my sons in Boston, Todd and David, work for IT companies in the e-world, they live the new reality that managers must adapt to and learn to shape – a constant reality check for a Dad in my business.

Don Marchand
Lausanne, Switzerland

Part One

**Competing with Information –
A Role for Every Manager**

1

Why Information is the Responsibility of Every Manager

In this opening chapter, editor **Donald Marchand** outlines the key elements of how information can be used to develop and sustain competitive advantage, providing an overview of this vitally important subject and a guide to the organization of the book.

Introduction

Information is the way people in business express, represent, communicate and share their knowledge with others to accomplish their activities and achieved shared business objectives. If knowledge - our experience, skills, expertise, judgment and emotions - resides primarily with people, then by using information, people can inform each other and be informed about the decisions, actions and results of their work in companies. It is through information about markets, customers, competitors, partners, internal operations and the mix of products and services offered by the company that managers and employees create business value and improve business performance.

Peter Drucker has called information "data endowed with relevance and purpose". Data exists all around us in the form of signals, events and situations, which people can choose to interpret as potentially relevant or not relevant depending on their purposes. This over-abundance of data challenges people in business organizations to manage their time and attention carefully since both of these resources are in scarce supply. Business organizations must focus their managers and employees on the relevant information to execute appropriate activities and tasks to implement their strategies and achieve results.

Companies compete with information to the extent that managers and employees seek, collect, organize, process and use the relevant information in decision-making and actions that lead to superior business performance in markets. Effective use of information is critical to how executives manage their companies and how businesses create value in their markets (Marchand et al., 2000).

Purpose of this book

The purpose of this book is to assist executives and managers in understanding better the ways information can be used and managed in companies to achieve business results. The perspective of this book is primarily people- rather than technology-centric. A basic assumption is that managers and their people shape the use and deployment of information in companies. Information technology (IT) practices and investments, while important to managing information in business, do not lead directly to improved business results. Although we will address the role of IT in enabling companies to manage information effectively in their businesses, we share the view advanced so eloquently by Tom Davenport (1997) that:

Information and knowledge are quintessentially human creations, and we will never be good at managing them unless we give people a primary role ... The status quo approach to information management, invest in new technologies, period, just doesn't work.

In addition, the perspective of this book emphasises the mindset and viewpoint of the general manager rather than the functional manager – the IT or information specialist. The basic intent of the book is to enable senior and general managers to understand how to use and manage information effectively to improve business performance for three reasons.

First, it is the unique responsibility of general or senior managers to develop an *integrative view* of how to manage people, information and IT in a business to implement strategies and achieve results. While IT and information specialists play important roles in supporting how a company uses information effectively, it is general managers who must understand how to integrate business processes, organizational structures, behaviours and values as well as the appropriate information uses and IT resources to achieve the company's or business unit's strategies. At the end of the day, general managers are responsible for both the results of their business units and how to achieve them.

Second, general managers are necessarily generalists rather than specialists who must approach information management with a *holistic perspective* and critical eye. They do not know and cannot be expected to know what IT specialists know about technology. While IT specialists may have a technology solution for every business problem, it is up to general managers to discern where and when IT can be deployed to enable appropriate use of information by people in the business. General managers must exercise their judgment in deciding when IT investments and applications are appropriate. They cannot assume that IT investments will necessarily lead to improvements in information management or that these changes will directly produce better business results. Thus, general managers must always balance the opportunities, risks and investments in IT with the capabilities of the people in a business to use information to run the business and improve performance.

Third, while general managers may not be expected to be information specialists in their business, they are expected to *create the conditions in a business for effective information use*. In this sense, the view from the IMD authors in this book is that information management is the responsibility of every manager in a business.

On the one hand, managers are expected to know and understand what information they need and use to make decisions and interact with people inside and outside the company. Peter Drucker (1999) has called this expectation *information responsibility*. For managers to produce the information required for their work, they have to address two broad questions:

- What information do I owe to the people with whom I work, and on whom I depend? In what form? And in what time frame?
- What information do I need myself? From whom? In what form? And in what time frame?

Thus, managers must become aware of how they use information to make decisions and act on an ongoing basis. If they do not know the answers to these questions, then it is doubtful that they can expect their people to understand their information responsibilities to each other.

On the other hand, managers must also understand how their organization uses information to achieve business results. This second aspect of information responsibility extends to the company or business unit and its capabilities to sense, collect, organize and deploy the appropriate types and quality of information so that people can execute their activities effectively. How effective is the business in using information to create value with customers, innovate with new products and services, manage risks or be efficient in operating business processes? Rarely will a company be good at all aspects of information use. So general managers must discern what the appropriate mix of information management capabilities is to support both today's priorities for running the business effectively and tomorrow's needs for competing with information in their markets. While the specific answers to these challenges will be different for each company, and perhaps for each business unit, the responsibility falls to general managers to understand how information enables their company to achieve superior performance today and compete in existing or new markets in the future.

Information management responsibilities exist at the level of the individual manager and business unit at the same time. Managers must understand how they use information with those around them and how their company creates business value with information. This dual role creates significant opportunity for managers to 'walk the talk' among people in their companies about the uses of information in decision-making in the business and in creating value for the business.

The business framework: strategic information alignment

This book is organized around a business framework of strategic information alignment that was developed at IMD and is used widely in IMD executive programmes.

> **"Each way of using information involves different types of information"**

The framework is designed around four fundamental ways of using information to create business value (*see* Figure 1.1). Not all companies are equally able to manage information along each axis, which accounts for variations in how companies use information to compete.

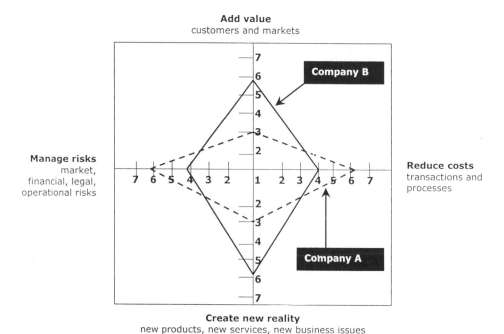

Figure 1.1: *How information creates business value*

Manage risks

The first and oldest way to create business value with information is to manage risks in the business. During the twentieth century, the evolution of risk management has stimulated the growth of disciplines such as finance, accounting, auditing and controlling that every company requires to manage information associated with financial, legal, market and even operational risks. Most managers today take for granted the fact that these forms of risk management are necessary to operate most businesses, although the capabilities to use information in identifying and responding to risks vary widely across companies even in the same industries.

Reduce costs

The second way of using information to create business value is to reduce costs. Here the focus is on using information as efficiently as possible to achieve the outputs required from business processes and transactions. This process view of information management is linked closely with the re-engineering and continuous improvement movements of the 1990s and the quality improvement movement of the 1980s. The emphasis is on lowering the total costs of cross-functional processes by eliminating unnecessary and wasteful activities and automating the improved processes. In addition, some companies have sought to mass-customize processes and products as a way of lowering product and process costs and providing more customized services to customers.

Add value

The third way of using information to create value is via the products and services offered to customers. Here the emphasis is on knowing the customer and sharing information with customers to enhance customer satisfaction. Many service and manufacturing companies focus on building relationships with customers, profiling customer behaviour and serving customers after sales with improved product and account management information.

Create new reality

Finally, companies can use information to innovate: to invent new products, provide better services, and use emerging technologies to create new business opportunities. Many companies are learning to operate in a 'continuous discovery mode', inventing new products quickly and using market and business intelligence to retain a competitive edge. Here information management is about mobilizing people to create new ideas, to apply them rapidly, and to share information and promote creativity throughout a company.

Every company pursues some combination of the above strategies, as we will explain in Chapter 2. For example, some companies (such as Company B in Figure 1.1) focus on using information to innovate and add value with customers on the vertical axis, while other companies (such as Company A in Figure 1.1) operate on the horizontal axis, where using information to minimize risks and reduce costs are key requirements. Companies will differ not only in how they use information to support their strategic priorities today, but will also shift priorities and requirements for using information in the future. These periodic shifts in strategic priorities, and the practices and capabilities to manage information, will create opportunities for companies to compete, based on their effectiveness in using information to achieve business results and improve future performance.

Benefits of the strategic information alignment framework

This book employs the *strategic information alignment* (SIA) framework as both a conceptual tool to assist managers in thinking about how they and their companies compete with information today and in the future and as a way of organizing contributions in the chapters to follow. We believe that managers in IMD executive programmes have found this framework useful for four reasons.

First, the SIA framework fills a perceived gap in management thinking and practice. It provides for the first time an integrative view of information use and how to align information use to strategic priorities in a business.

Second, the SIA framework takes a complex management topic and focuses managerial attention on the essentials of how to view business strategy and the required organisational capabilities to use information, IT and people to improve performance.

Third, the SIA framework can assist managers in developing a shared language around how they use information and what information practices will be needed for their business today and in the future. The framework can also help bridge the communications gap that often appears between general managers and IT and information specialists by focusing on information and IT priorities from a business perspective rather than a functional or technical perspective.

Finally, the SIA framework provides a road map for addressing the managerial answers to three key questions:

- *Why* is information important to competing in the business today and in the future?
- *What* priorities for information use and management are appropriate?
- *How* should managers implement their strategic priorities and achieve improved business performance through people, information and IT?

Organization of the book

Part One: Competing with Information – A Role for Every Manager

This book is designed to assist managers in addressing the three questions noted above. Chapter 2 sets the scene for the book by explaining the strategic information alignment framework and its use in defining the four ways companies can compete with information to improve today's performance, and to position the company for future market leadership. The chapter focuses on the development of information management practices relative to each strategic priority: minimizing risks, reducing costs, adding value with customers, and creating new reality. Managers must decide what mix of strategic priorities and information management practices their company will pursue and invest in both today and in the future. Variations in information management practices will occur not only across companies, but also across industries.

The chapter emphasizes the need for managers to develop the right mindset regarding the role of information management, information systems and information technology in their businesses. Over the past 20 years, most senior managers have considered the key levers for managing business change to be strategy, organizational structure, processes and people. *Strategy* gives a company direction and vision. *Structure* defines people's roles and responsibilities. *Processes* define the business activities, such as sales and marketing, manufacturing and distribution, and research and development. Finally, *people* are influenced by the organizational culture as well as their own values and behaviours, and these determine how people execute their tasks and how they link their own performance to the company's.

However, today many managers question this model. This is not because it has not worked in the past, but because, unlike the emerging model of managing business change, it does not make visible three key aspects of future change programmes.

- It places more emphasis on the creation and application of knowledge and information by people and how companies can enhance these processes (this is often referred to as *knowledge management*).
- It emphasises how companies sense, collect, organize, process and store information, and the importance of effective information use and management of information in a business.
- Information systems (IS) and IT have often been viewed as necessities or cost centres in the past, but not as levers for implementing business change. The traditional perception of IS/IT continues to exist in the minds of managers alongside the growing perception that IT is critical for future business success.

To develop the right mindset, Chapter 2 provides managers a *five-step benchmarking process* to follow in addressing how to enhance their information effectiveness and their company's information management practices to improve business performance.

Part Two: Putting Information to Work

The second part of the book explores contemporary challenges and approaches in using information to add value with customers, create new realities and innovate, manage business risks and reduce costs strategically across the company. The book addresses how information management practices are evolving in response to globalization, mass customization, one-to-one customer relations, continuous product innovation, new forms of risk, the need for low-cost operations and products, as well as the impacts of electronic commerce and IT.

> **"For the first time, this book offers managers a comprehensive view of how information can be managed more effectively across their businesses"**

A   Adding Value with Customers

This section provides four views of how to use information to add value and delight customers. In Chapter 3, Jacques Horovitz shows that two trends have converged and expanded the need for and use of information about customers. First, over the last 20 years, companies have moved from serving markets, to serving customers, to serving *each* of their customers. Information needs have shifted from market information to the behaviours and profiles of each customer. Second, many companies facing more intense competition have had to search for new sources of growth. Companies have discovered the profitability of serving existing customers better and increasing loyalty versus the costs of acquiring new customers. Horovitz then presents the *three steps in the customer bonding process* – conquest, satisfaction and loyalty – and explains how customer, product and service information can be used to increase customer interactions and satisfaction over the long term.

In Chapter 4, Jacques Horovitz reverses this approach, and examines techniques for improving the customer's knowledge – and hence their desire to buy and stay loyal. The three elements of support needed from the business are outlined: help for customers to buy, help for them to obtain what they want and use it effectively (service), and help for customers to adapt their usage to their evolving needs. Information is vitally important for all three of these areas. Leading on from this point, the chapter also explains how information has a central role in selling, for example, by helping customer decision-making, supporting transparency of pricing and highlighting availability.

In Chapter 5, Sean Meehan addresses the challenges of appropriately sensing information about customers in markets. He defines market sensing as all the actions engaged in by all members of a company which determine and refine individual or collective perceptions of the marketplace and its dynamics. For Meehan, market sensing is not a core capability that by itself leads to competitive advantage if done well. Neither is it 'owned' by any one function such as marketing. For market sensing to lead to business performance improvements, it must be driven by the right management mindset that influences how a company mobilizes itself to respond to the market and customer intelligence that it senses. He illustrates his analysis with the unique market sensing efforts of Daewoo to successfully penetrate the crowded UK auto market in the late 1990s.

Chapter 6 by John Walsh builds on the perspectives of Horovitz and Meehan concerning the importance of sensing customer information for better customer relationships. Walsh focuses on how interactive technologies, such as point of sales scanners and the Internet, can capture customer information online and continuously so that retailers can effectively target customers with the right product mix, at the right prices and at the right time. Walsh suggests that with volumes of customer information available interactively, traditional marketing research will be transformed and include not only more personalization, but also involve the use of simulations to learn about, and respond to, customers and test products and services. Will personal learning from customers disappear with the new interactive technologies? Walsh does not believe so since it will be even more important to talk to customers and understand their motives and attitudes when so much is known about their behaviours online.

B   Creating New Reality

In Chapter 7, Xavier Gilbert focuses on the processes for proactive learning by managers. In examining how entrepreneurs learn in start-up companies, Gilbert identifies *four pillars for rapid learning* that he represents as the wind, the forest, the fire and the mountain. The wind represents the energy invested in eclectic information gathering – being curious, receptive and challenging of one's beliefs. The forest represents the capability for managers to map their competitive landscape and not get lost in the trees. Cognitive maps are like the sailor's navigation plan – constantly changing with the wind, the seas and the weather. The fire represents the willingness to try things out and to learn from good and bad news. Finally, the mountain represents the opportunity for reflection as we look at the path we have followed and decide on the next course of action.

> **"Using information to create new business realities (such as new products, new services and new businesses) requires managers to rethink not only how they learn and use information to develop innovative business solutions. They must also understand what forms of organization best support creative knowledge work and how information about the external world can be continuously sensed and deployed for new product innovation"**

Each of these steps defines the learning cycle that managers must move through to renew themselves and their learning. For companies, the learning cycle must be developed systematically based on a 'learning architecture' that leads companies to excel in growing and using knowledge and information to compete.

Chapter 8, by Jean-Philippe Deschamps, differentiates information for *innovation* from information for operations and business process support. Information for innovation is softer, more externally focused and more forward-looking than information for operations. Innovation can be viewed as a business process with both a bottom-up and top-down dimension. When managers view innovation as bottom-up, information's role is more instrumental – it is the carrier of tacit knowledge among people creating new ideas and knowledge. When managers view innovation as a top-down process, information becomes a driver of the process.

Deschamps describes the innovation process in three major steps: first, managers must decide what market, competitor and technology intelligence to collect. Second, they must mobilize the people in the organization to search for the intelligence. Third, they must set up mechanisms to analyse and exploit the outputs of the previous two steps.

For Deschamps, companies must foster an *intelligence culture* that has the visible commitment of senior managers, the right incentives for people to engage in search-ing for and sharing intelligence, and a tangible sense of urgency for the people to engage in constant reassessment.

C   Reducing Costs

While cost reduction and productivity improvements have been on the minds of senior managers for many years, using information to reduce costs involves more than just better cost accounting or reducing 'head counts' and expenses. On the one side, it involves using information so precisely that a company wastes little money, time, energy or materials on meeting the customer's precise needs. In Chapter 9, Andy Boynton and Bart Victor call this business capability *co-configuration* or efficient per-sonalization. More and more companies are facing the dual challenge of being the low-cost operator in their industries and also the most customer responsive. Boynton and Victor suggests that companies must move beyond mass-customization where products are partly standardized (80–90%) and partly customized (10–20%) to meet the differentiated needs of customers on a one-to-one basis. This requires that com-panies sense, respond and adapt their products to the individual experience of each customer. They use the example of the Danish hearing aid company, Oticon, and their innovative ways of configuring their digital hearing aid products to each customer's unique needs and requirements. For Boynton and Victor, co-configuration is not just an ability to provide new value to customers. It is a new way of working by con-tinuously linking the customer, the product and the company to achieve maximum customer value and cost efficiencies at the same time.

The other key aspect of using information to reduce costs focuses on adopting systematic techniques for achieving meaningful cost-reductions across a company without diluting the capabilities of the company to compete. In Chapter 10, Bob Howell suggests that strategic cost-reduction can actually create economic value as a business activity rather than dilute it. He notes that up until the 1990s, many busi-nesses and industries lacked a real sense of urgency to reduce their costs. However, over the 1990s, companies such as Toyota have placed cost-reduction at the heart of their improvement efforts and strategic positioning in their industries. To do so, these companies have had to develop the management approaches and information to enable strategic cost-reduction programmes. Yesterday's cost accounting systems and management information systems are poorly equipped to support the combination of approaches that Howell suggest are needed to strategically become the lowest cost producer in one's industry. He presents a *ten-step plan for systematically improving the cost position of a company* over time in a way that creates rather than destroys business value.

D   Minimizing Risks

In Chapter 11, Stewart Hamilton emphasizes the importance of information in risk management – not only as a key element in control systems but also as a source of vulnerability and a resource to be protected. Hamilton highlights recent high-profile financial disasters and explains that the lessons to be learnt are not only relevant to the finance sector but are generally applicable to any business. Information systems are too often vulnerable to dislocating events – dramatic events that can have major consequences for the business as a whole. These dislocating events can be caused by factors from four key areas of change: process change, people change, organization change and IT/IS change.

Whereas Chapter 11 highlights the risks faced by management information systems and the need for effective control systems, Stewart Hamilton's Chapter 12 provides practical techniques for assessing, managing and controlling risk. The measures that can be taken to control risk are explored; these include accepting that risks exist, creating the right climate for risk management, and understanding the key elements of the risk management process. This process involves risk analysis, measures for risk avoidance and mitigation, and techniques for risk monitoring and control.

Part Three: How Your Company can Compete with Information

Part Three focuses on how managers can implement their strategic priorities and achieve improved business performance through better information use and IT practices in their companies, coupled with appropriate information behaviours exhibited by their people and themselves. Given the variations among companies in strategic orientation, we expect important differences in the ways managers think about their business activities and the information required to support these activities. In addition, differences in company cultures, work styles, value chains and local, regional and global organization will influence how companies can leverage information resources and knowledge residing in their people through their business processes and information systems. Finally, managers are further challenged by the rapid development of the Internet and electronic commerce on business-to-business and business-to-consumer activities. What does managing on Internet time really mean? How will e-commerce disrupt industry value chains and introduce new business models of competing with information and IT? How is e-commerce affecting our company's performance today and competitiveness tomorrow?

In Chapter 13, Don Marchand employs the strategic information alignment framework developed in Chapter 2 to focus managers on how to evaluate and diagnose the business value of their company's information management practices both today and in the future. Based on the four ways of using information to create business value and the 'cross' diagram presented in Chapter 2, Marchand uses the diagram to map information practices along each of the four axes: minimizing risks, reducing costs, adding value with customers in markets, and creating new reality. This exercise permits managers to develop a composite picture for a business unit or a company of how they perceive their information practices in relation to their strategic priorities today and in the future. The diagnostic results then illustrate gaps and changes in management expectations concerning information practices needed for future competition that must be improved. Next, Marchand describes *five practical steps for benchmarking* and developing improved information management practices that fit future performance priorities and expectations.

The reader at this point may ask: shouldn't managers have understood their information management practices in the past and how they could be improved through benchmarking practices inside and outside their industries? The answer to this question is not necessarily. As Tom Davenport has also observed, information management practices represent one of the *least* understood areas of company practices affecting business performance. Hence the need for using diagnostic and benchmarking techniques to make the process of evaluating information management practices in a company or business unit more explicit and systematic.

Chapter 14 moves from information management practices to the company's culture and social structures that influence how people make their knowledge explicit, and use information effectively to execute their activities. Piero Morosini observes that competing with knowledge and information is not about possessing these assets, but about using them. Effective use of knowledge and information depend directly on the company's values and behaviours of its people. A company's knowledge strategy should aim at creating unique ways that managers, employees, suppliers, partners and customers can learn from each other, and use information effectively to continuously create market value and implement appropriate actions. A company does so in two ways. First, by creating a unique social structure whose key elements include open business values, the right social players and networks, and appropriate guiding rituals and myths surrounding the effective use of information and knowledge to create business value. Second, a company must implement an appropriate information infrastructure that enables the social structure to work effectively. This infrastructure is more than IT networks and associated hardware and software. It involves creating both the IT and information management practices that best fit how people behave with information and knowledge in the company to improve performance.

Chapter 15 by Don Marchand focuses on the challenges managers face in moving to the 'second wave' of business process redesign and IT systems to support their company's demand/supply chains to customers. During the 1990s, manufacturing and service companies invested billions in replacing their legacy computer systems in advance of the year 2000 change by implementing Enterprise Resource Planning (ERP) systems that promised to provide seamless use of information across their supply chains. This was the first wave of business process redesign and IT systems in supply chain management. The second wave of ERP systems and process redesign post-Y2K promises to address the demand side of company value chains by providing better customer information management, account management, product information and services management for customers.

Although senior managers are generally supportive of this shift in ERP from the supply or product push side of the value chain to the demand or customer pull side, these same managers are concerned for three reasons. First, the track record of companies in implementing ERP systems and completing business process redesign projects has been decidedly negative. Clearly past performance during the first wave of ERP implementation is not an indicator of future success during the second wave. Second, the price of the second wave of business process re-engineering (BPR) and ERP systems may be too high, coming on the heels of already heavy investments aimed at replacing the legacy systems in finance, human resources, order fulfilment, production, logistics and inventory management. Third, senior managers may be more reluctant to mortgage their future strategic choices to large-scale, multi-year enterprise-wide ERP projects.

In a post-Y2K era, senior managers will need to re-evaluate both the first and second wave commitments to ERP and BPR to make sure that these investments are targeted at making their companies more competitive in their industries. To do so, Don Marchand suggests that senior managers will have to address five key questions:

1. What approach to demand/supply chain management is your company implementing?
2. What is the competitive value for your company to redesign and automate *similar* aspects of its demand/supply chain as your competitors?
3. Should the software for operating your company's demand/supply chain be bought and configured as a package, or should it be custom built?
4. What is the appropriate 'time to implement' BPR and ERP projects?
5. How will Internet/intranet/extranet use along the demand/supply chain influence customer, partner and supplier relationships?

Many senior managers are unprepared for the second wave of ERP and BPR projects in the post-Y2K era. Having lived through the first wave of these projects and IT systems, it is understandable that these same managers are reluctant to address these questions again. However, there has never been a time when BPR and IT are so closely associated with business performance, and so risky in their potential to destroy shareholder value, profitability and market credibility.

In Chapter 16, Don Marchand addresses the related challenge of operating demand/supply chain processes on a local, regional and global basis at the same time. Managers often ask the question: how can we attain maximum business flexibility to achieve market growth and profitability, while at the same time standardize business practices to lower costs, leverage scarce expertise and use IT to share information and knowledge across the company about products, customers and market conditions? Implementing the right balance between business flexibility and standardization is not a one-time choice for companies but a journey influenced by the product and service mix that a company delivers, and the business processes and information required to deliver these services and products to customers and markets. Under-invest in IS and IT and the company lacks the capabilities and infrastructure to compete on a local, regional and global basis at the same time. Overinvest in IS and IT and the company raises its operational costs to unacceptable levels in the face of competition. Marchand presents five approaches to going local, regional and global at the same time using IS/IT. He also discusses the criteria and trade-offs that senior managers must make to find the right balance between business flexibility and standardization over time for their company.

Finally, in Chapter 17, Don Marchand addresses the business and information management challenges that managers face in developing appropriate e-commerce strategies in their companies. He first explains seven important principles that are affecting e-commerce strategies today. He then focuses on the evolving business practices associated with four different forms of Internet use in a company (the four nets):

- Internet or business to consumer focus;
- intranets – the use of Internet technology inside a company;
- extranets – the use of Internet technology between companies; and
- industrynets – new forms of intermediaries aimed at disrupting the existing value chains of specific industries.

Marchand suggests that companies must develop the right mix of four-net strategies for their business context. The responsibility falls uniquely to general managers to determine how information and knowledge can be leveraged effectively in e-commerce.

References

Davenport, T.H. (1997) *Information Ecology*, p. 3. Oxford University Press, Oxford.

Drucker, P.F. (1999) *Management Challenges for the Twenty-First Century*, p. 124. Butterworth-Heinemann, Oxford, UK.

Marchand, D.A., Kettinger, W.J. and Rollings, J.R. (2000) *Information Orientation: The Link To Business Performance*. Oxford University Press, Oxford.

2

Creating Business Value with Information

In this chapter, **Donald Marchand** outlines the four ways that companies can compete using information. The chapter focuses on the value of information for creating new reality, adding value with customers, reducing costs and minimizing risks. It also emphasizes the need for managers to develop the right mindset for the role of information in building competitive advantage.

Overview

Today, senior executives want their companies to be 'learning organizations' where employees and managers are open to new knowledge, seek out best practice and use their capabilities effectively in the development of new products or in providing better customer service. New business practices, such as one-to-one marketing on the Internet, customer-focused supply chain management and electronic commerce, depend on the skilful use of high-quality information. New information systems tools, such as data warehouses, knowledge repositories and Java (the Internet programming language) are influencing how information and knowledge are used in companies. In addition, the world of information technology is alive with the possibilities of redefining how knowledge workers share multimedia information and collaborate using the Internet, intranets and extranets.

In the midst of this rapid change and new technologies, many general managers feel uneasy and ambivalent about how they will navigate through these business challenges. General managers in their forties and fifties – those born 'before personal computers' (or BCs) – are increasingly concerned about understanding the mindsets of the younger generation, or those born 'after computers' (ACs).

Do ACs truly have new insights about competing in the information age that BCs do not, or are they merely more comfortable with the new technologies? Clearly the mindsets of managers in their thirties and late twenties are attuned to the uses of personal computers, multimedia technologies and the Internet. These are the tools that will influence and define how information management can create business value for the foreseeable future. However, the knowledge of exactly where these tools will be used to differentiate successful companies from less successful competitors is not well established among either BCs or ACs, nor are the specific uses of information and knowledge that will enable companies to be winners in information age competition.

One fact is certain. Managing business change in the years ahead will require fundamental rethinking of business practices, strategies and implementation approaches as companies learn to compete with information and new technologies. In this chapter we will:

- Outline the role and value of information for managing business change.
- Differentiate between information technology, information systems and information management, and explain how information can be used to provide companies with a competitive edge.
- Explain the five-step process for benchmarking a company against current best practice in information management.

Making invisible assets visible

The traditional view of the role and value of information

Over the past 15 to 20 years, most general managers have considered the key levers for managing business change as being strategy, organizational structure, processes and people.

- *Strategy* provided the direction and vision for the firm.
- *Structure* defined the roles and responsibilities of people.

- *Processes* defined the tasks and activities that the business executed, such as sales and marketing, manufacturing and distribution, and research and development.
- The culture and values of the company, as well as its rewards for performance, influenced the motivations and behaviours of *people*.

Together these key levers became the leading model for managing business changes inside the company, as well as for providing management consulting services to companies. So, the question is what is wrong with continuing to view business change this way in the new millennium?

Like all mental models that are partial or incomplete representations of the real world, this model's strength permits general managers to focus on specific levers of change and not on others. Moreover, the model provides a lens on the world of business that is linked to its origins in the industrial age.

First, the model reflects an industrial age emphasis on the value of managing physical assets such as capital, labour, equipment and buildings. The focus in manufacturing and service companies is on products and physical processes for developing, transforming, distributing and selling those products. Information's role in the business is to control and monitor the physical processes, such as replenishment of stock in retail stores, or issuing insurance policy documents to customers. Service-based companies speak and act about their services as 'products'. Banks and investment companies call their mutual funds and savings programmes 'products' that require significant physical handling of records and paper documents.

Secondly, the role of information technology and automation focuses on labour savings in physical processes, whether those processes involve making televisions or processing paper and records for life insurance or medical care. IT is used either to replace physical labour or more efficiently to count things and move records and data around to where they must be used. Companies execute numerous transactions such as order processing, payments and deliveries that IT is well suited to automate.

Thirdly, the dominant way information is collected, processed and used by managers is for financial accountability and control. This model of business change views information as a tool for operational control of processes and people as well as the chief means of integrating mainly numerical information for management reporting. Managers are provided on a regular basis with management reports filled with ratios and calculations that reflect the need to measure and report on the handling of material, capital and people in financial terms.

These aspects of the traditional change model for the business are both its weaknesses and strengths. The strengths of the model lie in helping general managers focus on only those elements that contribute directly to success. Without exaggeration, this model of managing business change is responsible for the standard of living that is enjoyed today in advanced economies.

The role of information and knowledge in creating business value

The weaknesses rest with what the model does *not* reveal regarding the role of information and knowledge as direct sources for creating business value. Starting in the mid 1980s and accelerating in the 1990s, many managers and academics have questioned the more traditional model, not because it has not worked but because the model does not make visible four key dimensions of leading business change.

The emerging model is concerned with knowledge developed and applied by people. Information provides a vehicle for expressing, sharing and using knowledge, and the tools of information systems and technology are the enablers of business processes and networks among employees as well as with customers, suppliers and partners. This model for competing makes 'visible' in the general management mind three dimensions that have been largely 'invisible' in the traditional approach to leading successful business change.

This does not mean that strategy, structure, processes and people are less important than knowledge, information, systems and technology in implementing business change. Rather the focus is changed significantly by explicit emphasis on managing knowledge and information as key assets in the business using the new tools of information systems and technology.

Targets of competency development

The emergence of a new model for managing business change does not fully address the concerns in the minds of general managers about what they must do differently. In most companies, the terminology related to information management (IM), information systems (IS) and information technology (IT) is confusing at best. One indicator of this confusion is the abundant and diverse labels that are used to describe these activities in many companies, from MIS (management information systems) to IS (information services or systems) to IT (information technology or information/technology) to IM&S or I&S (information management and services or information and systems). This melange of acronyms can either be attributed to the quickly changing nature of the functions or activities described, or be viewed as a clear sign of the confusion in many businesses over how IM, IS or IT should be managed and to what ends.

As Figure 2.1 shows, IT refers primarily to the technology infrastructure of the firm from desktops and servers to local and wide area data, and voice and video networks. The primary business criteria for performance are reliability, responsiveness, ease of use and affordability relative to price/capabilities available from the information technology industry.

IS refers to the applications and database software that performs business functions, such as accounting and human resources, or supports key processes such as order fulfilment or product development. The business criteria applied to IS relate to the quality and functionality of the software, its flexibility and the speed and cost for its development and ongoing modification either inside the firm or by software providers.

Finally, IM relates directly to the content, quality and use of information necessary for running the firm, such as operational controls, customer services, and financial reporting.

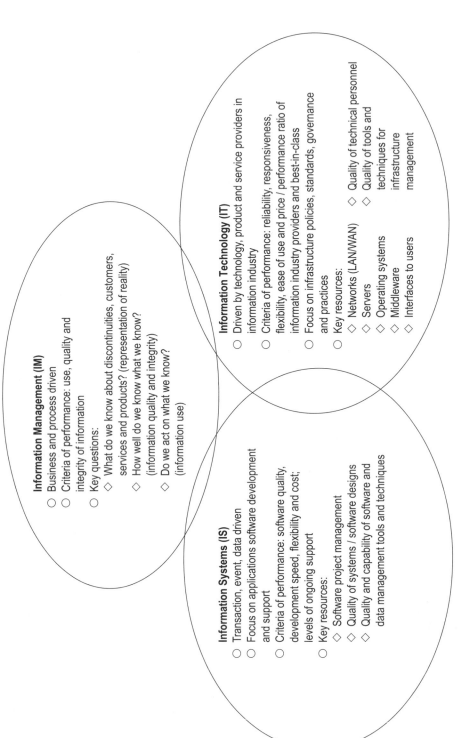

Figure 2.1: *Targets of competency development – why definitions count*

Thus, it is possible to differentiate the enabling IT infrastructure from the software applications to support business processes and the management of information in the business. This is important for general managers for two reasons. First, they can avoid the confusion in using the term 'IT' to encompass all the information that businesses create and use. How people use information and the decisions that they make in a business are as important as the tools that they use. The people and behavioural aspects of information use are often obscured when the IT label is all-encompassing.

Secondly, IM is tied integrally to business units since information use is closely linked to business activities and processes, whereas IS and IT may be shared responsibilities with internal technical support organizations in a company.

For some companies, IT infrastructure is managed on a regional or global basis by a technical support organization, or outsourced to service providers, while IM and IS are managed in business units or by product divisions. In other companies, IM, IS and IT are managed by regional or global business units in line with regional or global supply chains and processes. In still other companies, IM is a business responsibility while IS and IT reside with functional organizations controlled by finance or administrative departments.

How and by whom these activities are managed provides clear indicators about how well information is used in the company, as well as whether IS and IT are perceived as cost or support centres to be reduced or investment and profit centres to create business value.

Management with, not of, information

Even a quick look inside the offices of most general managers in companies provides abundant evidence of how they manage with, through and around the many documents, phone slips, e-mails on the PC screens, and faxes during an average day or week.

Most general managers are used to managing with information in their daily activities for three reasons. First, physical resources and processes such as customer service, product manufacturing, inventories and logistics, people and finances are no longer managed directly by managers but indirectly with information that represents these processes, activities and resources.

The need for speed of operations, broad geographic coverage, increased volume, lower operating capital costs and business flexibility requires companies to deploy communications networks and computers to manage information about physical processes efficiently, as well as to avoid physical handling of products or documents wherever information can be used to add value to customers. Express package companies such as FedEx and UPS often claim that information about the package is as important to customers as the package itself.

Secondly, the larger the business unit that a manager oversees, the more dependent he or she becomes on information to manage. A managing director of a company with 10 000 employees and 300 000 customers must manage with information about punctual deliveries, customer calls, complaints and surveys of customer satisfactions to evaluate the day-to-day performance of the business. The MD's direct, day-to-day human contact is necessarily limited with customers and employees alike.

Thirdly, human communication and collaborative teamwork require that employees and managers operate remotely across oceans, time zones and schedules, which increases the use of voice, video and messaging technologies in most companies. Thus, managers are more and more acclimatized to handling daily volumes of information and messages – e-mails, voice mails, faxes and standard mail – which would have been unthinkable just ten years ago.

In contrast to managing with information, general managers are far less concerned with the management *of* information. While the specific reasons for this attitude vary by company and industry there seem to be some common causes. Many managers, especially BCs, assume that functional departments such as finance and accounting or IS/IT are primarily responsible for the management of information. In this case, managers act as if all the company's relevant information should be managed by these functional units.

Other companies have a long tradition of delegating to functional departments such as marketing, accounting, product development, or even manufacturing, responsibility for managing information used by managers at all levels. In these cases, each functional unit manages its own relevant information but often cares little about sharing its information with other functions. In still other companies, managers assume that all employees and managers are responsible for the management of information. This attitude leaves everyone responsible for the information that they use as individuals, but no-one responsible for information used across business processes or functions, where individual ownership of information is often a barrier to information sharing outside an individual's direct areas of responsibilities.

Four ways of using information – the SIA framework

In examining the ways managers in many companies in diverse industries in the US, Europe and Asia Pacific think about and use information, and in reviewing the historical development of the corporation, especially during this century, I have concluded that there are four fundamental ways of using information to create business value. Moreover, it is increasingly clear that competing with information requires conscious choices by managers in companies to develop their firms' capabilities along each axis (*see* Figure 2.2).

Depending on strategies and market positioning, not all companies use information in similar ways, even in the same industry. Nor do all companies have the same capabilities to manage information along each axis, which accounts for wide variations in how companies use information to compete. These differences eventually create competitive or entrepreneurial opportunities for some firms in each industry to excel in managing and using information in their business system with customers, partners and suppliers.

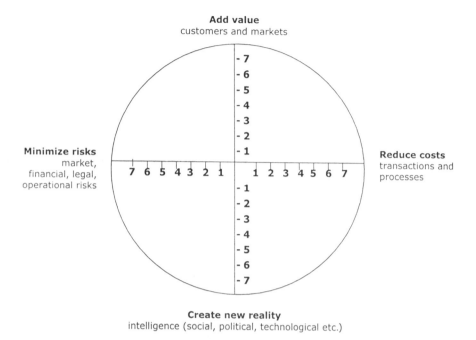

Figure 2.2: *Four ways of using information to create business value*
The practical applications of this diagram are explored further in Chapter 14.

Minimize risks

The first and oldest way to create business value with information is to minimize risks. The evolution of risk management in business has provided the stimulus for the growth of functions such as finance, accounting and auditing, which manage information, to account for orders and goods, finance future investments, hedge against the unforeseeable, budget over predictable periods such as quarters and years, and audit the books to protect against fraud and errors in counting. In addition, financial devices to control risk, such as bonds, stocks and options, have evolved as trading and capitalism developed in the industrial age of the nineteenth and twentieth centuries.

In examining the operations of the modern corporation today, it is easy to forget or overlook how much of the company's ways of using information are shaped or influenced by the controls needed to manage commercial, operational and financial risks. In fact, it is only when risk management controls break down or are violated, as in the case of Barings bank and the derivative trading activities of Nick Leeson, that it can be appreciated how much of the success of a company is dependent on a daily basis on the monitoring and control of risks. The central role of information in managing issues affecting risk is explored fully by Stewart Hamilton in Chapter 12, while Chapter 13 provides an insight into techniques for using information to control risk.

Reducing costs

The second way of using information to create business value is to reduce costs. Here the focus has been on improving business processes and transactions so that information used in processes, as well as to monitor processes, is as efficient and economical as possible to achieve the outputs required.

Historically, this way of thinking about deploying information began with Frederick Taylor's 'time and motion' studies in the 1930s and 1940s and has led through the scientific management movement of the 1940s and 1950s to total quality improvement (TQM) in the 1970s and 1980s and the evolution of re-engineering and process improvement in the 1990s. The common elements to all these movements has been a focus on first eliminating unnecessary and wasteful steps and activities, including paperwork and information movement, and then simplifying – and if possible – automating the remaining processes and transactions to reduce costs.

The search for continuous improvement embedded in TQM and radical re-engineering as represented by Michael Hammer, the acknowledged guru of re-engineering, both focus on the need to eliminate and simplify information use in processes and transactions to reduce costs and improve productivity. During the past ten years, many companies have focused on using information to reduce costs and minimize risks at the same time. Thus, their efforts to improve information management have advanced along both sides of the horizontal axis, often with mixed results as the high failure rates for radical re-engineering projects suggests.

Nonetheless, general managers in many commodity-based industries, or those threatened by increased commoditization of their products and services, have focused their business strategies and change management initiatives on improving business results on both sides of the axis at the same time.

Adding value

The third way of creating business value with information focuses on adding value to customers and markets. Here, the focus of information management is on knowing about, and sharing information with, customers, partners, suppliers and employees to improve customer satisfaction and relationships before, during and after sales.

The evolution here has been from companies that processed customer orders, with little or no interest in the ongoing satisfaction of the customer, to companies that seek information about customers before, during and after sales to create better relationships with customers to enhance customer loyalty, repeat purchases and satisfaction. (These issues are explored fully in Chapters 3, 4, 5 and 6, which examine how information can be used to delight customers and enhance sales.)

Historically, the focus on the customer is not new. The evolution of advertising and marketing in the late nineteenth and early twentieth centuries emphasized a need to collect for the first time systematic information to influence customer perceptions and purchasing decisions for the mass-produced products of the industrial age.

Companies began to collect information on customer responses to advertising and commercials as well as discount and incentive programmes. These uses of customer and product information continued to evolve into the 1980s, when information management to promote 'product push' to the consumer was replaced by a 'customer pull' view of marketing information as well as of customer services during and after sales.

This shift in marketing development from transactions to 'relationships' has led to an intense interest in 'knowing' the customer and managing customer services with excellent information about the customer. In addition, the customer pull view of the value chain has moved from a supply-driven emphasis to a demand-driven emphasis: this has placed a new focus on information management practices and systems that permit employees, partners and suppliers of the company to understand and respond rapidly to the needs of customers and end-users of products and services.

These changes have led companies to invest in point-of-sales, account management, customer profiling and service management systems that employ technologies such as point-of-sales terminals, hand-held scanners, relational databases and telecommunications networks to reach and communicate well with customers.

Creating new reality

Finally, firms can use information to innovate or create new realities – attract new customers, invent new products, provide different services and use emerging technologies. Historically, this use of information evolved in marketing departments, which were responsible for 'hearing the voice of the market' and suggesting new products, or in R&D departments, which were involved in sensing new technological, social and economic trends and coming up with new products.

Each of these departments relied on information professionals – especially librarians – to seek out or contract for market, competitor or technological intelligence and to pass this information along to the appropriate marketing or R&D units for their use. At its best, information use and management in these departments was focused on sensing the outside world and discovering distinctive trends and ideas that might lead to commercially viable products and services. In the 1990s, this fourth way of using information to create business value has led to the use of Internet technologies to share external intelligence across all departments and functions in the firm, and not just within specific departments such as R&D or marketing.

Whole companies such as Intel and Microsoft are now learning to operate in a 'continuous discovery mode', inventing new products in shorter timeframes and using market intelligence throughout the company to retain competitive edge. Within these companies, investments in information management focus on mobilizing people and collaborative work processes to share information and promote discovery and experimentation company-wide.

Companies that focus on using information to create new reality and add value with customers on the vertical axis contrast sharply with companies operating on the horizontal axis, where minimizing risk and reducing costs are key drivers of information use and management.

To compete with information today means that companies must focus increasingly on differentiating their uses and management of information from their competitors and find ways of using structures, processes and people, as well as IS and IT, to satisfy customers and promote growth.

BENCHMARKING

Five-step process for benchmarking an organization's use of information

While many companies exhort their managers to engage in benchmarking of best practices, not many companies focus their managers on benchmarking the best information management practices.

IM benchmarking may be done by *functional* areas of the business, such as finance and marketing, or by the *IS/IT* organization. In the latter case, the focus is usually on how new technologies, such as data warehouses or intranets, will impact on information access and availability. Rarely will a team of general managers directing business units engage in profiling their information management practices and examining best practices along the four dimensions inside or outside their industry.

To get started in positioning their company for competing with information, general managers should follow a five-step benchmarking process.

1. **Ask the question: what are the current ways the business unit (BU) uses information?** Mapping and evaluating current practices provides a baseline to assess the gap between where a business needs to be to compete effectively and where it is today.

2. **Compare and contrast the ways of using information with other business units in the company**. How does it compare against BUs whose market position and development is similar or different?

3. **Compare and contrast the BU's ways of using information with other companies inside and outside the industry**.

4. **Develop a clear view of what improvements need to be made in the company's ways of using information to close the gaps between desirable practices and current capabilities**. What capabilities need to be improved in information use practices to be the best in the industry or globally?

5. **Identify the changes in the business that will be required to implement the desired levels of information management practices in the firm**. What changes need to be made at the BU level, as well as at the corporate or regional levels, in strategy, organizational structures, key

processes and people, to achieve desired levels of information use and management with the highest probability of improving the company's competitive position?

The importance of management mindset

Leading a successful business requires a deep appreciation by general managers of the critical role of information as the means of sharing, expressing and communicating knowledge among people. Information use and sharing are vital to the processes by which people understand, represent and impact the realities of the business relations with customers, internal operations, product innovation, and control of internal or external risks to the business.

The importance of IS and IT cannot be underestimated for enabling a company to redefine how it uses information to move beyond processing transactions and management reporting to new levels of knowledge work among employees and with customers, suppliers and partners. On the other hand, information management involves more than new applications of systems and technologies and must include appropriate changes in the ways people use information to make decisions, take actions and collaborate with others.

Thus, in deciding how to compete, the mindsets of managers *do* count. For ACs, this may mean gaining better appreciation for the organizational and behavioural side of information management inside companies, where adopting new Internet-based technologies alone will not necessarily achieve business results. For BCs, this may mean that managing with information must also include a serious concern with the management *of* information in the company as the constraints of time, geography, space and organizational structures are redefined with global networks.

In both cases, the quality and integrity of the information that is used to run the businesses will increasingly differentiate winning companies. Excellence in information management will be 'the difference that makes the difference'.

SUMMARY

Creating business value with information

Five business capabilities act as the levers for business change: strategy, structure, processes, people and *information*. This invisible asset is emerging as a key resource in the search for competitive advantage. However, within the area of information there are a number of different definitions – and more importantly specific issues and resources – that need to be recognized and developed as distinct competencies. These include:

- **Information management (IM)** – this is business- and process-driven, and focuses on the *use, quality* and *integrity* of information.
- **Information systems (IS)** – these are driven by transactions, events and data, and are concerned with issues of software quality, speed of development, flexibility, cost, and levels of ongoing support.
- **Information technology (IT)** – the management focus here is on infrastructure policies, standards and practices; the key issues include reliability, responsiveness, flexibility (again), ease of use and price/performance ratio.

Information is therefore a tool that adds value, builds competitive advantage and should be used to *support* management – it is not simply an overhead or functional system that needs to be managed in its own right. This point may seem obvious but to many managers it requires a shift in management mindset. The management mindset has had to change to take account of the content, usage and quality of information, ensuring that it is *aligned with strategic priorities*.

This change in mindset can be approached by considering the ways that information can create business value. Information can be used for:

- *Adding value* to customers and markets.
- *Reducing costs* of transactions and processes.
- *Minimizing risks* of business by using information to monitor and maintain control systems.
- *Creating new realities* and innovating by leveraging understanding of key developments (for example, social or technological).

These four strategic priorities are the keys to the *strategic information alignment framework* outlined in the rest of this book. Our starting point is the first use of information: adding value with customers.

Part Two

Putting Information to Work

Section A

Adding Value with Customers

3

Using Information to Bond with Customers

Applying information to serve each individual customer
effectively provides a major source of competitive
opportunity. **Jacques Horovitz** explains the theory and
practice behind successful customer bonding.

CASE STUDIES: THE POWER OF CUSTOMER BONDING

Even in an industry fabled for its pace of change, innovation and visionary entrepreneurs, the rise of Dell Computer is astonishing. From a small, one-office operation in 1984, Michael Dell expanded his business to a turnover of $265 million by 1988, and $2 billion by 1992. Inevitably, Dell's competitors came to understand the secrets of his success and the industry eventually emulated Dell's business methods en masse, but the story of his company's initial growth and success is a master class in using information to understand and bond with customers.

In 1988 Dell Computer started competing aggressively with the market leaders, IBM and Compaq. Dell's strategy was to provide good-quality personal computers at low (but not the lowest) prices, backed up with friendly and reliable after-sales service. But the real key to Dell's success was to carefully target this product offering by getting to know, in detail, their customers. Large amounts of advertising were placed in new (and unfashionable) magazines read by computer experts, raising the business's profile with this key group. Combined with this was Dell's direct response advertising methods: in order to get the Dell product catalogue, customers had to either complete a detailed response card, or call a toll free number where they were asked the same, detailed questions. The Dell telephone representatives were highly skilled, trained to ask questions but also to listen to customers, recording their preferences and requirements in detail and then acting on them. Potential customers were flattered at the interest and level of attention they were receiving and responded in droves, enabling Dell to amass an enormous database of vital information about each individual prospect and customer. This information was then used to help customers, tailoring product and service solutions to each individual need, in a way that customers understood and appreciated.

Starting in Milwaukee in 1909, Harley-Davidson has enjoyed a long, successful history as the USA's foremost motorbike manufacturer. However, by the early 1980s their reputation and business were in serious trouble following a sustained onslaught from affordable, high-quality Japanese machines produced by companies such as Honda and Kawasaki. Following a management buy-out, Harley-Davidson tackled their product quality problems, using the techniques of Dr W. Edwards Deming (ironically, an American whose quality methods transformed Japanese manufacturing). The next challenge was to win back – and maintain – market share: they are now America's leading bike manufacturer, with an amazing 90% of Harley-Davidson customers staying loyal to the company.

There are several core methods that Harley-Davidson uses to bond with their customers; underpinning each has been an approach that uses information and understanding of individual customers to sell the spirit of riding a Harley, providing a knowledgeable, caring approach that also appeals successfully to customers' emotions. The managers of the business meet their customers regularly at rallies, where new models can be sampled with free demonstration rides. Advertising reinforces the image and perception of owning a Harley, appealing as much to existing customers to stay loyal, as to attract new ones. The Harley Owner's Group (HOG) activities are central to binding their customers to the company, and rather than providing trite or cheap *benefits Harley devotes considerable resources to ensuring that their customers receive benefits that they value. Membership of HOG is free for the first year for new Harley owners, thereafter a membership fee (approximately $40) is payable; over two thirds of their customers renew. True, it might seem easy to sell a product as exciting and appealing as a motorbike. But then Harley-Davidson also manages to get tens of thousands of their customers to keep on buying their machines, as well as paying to attend rallies where they enjoy themselves, make friends, provide valuable customer feedback – and even tattoo themselves with the name of the company! How many businesses achieve that?*

Both of these examples highlight the importance of customer bonding – developing solid bonds at each step of the relationship with the customer. To achieve this, the nature of bonding and the central importance of customer information must be clearly understood.

Overview

During the last twenty years businesses have moved from serving markets to serving customers, to serving each individual customer. As a result of this increase in focus, the nature of information needed for decision-making has shifted dramatically. In yesterday's world, information needs focused on macro issues such as market size, market volume, market growth and others; in today's world, information focus has shifted towards knowing customers – their needs and expectations, their satisfaction and repeat purchase behaviour (using averages – either global or for each market segment). In tomorrow's world, information will focus on each customer's individual needs, expectations, satisfaction, loyalty, behaviour and response to particular marketing stimuli. This sharpening in focus has already started, in part as a result of the opportunities afforded by technological advances, but also driven by the quest for greater efficiency, effectiveness and competitive advantage.

> **"Customer bonding not only enables businesses to compete more effectively, it also provides a valuable source of growth during times of intense competition"**

Parallel to this trend, many industries face the dilemma of where to find new sources of growth, as markets mature and competition intensifies. Companies need to balance the costs of acquiring new customers against the costs of keeping current ones. In most sectors today customer retention – or bonding – is vital to success, despite the presence of new customers. There are several reasons for this: it is cheaper to keep customers than to acquire new ones; available new customers might be limited, and the costs of attracting and retaining those new customers might be extravagant – especially for that part of the market that we call bargain hunters.

If we put those two trends together – serving each customer and focusing on existing ones – the need for information and its role in building a profitable customer base is expanding. In this chapter we will:

- Explain how to use information to enhance customer bonding, creating solid bonds at each step of the relationship with customers – the three-stage process for customer bonding.
- Outline how customer databases can be applied to enhance customer bonding.

The three-stage process for customer bonding

Customer bonding – the ability to attract and keep customers for a long time – is a step-by-step process that successful companies complete in the right sequence. It requires three acts, in the following order:

1. conquest
2. satisfaction
3. loyalty.

Customer bonding happens when all three acts are accomplished *well*, and this qualitative element is central to the success of the entire process. Satisfying the customer well does not merely mean performing well relative to competitors, it means meeting customers' expectations as completely as possible and, where feasible, exceeding them (*see* Figure 3.1).

Figure 3.1: *The three-stage process for customer bonding*

Stage one: conquest

Conquest is about capturing and gaining customers. It means proposing the right product or service to the right customer at the right moment. This involves *targeting*: attracting potential customers, matching the offer to their needs as closely as possible, and helping the customer buy what they want. Finally, conquest is essentially about having a good value proposition.

Stage two: satisfaction

Once the selling is done and the promise is made, it is the need to create satisfaction that will bring continued success. Satisfaction means ensuring that what was promised gets delivered, that problems are solved, that future needs are anticipated and that, where possible, customer expectations are exceeded and customers are delighted.

Stage three: loyalty

Unfortunately, satisfaction is sometimes simply not enough to keep customers. Some may want another 'experience' to compare; some may get lured by cheaper prices as the product's value is not perceived as being sufficiently distinctive or competitive; and some customers may want multiple sources of supply to minimize their risks. Among all of these reasons, the one that we can control most effectively is the reinforcement of satisfaction through loyalty-building instruments, such as rewards, recognition, customer involvement and commitment, and strong individual relationships over time.

Implementing the three-stage process for customer bonding

Success cannot happen by starting with the third act. A frequent flyer program that rewards passengers of an airline who are otherwise ill-served is not going to keep them loyal. It will just be seen as a discount. A tour operator who has excellent vacation resorts but sells a holiday where there are lots of young children and families to a single adult is not going to win the bond of the customer, regardless of the high standards delivered in the resort. Conquest was flawed. As customer bonding requires three sequential acts, each requiring a different set of objectives, activities and decisions to be made, the need for *information* (type, sources, usage) will be different for each act. This is what we are going to see in the next section.

Using information for successful conquest

Two key pieces of information are necessary at the conquest stage, as they help to understand and know the customer: information for *targeting* and information for *customization*. Information for targeting enables us to identify those customers that have the best fit with the offer, as well as helping to communicate and attract them. Information for customization highlights the differences in their needs, allowing the offer to be adapted or customized to ensure successful conquest of each clearly-defined market segment. As a result of these two aspects of information – targeting and customization – there are four different elements of information content, as shown in Figure 3.2.

Although the purpose of this chapter is not to describe market research methods, it is useful to consider different ways in which information can be collected for each of the four quadrants (*see* Figure 3.3).

As targeting increases and we are moving towards customized solutions, more detailed information has to come from each individual customer – not just who they are but how they behave and react to different stimuli.

Perhaps one of the greatest advantages of the Internet is the ability to electronically capture detailed information about current and potential customers. Many commercial websites routinely capture data about customers' lifestyles, preferences and – most significantly – their buying habits, and this trend is set to increase in scope

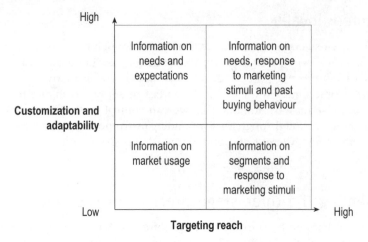

Figure 3.2: *Information requirements for effective targeting and customization*

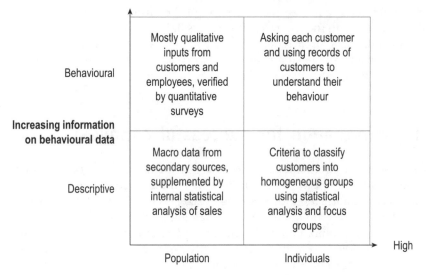

Figure 3.3: *Market research sources for customization and targeting*

and sophistication as the ease of electronic commerce increases. This information can prove invaluable in all three stages of the customer bonding process: it aids conquest by enabling the sale to be made at the right moment, to the right person in the manner that they prefer. Satisfaction is achieved by using the information to anticipate future needs, as well as speeding up the delivery process for many items (notably information). Loyalty can be engendered by regularly interesting and involving the customer in the website, and building a strong, individual relationship – for example, through the use of e-mail as well as competitions, news and special offers.

Using information to ensure that customers are satisfied

At this stage, the customer has bought our product and service and we need to ensure that the promises made while selling are met – ideally exceeding expectations and *delighting the customer*. Four types of information are key to achieving customer satisfaction:

1.   Information that enables us to adapt service delivery to specific customer requirements.
2.   Information that provides feedback from unsatisfied customers, highlighting areas for improvement, using the information for future relationships as well as solving problems.
3.   Specific information that assists us to delight each customer.
4.   Information verifying that service delivery corresponds to the required standards.

Using information to adapt to specific customer requirements

Not all customers want to be served the same way. In a restaurant, some are in a hurry, some are not. In a bookstore, some just want to buy from the top ten, some would like to browse and find something eclectic. When buying insurance for a business, some customers simply want to know the bottom line, others want detailed explanations of the terms of the policy.

If we can somehow know what each customer requires in terms of adaptation for service delivery once the offer has been bought, then the chances of satisfying the customer increase. We can ask, observe, or let the customer choose through well-designed orientation panels. In the first two instances (ask or observe), the role of information is significant. For instance, from a satisfaction viewpoint industrial customers are often segmented into two segments: hassle-free and value-added. In the first category, all that the customer wants is zero hassle: all of the merchandise gets delivered on time, the bill is error-free, there is no quality issue and it works. In the second category, the customer also needs help in using the product, for example to improve productivity or assembly. Through a simple series of four or five questions, the department in charge of delivery or after-sales service (or, in smaller companies, the salesman) will be able to identify whether a particular customer is looking only at a hassle-free relationship, or also wants an element of added value. As a result, the salesman will be better able to adapt the service needs, even selling additional after-sale contracts for 'extra comfort'. (Typical questions might include: how can we help? What elements are particularly important (or what features are you looking for in particular)? How often do you buy? Will you require any additional support? Can I explain about our after-sales service?)

Clearly, asking customers questions so as to have information on how they like to be served is not always possible. Imagine a waiter who asks every customer whether they are in a hurry or not when they order a coffee, simply to know whether he should bring the bill with the coffee or when the customer asks. One could argue – wrongly – that the safest solution is to bring the bill with the coffee all the time – which will upset those who want to take their time and think the waiter wants to get rid of them quickly. As an alternative, the waiter may *observe* the customer's behaviour: does he look at his watch? does he have money in his hands when he orders? and so on. When this information is recorded for future contacts with the same customer, it becomes an *information-based customer satisfaction enhancement*. This is what has made the Ritz Carlton hotel chain, for example, world-renowned for its attention to customer satisfaction. All staff are trained to observe, discreetly asking questions and recording preferences on customer files so that next time they visit customer satisfaction can be even greater. If I order a tomato juice, next time there will be more tomato juice in my mini-bar; if I come from a specific region, next time I come to my room the TV channel in my bedroom will be tuned to my home base.

Using feedback from satisfied and dissatisfied customers

Of course, knowing what makes a customer satisfied (or dissatisfied) – and the relative importance of each factor in the customer's current or future buying behaviour – will help to improve satisfaction. Whether individually or by sample, any measure of customer satisfaction will help to highlight the priorities for improvement, as shown in Figure 3.4.

Figure 3.4: *Assessing information on customer satisfaction*

An interesting situation arises in the lower right quadrant, where current levels of satisfaction are high, but the relative importance to overall satisfaction is low. Selecting the best approach may mean redirecting resources to other priorities that are more valued by customers; or if the trend is for that particular area to increase in relative importance in the future then it might be worth keeping current levels of satisfaction high.

Angry customers – a special case

Angry customers are often the best allies of a firm: they provide free information for improvement and in general are the most loyal. Putting both reasons together means that the information provided by angry customers should be used actively to enhance customer satisfaction.

In order for the information provided by customers about poor quality to be used internally, there is a need for a clear and effective process. First, information on the reasons why customers are unhappy needs to be collected (only 10% of unhappy customers complain formally to the top of organizations). 90% of this information lies with distributors, front line personnel, and the field sales force, or is supplied on the telephone rather than in writing. For example, while studying the complaint process at a major automobile manufacturer, consultants from IMD found that only 7% of the information reached the top level of the organization – the rest lay with the dealers or regional managers. In another case, a formal survey of all customers of a tourist business showed that two-thirds of customers (about 120 000) had complained – whereas the company had formally received 'only' 10 000 letters of complaint.

You also need a mechanism of feedback to the appropriate department to resolve the problem and implement improvements quickly. For instance, at KAO, a Japanese cosmetics firm, all incoming calls at their central customer service department are immediately sorted and dispatched to 150 sites within the company (R&D, marketing, production, distribution) so that problems can be solved more quickly. In addition, some companies use special panels of customers who volunteer to give feedback quickly in order to solve problems faster. For instance, automobile manufacturers will use taxi drivers for feedback, since taxis do as much mileage in six months as an average driver would do in three years. The two information requirements for complaints handling are illustrated in Figure 3.5.

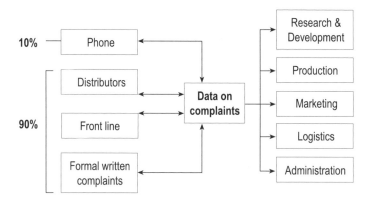

Figure 3.5: *Key information flows for effective complaint handling*

Using information to ensure customer delight

The next type of information needed to ensure customer satisfaction is that which enables the customer to be *delighted*. Delight occurs when the customer experiences a pleasant, unexpected surprise. Delight may also happen when the customer achieves an important target set together with their supplier or partner. In the first instance, only an intimate knowledge of a customer's needs, preferences and circumstances will help create a positive surprise. For instance, a customer who complains about a product defect six months later receives an invitation to see how – thanks to their remarks – the production process has been changed to prevent the problem. In the second instance (where the customer attains a significant target) information may be required on the performance achieved by the customer even before they know about it, so as to congratulate them for achieving a particular target. For instance, insurance companies will often encourage customers to avoid claiming in the last months of their policy so that they can keep their bonus rate.

Using information to verify that quality standards are being met

Quality is often defined as a level of excellence based on the needs and expectations of our target customers. However, the quality level has two aspects: as the customer

> "Customer information combined with internal business data is vital in managing performance and sustaining loyalty – it helps managers to control the gap between actual and perceived performance"

perceives it and as it is in reality. As mentioned previously, the level of complaints and measurements of satisfaction will provide the necessary information about customer satisfaction. But what about the quality in reality – both its level and the frequency with which it is achieved? Here, we need a different set of information relating directly to internal processes, such as delivery dates, failure rates, queuing rates, breakdowns, defects and others. These quality indicators, which can be computed directly from the business operations, also need to be supplemented by the 'softer' aspects of quality standards. Unlike those quality indicators on which information can be collected mostly automatically from the service delivery process, softer issues require direct observation with checklists, a technique that is often called the *mystery shopper technique*. An example of this is the Meridien hotel chain, which pays some customers if they agree to complete a 900-item checklist that lists all of the quality standards that the chain has defined for its luxury hotels.

Loyalty building and the need for even more information

Surveys of customer satisfaction show that to guarantee repurchase it is sometimes not enough simply to provide excellent customer service. Only very or completely *satisfied* customers will stay loyal and buy again. Assessing both the intention to

> "There is often a key aspect of customer satisfaction that, once attained, will boost the intention to repurchase"

repurchase for your industry as a whole (or key competitors) and your business in particular can be difficult, but using information in this way is a powerful means of monitoring service levels. It can highlight directly areas for improvement, removing complacency or ignorance about customer satisfaction and providing firm targets for the future.

Developing a successful customer loyalty scheme

There is a wide range of different alternatives to promoting loyalty, and a variety of schemes have been put into place. However, conditions for success generally include:

- Proposing meaningful benefits to loyal customers.
- Providing a good mix between tangible benefits (such as points, freebies and discounts) and soft benefits (such as service or value); tangible benefits are a necessary condition for success, but are not sufficient on their own.
- Completing a cost/benefit analysis to see whether the cost of providing the benefits is offset by increased loyalty and repeat business.
- Continuously upgrading and refreshing the scheme in order to keep customers motivated to stay.
- Communicating effectively, in a way that is adapted to different customer preferences, in order to continuously promote the benefits, get feedback and continuously refine and improve the process.

Customer loyalty schemes also require sophisticated information databases, including details for each customer of:

- Buying behavior (what, when, how much and, if possible, where and why they bought).
- Communication preferences for each customer (e.g. mail, e-mail, fax, phone, visits).

In addition to customer details, the information database also needs to provide:

- Constant updates on customer usage of loyalty benefits so as to promote, refine and extend the most popular benefits, developing and sustaining the overall success of the scheme.
- Cost/benefit effectiveness (global and per customer) of schemes.

CASE STUDY: CUSTOMER LOYALTY SCHEMES

Many industries are characterized by the fight not only to attract customers, but to retain their continuing support and loyalty once captured. This is clearly the nature of certain industries, such as computer games or mobile phones, where an 'installed base' of customers is an essential prerequisite for future revenue streams and profitability. In these industries, the importance of building market share is paramount. However, a stunning example of information used to enhance customer bonding and so improve competitiveness has been the worldwide growth of customer loyalty schemes.

Loyalty schemes have long been a feature of marketing programmes, with notable schemes including Green Shield stamps and, more recently, Air Miles. However, the growth has been in the number and types of firms (or groups of companies) offering loyalty programmes, as well as the diversity of those programmes. These have ranged from bookstores, such as WH Smith in the UK who have a sophisticated database of 3.9 million customers, through to credit card companies and telephone operators such as MCI in the USA, who have pioneered the friends and family discount for up to 12 contacts around a single customer. This single measure, undertaken with relatively modest advertising expenditure (reportedly one-twentieth of that spent by the market leader, AT&T), resulted in MCI gaining 4% market share at a time of fierce competition.

Currently the retail sector is gripped with a wave of customer loyalty programmes as supermarkets, clothing chains and other retailing businesses battle to build and maintain market share, using the weapon of added benefits (usually discounts or goods in kind) to gain loyalty and repeat business. The expansion into Germany and Britain of Wal-Mart, the US-based giant that competes aggressively on price and is currently the most successful retailer in the world, has intensified the battle for market share. The two main defences available to Wal-Mart's rivals in this battle for market dominance seem to be mergers and customer bonding through loyalty programmes. Once these weapons have built (or stabilized) market share, it seems likely that the next step will be to pass on economies of scale to consumers and compete aggressively on price – a strategy that has certainly worked for Wal-Mart.

The inventiveness of loyalty programmes is constantly surprising, providing insights into the brand values of the company as well as the threat that they pose to competitors. For example, the ingenious use of loyalty schemes for customer bonding is highlighted by the case of Virgin Atlantic. In order to reduce the time that it takes to get new customers, Virgin offers privileges to those involved in competitors' loyalty schemes: Virgin will offer a free companion ticket to any British Airways frequent flyer who has accumulated 10 000 miles! This approach provides the added advantage of reinforcing perceptions of the Virgin brand as being dynamic and flexible – if somewhat bold and outrageous.

BENCHMARKING

Assessing your business's bonds with its customers

Understanding how effectively your business relates to current and potential customers is an important first step in enabling you to develop a clear benchmark and set achievable targets for the future. The questions below will help to assess current realities and highlight areas for further development.

Organizational culture and structure

- Are the people liaising with customers empowered sufficiently to help them?
- Are customer complaints handled quickly, and are there processes in place to prevent problems recurring and to follow up complaints once the situation has been resolved?
- How are service quality problems resolved (how quickly, by whom and at what cost)? How could this be improved?
- Do the people developing the product offer (including all aspects of the product such as pricing and delivery as well as product benefits) have a good value proposition? How is this arrived at?

Issues of speed and efficiency are particularly important for service businesses (such as hotel chains), where frequently made claims of empowerment and customer service have to be realized quickly and routinely.

Personnel and skills development

- Are the people liaising with customers skilled at listening and recording customers' needs? This can be used for market sensing (see Chapter 5) as well as to enhance the sales proposition and to develop customer loyalty schemes.
- Are the right people in the right place at the right time?
- Is additional training needed? For example, would front-line personnel benefit from greater product knowledge?

Brand perception, marketing and customers

⟫ What do customers value most about your products? (It may help to list them in priority order.)

⟫ How can these benefits be extended profitably?

⟫ What do customers *dislike* about your organization or products? How can these issues be removed?

⟫ How many customers are retained (i.e. buy more than once)? How can this retention rate be improved – what would be a realistic target and timescale?

⟫ What contact does your organization have with its customers, and how well is this managed?

⟫ Are there any additional communication channels that could be used to link with your customers?

⟫ How can you involve your customers in the business on an ongoing basis (for example, through reward schemes or piloting new products)?

⟫ How does your organization monitor customer satisfaction?

These factors all influence and enhance customer loyalty schemes, adding value for customers. To ensure that schemes remain dynamic and in touch with what customers want it is vital to establish systems that easily capture market data. This issue is explored further in Chapter 5.

Innovation

⟫ How innovative is the business? For example, how often are new ideas generated to improve service to the customer and to differentiate the business from its competitors?

⟫ Who generates new ideas? Those with a close understanding of customer needs, or others?

⟫ How quickly, successfully and cost-effectively are new ideas implemented?

⟫ How effective is the process for anticipating customer needs?

Information systems

⟫ How detailed is your customer information? Does it *really* tell you what you need to know, or could it be improved?

⟫ Do people in the business share the same information?

⟫ Do the views of customers flow quickly to the right parts of the organization?

⟫ Does everyone that needs it have access to the necessary information?

⟫ How often is information relating to customers updated and distributed?

Customer database development

As companies see the power of having more direct data in helping to conquer, satisfy and keep customers, their response is, of course, to build common databases for all three needs. This is important as it will help the different departments in charge of conquest (marketing and customer service, sales), satisfaction (logistics, operators, after sales) and loyalty (marketing again) to access consistent, valuable information, digging into the datamine on a continuous basis. Typically, a customer database satisfying these three needs will have the following features:

- Segmentation of customers, including one segment detailing customer needs, wants and expectations.
- Best time and preferred means for communication per customer or segment.
- Behavioural patterns of customers, typically including response rates to marketing stimuli (such as special offer promotion); purchase patterns (amount, frequency, timing); any seasonal patterns or influences; the relative popularity and success of different sales channels (direct, indirect); location; buying intensity; and other relevant patterns.
- Demographic details of buyers, including profile, usage and addresses.
- Incidents and contacts with customers. Types of problems, how they were resolved and the satisfaction with the response are all highly relevant.
- Measurements of satisfaction, shown globally as well as for each segment and each individual.
- Scoring systems for each customer allowing selective targeting for new communications and new marketing stimuli, and helping to predict future behaviour. For instance, Laura Ashley discovered that those who buy new curtains are likely to change other parts of their interior design.
- Prospects of future business from each customer, possibly grading customers according to demographics, closeness or likelihood that they will reorder. A clear example of this is the seminar and conference business, where past delegates and customers are given a significantly higher priority as 'warm' or 'hot' contacts than the more general pool of potential customers.

Less than three years ago, only 10% of the Fortune 500 had such databases, and 50% of them were only in the process of compiling it. For 70% of them a database was perceived only as a mailing list. Some companies, such as Kraft who have 30 million customers in their database, have understood the gold mine. For example, American Airlines has 32 million customers and 60 companies participating in reward schemes. Microsoft UK established a database for its 30 000 customers who bought into their advantage loyalty program for an annual fee of £34.95: this scheme alone generated 111% of the revenues from Microsoft UK's non-card members.

Examples of databases used for successful customer bonding

Developing customer databases uses normal transactions as a starting point. However, some companies have gone much further and developed some ingenious, distinctive and popular marketing tools to gain access to customers. For instance, food manufacturers such as Unilever and Nestlé who are not in direct contact with consumers use promotions such as free samples to get addresses.

However they are acquired or built, customer databases can be used for conquest, satisfaction or loyalty. For instance, Nestlé's Casa Buitoni Club has 80 000 names of people who like pasta, with each member receiving a newsletter every quarter with recipes, as well as the opportunity to enter a competition providing free holidays in Italy. Nestlé claims that the Casa Buitoni Club has increased purchases of their pasta by 15%. Other examples of effective customer databases used for conquest, satisfaction and loyalty include:

- *Sotheby's*, the successful auction dealer, employs people whose role it is to wine and dine their prospective customers. This enables them to gain detailed records on customers' tastes as well as issues of inheritance, allowing them to propose legal advice and evaluation services. In addition, they ask each customer about their interests so they can invite customers to specific auctions based on their interests.
- *Procter & Gamble UK* markets the Pampers brand of babies' nappies by sending individualized birthday cards to babies (i.e. to 3% of the population).
- *The Financial Times* has expanded its business beyond newspapers to include publications, conferences, electronic online information and newsletters. In 1995 it started investing £250 000 to get on file 500 000 customers common to all businesses, so as to increase cross-buying.
- *British Airways'* Caress (Customer Analysis and Retention System) approach to customer complaints is *paperless*, scanning letters or inputting customer phone calls into a databank and then responding after five days, rather than the previous response time of 55 days.

Figure 3.6 highlights the information flow for all three uses (conquest, satisfaction and loyalty).

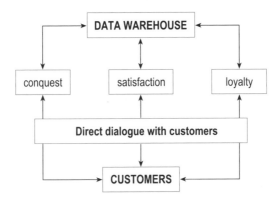

Figure 3.6: *Information flows for customer bonding*

Developing a database for all three parts of the customer bonding process – conquest, satisfaction and loyalty – will enable a business to improve its direct access to each customer through the customer's preferred channel, and will also provide a dialogue (or feedback) to fine tune its communications and general operations.

 **SUMMARY**

Using information to bond with customers

Customer bonding is a complex process that needs to be approached methodically, in the right sequence. That sequence involves *conquest* (proposing the right product), *satisfaction* (delivering well) and *loyalty* (keeping the customer satisfied).

Conquest

Two pieces of information are essential here. First, information for *targeting* that ensures that the right customers are communicated and attracted in the most effective way, and second, information for *customization* so that the differences between each individual customer are understood and accounted for.

Satisfaction

Four types of information are needed to achieve customer satisfaction:

1. Information enabling the business to adapt to specific customer requirements.
2. Information providing feedback from customers, highlighting areas for improvement, enhancing future relationships as well as solving problems.
3. Information ensuring that the business delights each customer.
4. Information verifying that service delivery corresponds to required standards.

Loyalty

Many diverse factors affect loyalty, but the one that can be controlled by the business most readily (and effectively) is the reinforcement of satisfaction with loyalty-building instruments. This in turn requires an understanding of the rewards that are likely to bring the greatest benefit: involving customers, gaining their commitment and developing strong, individual relationships.

Customer databases are vitally important as a tool for customer bonding, rather than simply as an end in themselves. As Michael Dell (founder of Dell Computer) emphasises: "The real value of a customer database is in providing a familiarity with the customer – a comfort level that personalizes the relationship. This is how information can really be used to bond with customers".

BEST PRACTICE

Techniques for successful customer bonding

There is a wide range of practical measures that can be adopted to enhance customer bonding, and inevitably many of these are specific to individual industries, as well as being dependent on the size and state of development of each business. The following checklist provides practical ideas for improving the business's bonds with its customers.

Key ideas

- Develop a dynamic, comprehensive database of customer information that enables your business to relate well to its customers (current and potential).
- Look at each stage of the bonding process and consider how you can:
  Conquer – capturing and gaining customers by *targeting* and *customizing*.
  Satisfy – by adapting product offerings, using feedback, delighting customers and maintaining quality standards.
  Develop loyalty – by developing loyalty-building programmes that enable strong individual relationships to be developed over time.
- Understand your competitors: what is it that attracts your customers to them?

Action checklist

Assess the current position   Understand how the business currently relates to its customers, what information is available and where the main areas for improvement lie. Discussing issues – concerns and opportunities – with customers is a good place to start (one adopted by businesses such as IBM and Harley-Davidson). (Key questions for assessing the current position are detailed in the *Benchmarking* section above.) In particular, consider each stage in sequence:

- *Conquest* involves targeting potential customers with a good value proposition.
- *Satisfaction* means delivering what is promised and, whenever possible, delighting customers.
- *Loyalty* requires constant reinforcement of customer satisfaction using rewards, customer involvement and effort to build strong, *individual* relationships over time.

Establish a clear, effective process for dealing with customer complaints
Few things are as damaging and undermining to customer relations as lacking information. Without the right information, mistakes recur, corrective action is late, wrong or simply non-existent. This process has two stages: first, information on why the customer is unhappy needs to be collected, and second, there needs to be a swift and effective feedback system ensuring that the problem is resolved and prevented from recurring.

Build a detailed customer database   Information about customers needs to be:

- as detailed as possible;
- used and updated regularly;
- widely understood and accessible to everyone in the business who may benefit;
- segmented, including a segment on customers' needs, wants and expectations.

Relevant information typically encompasses behavioural patterns, demographic data, measurements of satisfaction, modes of communication, scoring systems for each customer to help predict future behaviour, and prospects for future business.

Set targets for improvement   Specific targets can be valuable across the whole process of enhancing customer bonds. Targets might include goals for repeat business, improved information from customers or reducing customer complaints. They can also help to mobilize others in the process of developing customer bonds.

Address organizational issues   Information needs to be shared throughout the organization and this may require adjustments to the organizational structure and attitudes, as well as adapting processes.

Implement reward schemes   These are vital for building strong bonds with the customer and for developing loyalty. In order to find out what benefits customers would value most, it is advisable to ask them. Rewards also need to be targeted to each individual as closely as possible, *delighting* each individual.

Ensure that the process is dynamic   The three-stage bonding process needs to be methodical and self-sustaining. For example, customer loyalty cannot be developed without the two preceding stages being completed well. The key to ensuring that the process is efficient and dynamic is to collect, analyse and act on detailed information.

4

Information as a Service to the Customer

Chapter 3 focused on techniques for improving the
business's knowledge of the customer as a means of
creating loyalty and achieving successful customer bonding.
In this chapter, **Jacques Horovitz** reverses the approach,
outlining techniques for improving the customer's knowledge
to want to buy and stay loyal.

CASE STUDY: THE ROAD TO SUCCESS – USING INFORMATION TO SERVE CUSTOMERS

From 1989 to 1991, Ryder, the largest truck leasing business in the world, suffered a steady decline in their business. This was in common with the rest of their industry, which was also suffering the effects of recession; however, in the market for truck rental by consumers and small businesses Ryder slipped to second place. Their response included a range of significant measures, but chief among these was an understanding of the need to use information more effectively to serve customers.

The Ryder approach highlighted three key influences affecting loyalty from the customer's perspective:

1. *The need to help the customer buy – for example, by producing a brochure explaining explicitly why they should buy Ryder's insurance covering damage to the truck, as well as providing another brochure offering other supplies and accessories. Ryder also recognized that customers would want to compare them with their competitors, so they produced a truck comparison chart, highlighting their competitiveness and reassuring potential customers.*
2. *The need to help the customer use the service – Ryder provided a free guide, published in Spanish and English, to moving (entitled* The Mover's Advantage) *to every customer and potential customer.*
3. *The need to help customers to continuously adapt their usage – as well as ensuring that each outlet was well-ordered, displaying a strong sense of corporate identity and commitment to customer service. Ryder also ensured that there were additional products and services available at their outlets. This included information about the advantages of towing using Ryder's towing equipment, and details of longer-term discount rates to attract customers back.*

Furthermore, the benefit of these measures to customers was monitored closely with a customer satisfaction survey, placed prominently in each truck cab. Quite apart from checking that customers were satisfied, they also served to highlight Ryder's renewed commitment to service, enhancing future sales prospects. The measures that Ryder adopted also helped the customer to buy by readily providing information, establishing credence with customers (for example, by featuring testimonials in marketing literature) and by providing peripheral clues as to the quality of the business. For instance, each outlet was inspected monthly (not quarterly as before) to ensure that items such as literature, banners and signage were well laid out and appealing, enhancing the customer's perception of the business as well-organized and professional.

These measures were among a range of actions taken by Ryder, and their overall approach helped to turn around their business during a time of recession, returning the company to the number one position in their industry.

Overview

When we think of information and information management we mostly think about the *type* and *amount* of information that we need to make better business decisions;

we then build information systems and processes around our needs. IT people are rarely asked to think about information that would add value to the service that we sell. In fact in most companies this kind of information is left with the marketers or the operations people.

However, as we move into the digital economy, information as a means to help the customer buy and use our product should be thought of as a natural *co-product* or benefit of information management, rather than as a by-product. What will serve the customer can also serve us, as long as we are providing products and services where cognitive and rational arguments prevail for customers when they buy from us, use our products and services or have any contact with the business.

Companies that are providing products and services only through the Internet have to consider this dimension thoroughly, as it's the *only* way that they can help the customer buy. (For this reason, several notable examples from the e-commerce industry are included in this chapter, and indeed throughout the book; for a specific review of the techniques for building e-commerce capabilities, *see* Chapter 17.) The framework used in this chapter is similar to that used in the previous one on the use of information for customer bonding, except that here it is reversed. Our focus is not about improving our knowledge on the customer in order to create loyalty, but on improving the *customer's* knowledge to want to buy from us and stay loyal, two facets of the same coin. In this chapter we will:

- Outline the key influences affecting loyalty from the customer's perspective.
- Explain techniques for using information to sell, by improving customers' knowledge and their desire to stay loyal.

Understanding the customer's perspective

From the company's viewpoint, trying to keep customers for life is done in three steps. The first is *conquest* – attracting and capturing customers with a good value proposition (i.e. one that corresponds to customer needs) – and is well communicated to target customers. The second step is to s*atisfy* customers through good-quality products and services, speedy recovery in case of problems, and delight. The final part of the bonding process is to *retain* customers through recognition, rewards and working at maintaining good relationships.

However, from a customer's perspective, wanting to stay loyal also involves three stages where help from the business is valued:

- *Help me buy* something that corresponds to my needs at the best price (*helping customers buy*).
- *Help me to get it and use it* without problems or glitches (*serving customers effectively*).
- *Help me to continuously adapt* my usage of the product or service to my evolving needs, at the best cost (*helping customers to adapt their usage*).

The question then arises as to how information can help the customer achieve these aims, and how the design and management of information in a company can include the customers' point of view?

Helping customers buy

For customers there are three modes of search for deciding which product or service to buy:

1. *Information search*, by which customers try to collect information on product features, services, prices, benefits and costs of usage.
2. *Credence search*, by which they try to get a feel for the value of a product by knowing the reputation of a company through past customers and testimonials.
3. *Experience search*, with customers preferring to try a product before purchase by testing it or using it on trial, and then basing the judgement to buy on their feeling. Other peripheral 'clues' are also relevant: for example, the store is clean and well organized, therefore the merchandise must be good. The contract is well written and easy to understand, therefore the software that is specially designed for us will also be user-friendly.

Clearly, information has a major role to play in the first two modes. The following concerns are usually present in the customers' mind when they use a 'rational' search to buy a product or service.

●   Is it for me?
●   How much does it cost?
●   Can I choose easily? Can I be helped to decide?
●   How does it compare to other offers?
●   Is it available?
●   Can I try it?

The first question – is it for me? – is the toughest one from the information viewpoint because people do not simply buy products and services; instead, they buy *benefits* corresponding to their needs, or *solutions* to their current problems or challenges. Information can help answer the question by adding value to the product or service.

CASE STUDIES: HELPING CUSTOMERS TO BUY

An example of a business making an extraordinary effort to help customers buy is the famous case of Pioneer, who produced a seed for sale to farmers. Farmers don't just want seeds– they want to be helped with precision farming, and this includes issues such as managing yields as well as financial risk (which crops to produce according to crop prices). Other issues of concern to farmers include achieving optimal land usage, searching for the best markets for a particular crop (for example, a business such as Kellogg requires a specific kind of corn for its Cornflakes), using precision satellite weather forecasts to avoid disasters, and obtaining information about the use of chemicals and biotechnology products. Finally, as farmers had become businessmen they needed to know about credit and financial services. All these factors led Pioneer to provide information services as well as seeds; for instance, every farmer can connect by computer to satellite weather forecasts provided by Pioneer. In addition, the results of 100 000 side-by-side yield trials made by Pioneer with its competitors are also given to its customers.

Another example of a business using information to help customers to buy is SKF ball bearings operating in the replacement component market of the automobile industry. SKF has developed a kit that includes not only the ball bearings but also provides information on the type of model that it fits, as well as instructions on using them.

Enhanced value is therefore the first way in which information can play a role. In this case the information added to the product enhances the benefits for the customer. It provides a solution, not just a product. Information also helps customers to look at what they buy and how it will be used in the value chain.

When Dupont realized that it was not selling enough fibres for use in the carpeting industry, it decided to look at the whole value chain: carpet manufacturers, wholesalers, distributors (retailers) and customers. It found that many customers preferred tiles or wooden floors for ease of maintenance and durability, but also because of unsatisfactory experiences with retailers including inconvenient locations, unimpressive carpet ranges, lack of samples and unreliability for delivery and fitting. Dupont changed its division from carpet fibre to flooring systems and started to think more of the decorative and fashion features of carpets, rather than its functional ones (robustness, stain resistant, durable, noise and heat insulating). As a result, it developed information for the whole value chain, including new information and advertising for customers on how to buy and maintain carpeting, and the Dupont hotline for retailers provided answers on consumer questions. Dupont's expertise on products, selling and understanding consumers was also available to retailers on video. Dupont provided information on market trends for carpet manufacturers, wholesalers and retailers.

Serving customers effectively

Several questions are usually on the customer's mind once they have bought, including did I make the right choice? When am I going to get it? Is it ready? What do I need to know to use it properly? If there is a problem, will I know? Will they repair their mistakes? These questions can be answered using information in two forms: the customer gets answers to these questions either if they ask (reactive) or if the supplier provides the information (proactive). Also, the customer can retrieve answers to these questions (self-retrieval) or the supplier can give them. Thus four types of customer service information system can be designed, as shown in Figure 4.1:

	retrieval by customer	retrieval by supplier
reactive	self-service	helpful
proactive	smart	thoughtful

Figure 4.1: *Customer service information systems*

Self-service customer information systems

In the self-service mode, the customer will have to somehow figure out what they need to make it work and who needs to be involved. The problems with this approach are highlighted by the example of buying toys for children, only to find out when you returned home that you needed batteries and they are not in the box. The retailer did not tell you because you did not ask, and the manufacturer did not proactively put a battery in the package or train the retailers. The information was missing and the result was disappointment and annoyance; it destroyed part of the value of the product, at least for a while. A similar example is when you try to buy a computer together with software, a fax modem, printer and other peripherals all connected with a telephone and plug. Find me any of the actors involved (telecom company; PC, software, printer and cable manufacturer and retailer) that can give full, complete information about the *whole* range (including connection to an Internet provider, explanation about line charges or proactive guidance about the additional memory necessary for the types of applications needed) and I will pay double!

Smart customer service information systems

The smart mode is still on the customer side, but the supplier has proactively made available all of the information necessary for the customer to retrieve. For example, FedEx *supertracker* allows customers to track their parcels and know when they have arrived and who they were given to. Based on customer satisfaction survey results, Disneyland Paris has designed maps of its park in six different languages to help guests of different nationalities find their way. It also includes suggestions to help people use their time in the park most effectively, so as not to be in areas that are too crowded. It has been noticed, for instance, that most people go anticlockwise around the park, so one suggestion is to go the other way.

As well as written form (documentation), smart mode can also be supported in electronic form. For example, at a Hertz rent-a-car station you key in where you want to go and the computer will print directions to get there. I call it smart because it is a *good* service which is cheaper for the provider since the customer has to do the effort, but the provider has thought in advance of what information will be needed by the customer to effectively use their purchase.

Helpful customer information systems

Helpful customer information systems represent the majority of the designs. The customer wants to know issues such as when is it going to be delivered, how to use the machine, why it is broken, why they cannot fully use its features and so on, and they call a hotline – a central call centre or helpdesk with an individual that provides the answer. What the customer does not ask they do not get an answer to. Some companies are even smart over the short term, offering their customers a fixed number of answers before they charge. This system works well with more sophisticated customers (i.e. those that do not need the supplier very much). However, it usually causes dissatisfaction over time with many other customers, as their perceived value of the service goes down at a rate directly proportional to the time and energy they have to spend calling the help desk.

Thoughtful customer service information systems

Thoughtful customer information systems are both proactive and provided by the supplier. *Before* you have to call they will tell you what is wrong. *Before* you have to connect, they will tell you what you need to get from complementary suppliers (for example, for your home PC). For example, Amazon.com sends you suggestions of books to buy based on your reading profile; Robeco proposes investments based on your investor's profile. At Peapod.com, the Internet super-market, your usual lists come on screen so you don't have to repeat what you normally buy (such as baby food and nappies, which are not going to change dramatically from one week to the next). Thoughtful information for customers is, of course, the most sophisticated system, requiring almost one-on-one knowledge of customer needs. However, only on rare occasions are they used by manufacturers who see defects in their products according to the frequency and intensity of spare part changes. They wait until the customer complains or notices the problem to change it.

Helping customers to adapt their usage

Customers' needs constantly shift and evolve, and from the customers' perspective any help in adapting their usage to meet these evolving needs will enhance their loyalty. Loyalty from the customers' viewpoints is based mostly on the constantly renewed perceived value of keeping the same supplier. The type of questions that are on the customer's mind are: do I *feel* recognized? Do I *feel* rewarded for staying? Do I *feel* that I get greater or new value as my needs evolve? Am I constantly reassured that this relationship is the best for me?

Of course, information has a key role to play for the customer to say yes to these questions. However, since the questions include feelings – not just objective facts or data – it won't be enough on its own, but it certainly provides a good foundation. For example, if customers receive offers for products and services that are too general for their needs, how can they feel recognized? If you are a guest in a hotel staying with young children, what is the sense in the hotel proposing a golfing week outside the school vacation period? Why do many medical centres not remind people when they need a new eye examination or check-up, yet last time they mentioned that it would be wise to do it every two years? I don't *feel* they care. I don't *feel* they know me.

Loyalty from the customer viewpoint therefore has to do with relationships, not trans-actions, and the job of the supplier is to maintain the relationship, partly through information provided to the customers. This use of information can take many forms; some popular ideas include:

- Offering customers something new especially for them (added value, new products and services, special offers).
- Supplying customers with details of other people who had the same problems and how they solved them.
- Reminding customers what they have to do – and when – in order to take full advantage of their purchase (e.g. maintenance, service visit, check-up).
- Supplying customers with a competitive analysis or customer sales survey highlighting product and service superiority.
- Providing a special offer for customers who we know do a lot of business with us.

However trivial some of this information may seem, it is invariably not provided. This tends to be because relationship management is rarely promoted: sales people are often rewarded on the basis of the *new* customers that they attract rather than existing ones that they keep.

Using information for selling

Information is a vital tool for selling and can be employed to enhance customers' knowledge, understanding and overall loyalty. Some of the key applications of information for selling include using information to:

- help customers' decision-making;
- enable customers to compare offers;
- support transparency of pricing;
- highlight availability.

Information to aid customer decision-making

Customer concerns such as 'Can I choose easily and can I be helped to decide?' are resolved with the use of information. At the online bookstore Amazon.com there are

> "'Traditional' non-e-commerce companies are far behind in providing information to help customers choose or decide, compared to companies selling on the Internet"

many possible approaches to help find a book, and in this significant respect it is far superior to the classical bookstore in which the books are usually assigned to a single theme. Sample chapters are also available as well as reviews by critics and other customers, supporting both the credence and experience of searches. With Microsoft and other software companies selling through the net, it is possible to download software and try it before it is sold commercially. However, much less common are instances where the supplier provides tools for diagnosis or testing in order to help the customer choose. Opportunities for such tools clearly exist; they include self-diagnosis tools and assisted diagnosis tools.

Self-diagnosis tools

Whether the customer is buying insurance, selecting a vacation or choosing the right milking equipment for their farm, it is possible to design a diagnostic tool that will get the customer to the product that they need. This works by getting the customer to answer simple questions that are scored and lead to an optimal solution.

CASE STUDY: CLUB MED AND THE KEY TO HAPPINESS

The Key to Happiness was a self-diagnosis tool developed for Club Med customers. The business had found that over 40% of customer dissatisfaction was linked directly to customers being recommended (or allowed to choose) the wrong type of location for their needs. For example, a family would unwittingly choose a resort designed for singles, or a couple wanting to discover the local customs would mistakenly visit an empty island. Further studies showed that in fact there were six customers segments: the tubes *who like to be comfortable and with their family; the* celebrators *who like to party;* epicureans *who prefer a high level of comfort; the* cultivated *who like to discover the country – its culture, history and charm; and* activists *who want to get in shape and enjoy sports. The key to happiness was a self-serving system designed to help customers, using questions to find out which of the six categories best suited the customer and which village would serve them best. It was available in each Club Med retail outlet.*

Assisted diagnosis tools

In this case, the information is collected transparently by the supplier, with the best or optimal options provided to the customer. For example, mobile phone sales people increasingly ask potential customers about their likely usage; whether calls will be local, national or international; whether usage will be high, medium or low; and the type of features that they would like with their phone. They are then able to help the customer decide which option is the most suitable for them.

Information for the customers to compare offers

Of course, customers can collect information on what the competitor is offering in terms of features, benefits, price and other key issues. However, this is time-consuming, cumbersome and sometimes limited. The real challenge is for a *competitor* to provide this information. Clearly, the business following this path has to be confident of their value proposition, but it certainly adds value to the customer. Another way to approach this issue is to list the criteria by which the overall purchase should be judged, detailing the *total cost of possession*. For example, one of Club Med's most successful advertising campaigns in the 1970s detailed what its price per day included (room, full board and wine, activities, entertainment, instruction, kids' club), and then invited its customers to ask competitors to give the prices of all the extras listed and compare. FNAC, a 'consumerist' retailer of photographic and audiovisual equipment, has, since inception, provided their views of the branded products that they sell in a newsletter available at the counter. They use objective measurements through their own testing laboratory and share this information, clearly taking the viewpoint of the customer as opposed to the point of view of the supplier and the type of margin it could offer.

Price transparency

Transparency of pricing is at the heart of this comparison of competitors' offers. Again, not many companies are eager to do that. Among the worst here are professional service companies (such as consultants and accountants) which provide a total amount, or an amount of man-days with a standard price per man-day. Often the customer never knows who will be in the team, whether the amount of time is correct, or how the bill was calculated. As a rule of thumb, one could argue that those who provide neither price transparency enabling comparison between prices, nor information on how the price is arrived at, have a lower sustainable competitive advantage than those who do. GE has started such a program. For each component needed from its 25 000 suppliers, its trading network system can get quotes in a matter of hours from the two or three suppliers worldwide that would best fit its requirements.

> **"Through the digital economy it becomes easier for customers to scan different offers, to the point where if the supplier does not help in determining price comparisons customers will do it for themselves"**

Interestingly, greater price transparency has been cited as one of the major benefits to consumers that will result from the full introduction of the Euro into the 11 participating EU member states. Price differences for the same product (quoted for the first time in the same currency) between the 11 states will, it is believed, need to be explained to consumers or removed.

Availability

Finally, as far as helping the customer to buy is concerned, information on *availability* is a key concern as well as a potential source of competitive advantage. Hewlett Packard devised a system available on computer to all its account managers selling to large distributors in Europe, so that they could immediately tell their customers how long their order would take to deliver, as well as tracking orders that had been received. Electronic data interchange (EDI) allows direct or assisted interfaces between customers and suppliers, reducing the cost of the supply chain for the customer and without the need for confirmations or waiting time, as well as enhancing customer value. This is achieved by reducing uncertainties and answering questions such as where do I stand? Where is my order? When can I get it?

SUMMARY

Information as a service to the customer

From the customer's perspective, loyalty requires three elements from the business:

- help for customers to *buy*;
- help for customers to *obtain what they want and use it effectively* (serving customers);
- help for customers to *adapt their usage to their evolving needs, at the best cost*.

Information helps customers in all three of these areas. It is valuable in helping customers buy by supporting their search for *information*, *credence* and *experience*. It helps serve customers effectively by providing the right information at the right time, in the right manner. This is highlighted by the four modes of customer service: self-service, helpful, smart and thoughtful, depending on whether information retrieval is reactive or proactive, and undertaken by the customer or supplier. Finally, information is an essential tool for building loyalty. Its significance has already been highlighted in Chapter 3, but from the customer's viewpoint loyalty is concerned with *relationships*, not transactions. The key to success here is to understand individual customers as closely as possible, tailoring offers not only to attract new customers but also to most accurately meet existing customers' needs.

Leading on from this point is the central role of information for selling. This can be achieved in many ways, including:

- helping customers' decision-making;
- enabling customers to compare offers;
- supporting transparency of pricing;
- highlighting availability.

One of the most significant tools – or battlefields – is the Internet, which is being used with increasing effectiveness for all four of these tasks.

Figure 4.2 summarizes the different elements presented in this chapter.

Most of this information is not built into the information systems of a company, but needs to be consciously designed and developed. Each element can in fact be seen as a separate module with different components:

- a customer database that includes details of second and subsequent purchases;
- a competition and industry database;
- a link between our products and services and each individual customer;
- a link between added-value information and each customer in the database;
- a link between production, logistics and each customer.

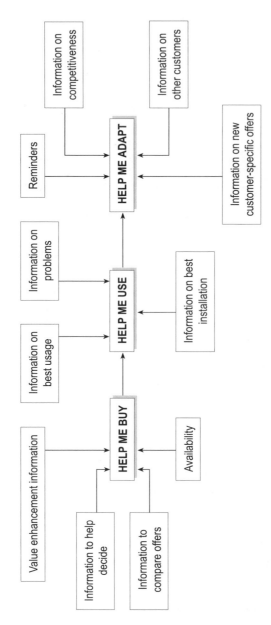

Figure 4.2: *Customers' information needs*

BEST PRACTICE

Using information as a service to customers

Developing links between all functions and customer queries

There is both a positive and negative aspect of enhancing customer knowledge for decision-making. The positive aspect, as mentioned, is that customers will be aware and able to buy, as well as feeling satisfied and more inclined to stay loyal. The other side of the coin is the negative factor: lack of information may result not only in lost sales but in other factors too, such as an erosion in brand loyalty and increasing frustration. The need to enhance customer knowledge can become manifest in myriad ways – many of them seemingly minor. For example, why is the head-office switchboard often not able to give the address of the store near you? It is therefore important to establish two links:

- a link between marketing information, technical service and each customer; and
- a link between feedback from unhappy customers, defects and each customer.

As the cost of information storage decreases the time that it takes to retrieve information is also reduced; it should, therefore, be fairly easy to build these linkages, as long as the people responsible for information systems understand it is a priority and integrate it into their design.

Techniques for using information for selling

Consider how best to aid customer decision-making, remembering the customers' desire to choose easily and be helped to decide. Diagnosis tools that collect and rationalize information, completed either by the customers themselves or the supplier, can be practical ways of ensuring that customers reach the decision that is best for them quickly and easily.

Comparing offers and ensuring price transparency not only helps customers to buy, but can also provide a valuable measure of confidence and reassurance that can be important for future business. That is the positive view: the other side of the coin is the need to recognize that if your business does not readily provide this information then your competitors may; or the customer will increasingly be in a position to find it out for themselves, without the added value of your help.

Measuring customer satisfaction on information issues

Of vital importance is the measurement of customer satisfaction on information issues. I often design questionnaires of customer satisfaction according to the three phases of concern to the customer described in this chapter: buying, using and adapting. Questions that might be included in questionnaires include:

- How satisfied were you with the information that you received to help you decide?
- How satisfied were you with the answers to all the questions you asked?
- Did you perceive that the proposal had superior value compared to competitive offers?
- How satisfied were you with the information provided to install the equipment (or to use the equipment)?
- How satisfied were you with problem identification on your installation?
- How satisfied were you with the information provided about new products?
- What additional information would you like to receive?

Once asked, this information needs to be carefully analysed, updated and above all acted on to ensure that the customer is best served by the use of the information.

5

Releasing the Power of Market Sensing

Market sensing is not a distinctive core capability and it does not guarantee competitive advantage. Instead, it represents 'table stakes' at a time when expenditures on activities designed to better understand customers are growing rapidly. In this chapter, **Sean Meehan** explains what market sensing is, what represents best practice, and how organizational capabilities must be aligned to leverage sensing effectively.

CASE STUDY: DAEWOO WINS THROUGH RESPONSIVENESS TO THE VOICE OF THEIR CUSTOMERS (IMD, 1998)

In 1993 Daewoo embarked upon an aggressive international expansion. It aimed to be at least the tenth largest car company in the world by 2000. West European markets were key targets. The UK launch was planned for April 1995, and a market share of 1% was to be attained by March 1998. Although this may appear a trivial target, such a share had never been achieved by a new entrant in anything like that timeframe. Additional challenges for Daewoo were that:

- *The two launch models were reboxed third-generation Vauxhalls.*
- *The market was crowded with well-established players who achieved wide coverage in terms of product range, geography and share of voice. The big three manufacturers (Ford, Vauxhall and Rover) accounted for over half of all new cars sold.*
- *Its two models were aimed at segments representing only 60% of UK sales. With no EU manufacturing facility, Daewoo was effectively excluded from the very substantial fleet market. Furthermore, with no diesel models, the available market shrunk by an additional 22% of the UK market.*
- *Daewoo brand recognition was virtually zero and the country of origin (Korea) had not established any positive reputation for product quality.*

In spite of these obstacles, Daewoo achieved its target in less than one year. *Central to Daewoo's success was their approach of creative* market sensing *and being highly responsive to what it had learned in the market place.*

In addition to their early market research, Daewoo successfully integrated a policy of customer orientation into its positioning. For example, pre-launch advertisements not only heralded Daewoo's approach but were also used to solicit opinions about exactly what people wanted (and what they did not); they were used to highlight Daewoo's customer-focused approach, and also to build a database of sales leads that had responded to the campaign. This database alone yielded 12% of the first year's customers, and their targets were achieved early largely as a result of the extent to which Daewoo developed, refined and sold their value proposition, using creative market sensing.

Overview

Perhaps the most common understanding of market sensing is market research, often carried out by specialist agencies or in-house departments. Market research is frequently undertaken in order to better understand a market prior to entry with a new product or service, to interpret an important shift in demand conditions, or simply to continuously monitor and track the sensitivity of target groups to media and other signals.

Resources committed to understanding the marketplace through market research are growing unabated. An annual ESOMAR (1997) study reported that worldwide turnover (revenues) of companies or institutes engaged in the business of providing market research for clients rose by 18% in 1997. Moreover, this is simply an indicator of growth – companies spend at least a further 25% on salary costs of in-house experts, systems and management time directed to the learning task. This suggests that managers know that they should be better informed about their markets and are investing in doing just that. However, it may be the case that with more and more data about the market being generated and interpreted there are fewer and fewer meaningful insights to be gained from formal market research investigations.

However, market research is only one aspect of market sensing. Understanding market sensing in terms of the formal gathering of data through market research is perhaps inadequate and distracting, in spite of the vast sums reportedly being spent on this activity. It is more helpful to think of it in terms of what it takes to inform and replenish a manager's *mental model* of the marketplace in which they operate.

> **"Market sensing includes all activities that help firms to understand the market. It is everyone's responsibility, and encompasses *any* factor that relates to the current and future market situation"**

A mental model is simply an understanding that a manager carries around in his head about who his customers are, what drives their purchasing behaviours, whether in general they are satisfied or not (and why), and how their competitors are placed. Market sensing, therefore, should not be thought of only in terms of formal activities such as conventional market research studies, but should also embrace all activities that modify a manager's mental model of the marketplace. My definition is:

Market sensing refers to all actions, formal and informal, systematic and random, active and passive, engaged in by all members of an organization, which determine and refine individual or collective perceptions of the marketplace and its dynamics.

Two particular aspects of this definition are important. First, market sensing as a process is all-inclusive (i.e. formal *and* informal, systematic *and* random, active *and* passive). Second, it is not owned by one specific function, it is everyone's concern. In particular, it is not the job of the marketing or the strategy department to ensure that the business has achieved an accurate understanding of the market. In fact, those companies who seek to push ownership of this responsibility into one function or department are missing the point. It is critically important that knowledge about marketplace dynamics (and in particular those that are changing) circulates around the firm so that all managers behave in a manner consistent with the newly understood realities of the market. In this chapter we will:

- Outline how market sensing works in practice to create competitive advantage and enhance performance.
- Explain the two main pitfalls of market sensing and how to avoid them.
- Explore the central importance of responsiveness to successful market sensing.

The power of market sensing

So, does market sensing work to enhance performance? Intuitively, yes. The knowledge of marketplace dynamics gained through market sensing is a little like motherhood. It is hard to argue that it isn't good or that more of it isn't better. Many managers hold the view that as market sensing leads to a better understanding of how target customers perceive value it should enhance performance in terms of sales growth, market share and profitability, as illustrated in Figure 5.1.

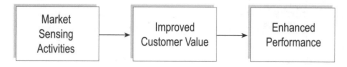

Figure 5.1: *Market sensing as a means of enhancing performance*

It is fair to suggest that firms who get it right in terms of market sensing will today enjoy significant competitive advantage. Successful market sensing provides firms with tremendous insights enabling them to understand customer motivations, buying patterns and value equations. Similarly, they fully understand the relative merits of competitors' offers and, perhaps more importantly, their strategic intent. They can therefore position their offering so as to enjoy positive performance: creating sustainable customer value and providing real economic benefit to shareholders and other stakeholders (such as employees and the community).

Potential pitfalls of market sensing

While most companies engaged in market sensing achieve superior performance – meaning enhanced returns from the market – some do not. Before addressing the question of how market sensing enhances performance, it would perhaps be beneficial to consider why and under what conditions some firms engage in market sensing without enjoying any positive performance outcome. There appear to be two reasons why some firms see no performance enhancement arising from such investments: data infatuation and, counter-intuitively, customer focus.

Data infatuation

Having woken up to the power of market intelligence, senior management rewards and endorses those projects and initiatives that are, or appear to be, supported by 'thorough' analysis. Line management learns the political value of such analysis and embarks upon a frenzy of research initiatives designed to support (or at best refine) some predetermined course of action. I have recently observed two competing divisions issuing divergent recommendations on the foot of the same piece of research. One division had clearly overstated the power of the findings of a marginally complex analysis (i.e. the recommendations were not really supported by the analysis, but in the absence of an opposing case the interpretation was accepted).

Following my review, a discussion about the use of market research ensued, with the organization reaching several key conclusions:

- Much of its research was carried out on a one-off basis responsive to very focused questions posed by specific business units, without much consideration for insights gained previously from other business units.
- The research questions were insufficiently open and objective and thus didn't offer much opportunity for learning, focusing instead on specific answers to predetermined questions.
- In practice it was very subjective in how it interpreted research results, often fitting the results to its preconceived ideas.

All of these factors left the results open to manipulation, serving the confirmatory purposes of the researcher without adding significantly to the institution's knowledge of the marketplace. This experience could be drawn from many businesses who learn that being more informed is not necessarily the same as being a smarter organization.

Customer-focus at the expense of competitor awareness

Whilst it is true that the more you know about how your customers perceive your offer and your performance, the better, this well-intentioned sentiment ignores a critical dimension – your current and potential customers' perceptions of competitors' offerings. It is through a real, if often subconscious, evaluation of competing value propositions that buyers discriminate. Therefore although it is crucial to participate in learning about customers, you must similarly learn about competitors.

Most companies can justifiably claim to undertake some rudimentary form of competitor monitoring. All too often, however, it is undertaken periodically by an analyst relying on secondary data sources. The output of the activity is rarely, if ever, shared beyond the top management team. The limitations of such an approach become apparent when contrasted with the more progressive vision of the managing partner of a well-known management consultancy, describing his vision for a newly instituted competitor monitoring system:

"I need to understand how my competitors think. Our investments in monitoring and understanding our competitors will be justified only when we can predict our competitors' moves."

His firm's 'new' (in the early 1980s) system continues to mobilize all of his several thousand partners and managers who are meeting with customers, competitors, suppliers and others, all of whom may have something small to report about one of a handful of pre-identified competitors. His rationale was that by setting up a system into which small pieces of information could be entered easily, trends and patterns of behaviour would become apparent. What in isolation may seem insignificant may become important when put in the context of other 'insignificant' data. Reports today suggest that he is more than satisfied with his return on investment.

Some businesses, therefore, are hindered by a restrictive view of market sensing, limiting it to market research, mostly with a focus on customers without thinking too hard about customer value and therefore about competitors. Other companies, however, do get it right on the sensing dimension and still fail to achieve the expected return from having developed this competency – why?

Responsiveness to market intelligence

My research suggests that much of the performance difference among firms that are active market sensors arises because they respond quite differently to their newly acquired intelligence. Put simply, advantage accrues to those firms able and willing to act on their market intelligence. Sometimes this can have major consequences, including:

- restructuring entire organizations;
- more frequently, cannibalizing an existing successful product with a lower margin substitute;
- hiring different types of people with different capabilities than the organization is used to.

Clearly, these are more difficult decisions than simply deciding to develop a market sensing capability. The realignment required to be truly responsive to the voice of the market can often be so great that it requires significant courage, persistence and an appetite for change. Market sensing's impact on performance is therefore indirect, acting through a responsiveness dimension (*see* Figure 5.2).

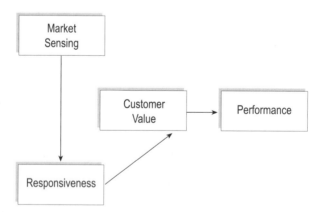

Figure 5.2: *The impact of market sensing on performance relies on responsiveness*

In a sense, responsiveness embraces the notion of aligning human and capital resources with the market opportunity (or in this context, realigning those resources). In many cases, companies are so utterly embedded in their and their competitors' way of behaving in a market that they cannot break out of the box and respond to the opportunity they have perceived. This certainly was not the case with celebrated rule-breakers such as CNN, Dell, First Direct and IKEA who, by focusing on how they could create new value by serving a market segment in a specific manner, could create and share that new value with the customer group. Daewoo Motors' successful entry into the highly competitive UK market offers a vivid account of how not to get shackled by industry norms. It shows that by listening to the voice of the market (using unusually creative techniques) and responding to it by aligning all elements of the product offering, your value proposition has instant appeal even in the face of entrenched competition.

Creative market sensing

Daewoo's approach to market sensing

An impressive example of the power of creative market sensing was shown by Daewoo's entry into the competitive UK car market in 1995. Their challenges and targets were significant, notably a 1% share of the UK market within three years, yet this was achieved within one year in spite of the handicaps mentioned earlier. Daewoo's early research found traditional buyers of medium-sized vehicles to be increasingly interested in functionality, style and price, and less interested in mechanical details. More importantly it found that buyers did not enjoy the buying experience. They disliked the inevitable haggling process with the dealer whom they considered too pushy. Additionally, buyers felt cheated on service, both in the process of buying a car and in terms of after sales service. They also felt that the claims of after-sales service benefits by established players lacked credibility. In short, the customer-focused car brand didn't exist in the minds of Daewoo's target market. It was clearly an available market position, provided that the

> "For Daewoo, market sensing provided precise, unique insights into the market that were so valuable they not only indicated where enhanced customer value lay, but ultimately provided a platform for a highly distinctive advertising campaign"

offer was right. The market research findings suggested to Daewoo that it should set up a wholly owned dealer network with all the service quality control that that implied.

Daewoo integrated its policy of customer orientation further into its positioning. Two advertisements, which were key to its pre-launch activity, successfully solicited additional input from prospective customers. One advertisement proclaimed:

After 15 years of making cars all over the world, Daewoo is coming to Britain. And as part of that process we are looking for guinea pigs to test drive 200 Daewoo cars for a year.

It invited viewers to call and explain why they should be one of the 200 selected. Daewoo viewed this as an opportunity to:

- Seek ideas by asking people what they disliked about the process of buying a car and car ownership, and what they wanted from a new company.
- Demonstrate that they are, in fact, customer-focused – after all, they were seeking real input into the design and enhancement of their value proposition. They believed this would set them apart from other manufacturers from the outset.
- Build a database of highly predisposed respondents to this campaign who would feel more 'ownership' of this brand and hence more rapid sales growth when the car went on sale.

In total 200 000 viewers responded, supporting their view that there was a market position available. 65% returned completed detailed questionnaires, yielding the largest response base to a survey by a car manufacturer ever in the UK. Examples of some of the important insights it provided were (Duckworth et al., 1996):

- 57% agreed that buying a car should be fun but always ends up being a hassle.
- 95% wanted longer, more comprehensive test drives than they currently received.
- 63% found showrooms intimidating and felt that the dealer always comes out on top.
- 95% believed dealers should be more like other retailers and less like car salesmen.
- 84% said that the dealer's attitude is as important as how they feel about the car.

And once they owned the car:

- 57% claimed that they did not trust the motor trade when it comes to servicing their car.
- 60% said that service deteriorated after buying a car.

We can be fairly sure that other car manufacturers were at least aware of the gist of such findings. Their investment in the prevailing infrastructure and channel system of 'independent' dealers, however, would make it very difficult to respond with confidence to fix the problem. They were handicapped in their ability to realign and respond to the voice of the market. This presented Daewoo, a new entrant, with a unique opportunity.

The Daewoo response

Daewoo rejected the option of recruiting unaffiliated dealers – they would have had a major retraining task and they were not convinced that this would produce the change in behaviour needed. Establishing a limited number of their own outlets was attractive despite the capital costs involved: they would not lose commission to a third party dealership. Salespeople were hired from outside the industry to avoid perpetuating perceived bad practice. Salaries were not dependent on volume and prices were fixed. Haggling was futile as the quoted price was all-inclusive, representing the total financial cost of ownership in the first three years. Some non-financial benefits were also included in the offer: Daewoo would bear the time and inconvenience costs of repair or service. Collectively, these actions put in place tangible evidence of the fact that Daewoo was serious about responding to the issues they had learned through their market sensing activities.

Daewoo was crystal clear about their value proposition and it resonated in the marketplace. Within six months it had become the most successful new entrant into the UK's crowded new car market. In its first full year its market share reached 0.92%, almost achieving its three-year target of 1% which had been considered bold and unrealistic by many insiders and observers alike. Its remarkable success cannot be explained solely by its particularly creative and noteworthy approach to market sensing – car companies are amongst the heaviest users of market research; rather it is the *degree to which it responded* emphatically to what its customers told it in research.

Daewoo was clear about its value proposition and how its offering was distinct from its competition. It was also clear on which dimensions not to compete. What is particularly interesting about this story is that the method of recruiting respondents secured, engaged or involved people who all shared a common perspective on the motor trade. In a sense, these respondents were contributing to the success of the brand from the outset. In fact, in addition to recruiting market research respondents, Daewoo's advertising also helped to drive brand awareness and support the task of positioning as a customer-friendly brand.

CASE STUDY: TESCO AND THE IMPORTANCE OF RESPONSIVENESS IN CHANGING THE MANAGEMENT MINDSET

Tesco, in the early 1990s the number two food retailer in the UK behind Sainsburys, needed to find a distinctive issue on which it could take on the market leader and win. On the issues of value and choice they could hold their own, and the issue they chose to compete on was the shopping experience. The key to Tesco was not simply to be seen as being on the customers' side but to translate that into what the customer wanted – an improved shopping experience. Tesco therefore introduced the hugely effective 'Every little helps' campaign delivering a range of innovations. These included one in front (opening a new checkout if there is more than one person in front of the customer in the queue); privilege parking close to the entrance for parents with small children; baby changing facilities; bag packing at the checkout (an innovation for the UK market); the ability to return any item of food for whatever reason; and several other popular features.

This example highlights the competitive advantages that market sensing can generate. It is no coincidence that for Tesco, responding to the process of market sensing led to improved customer service and a better buying experience. The impact of this approach was enormous and it played a major factor in Tesco becoming the UK's leading food retailer in the latter half of the 1990s. The approach enabled the company to enhance its offer to the consumer and the philosophy behind 'Every little helps' also provided a platform for a highly successful advertising campaign. In the highly competitive business of food retailing, market sensing provided Tesco with a valuable advantage, until their competitors were forced to adopt similar measures.

BENCHMARKING

Assessing market sensing within your organization

Assessing your organization's market sensing abilities is valuable in understanding both *where* and *how* to make improvements. Key issues to consider include understanding the extent to which an informed, dynamic, mental model of the market guides *all* manager's actions. It is also worth considering how well information about the marketplace flows around the organization. For instance, is understanding of market realities consistent and co-ordinated?

An over-emphasis on gathering and measuring data at the expense of analysis and action can afflict many organizations, and it is worth considering the extent to which this *data infatuation* may be present. It is also important to consider whether market data is used merely for political purposes, justifying predetermined courses of action. If so, the research methods may be inadequate and skewed, possibly resulting in inaccurate and flawed results.

Market awareness and understanding needs to continually guide managers' actions, therefore it is fundamentally important that market intelligence is accurate, realistic and unbiased. Furthermore, if the data provides unique insights that are not readily available to competitors then that can provide a valuable basis for action that delivers competitive advantage. As a result, it is worth considering:

▸ How *unique* are the insights into the market that are influencing your organization?
▸ How are competitors perceived in the market?
▸ How well are competitors' actions monitored?

The key is to view competitors from the customers' viewpoint, ensuring a customer focus (as illustrated by Daewoo and Tesco) rather than adopting a dismissive or superficial approach to the realities of the market. Understanding these realities does not simply mean focusing on customers, but understanding the competitive situation and how it evolves as well.

> **"Understanding and 'sensing' the market is clearly important, but to be effective means being willing and able to *act effectively* on market intelligence"**

The organization's responsiveness to market information and its creativity is another vital area to consider. In particular, how *responsive*, flexible and prepared to change is your organization to the needs of the customer and the realities of the market (notably competitors' actions)? Coupled with this is the issue of how *creative* your organization is in its response to market data. This can be achieved in a variety of ways, and regularly meeting and talking to customers – a valuable source of good ideas as well as guiding insights – is one of the most effective. The Daewoo case highlights the value of being prepared to turn a business on its head in order to respond to market insights. Organizations need to be flexible and adaptive, but they also need to generate ideas based on market intelligence that will enhance competitiveness. To ensure responsiveness it may therefore be necessary to consider:

- restructuring the organization;
- modifying product development strategies;
- hiring people with different capabilities than the organization (or the industry) is used to.

These changes are examples of the actions that may be required to align the organization to the realities and opportunities of the market. As a result of their scope and complexity, a major process of organizational change may be needed to enhance competitive advantage.

What makes a firm responsive to the voice of the market?

The Daewoo example illustrates that the relationship between market sensing and customer value (and thus superior business performance) is indirect – through responsiveness including, where necessary, realignment of the business. For most businesses the alignment issue is somewhat less dramatic than for Daewoo. Usually firms seek to steer behaviour of all employees by actively encouraging and reinforcing action that is seen to be customer-sensitive. Informal rewards such as peer recognition appear to be much more likely to reinforce the desired behaviour than more formal mechanisms such as financial bonuses. Of greater importance than reward systems are the extent to which the business's efforts are co-ordinated between departments. That is, the organization as a whole is focused on creating customer value: the finance, manufacturing and R&D functions are as concerned with creating customer value as is the marketing function.

One of the most interesting questions is *why* some firms develop an infrastructure that emphasises market responsiveness. It seems that the managers' beliefs and values – their collective mindset about what really matters and how they want things done – are key determinants of whether these mechanisms and structures really are effective, both in terms of generating market understanding through market sensing and being responsive. Our evolving model of how market sensing works to impact performance should therefore encompass the critical antecedent role of the management mindset (*see* Figure 5.3).

Evidence from my own research suggests that management teams in high-performing companies are characterized by a passion for experimentation and learning and for a healthy disregard for prevailing industry norms. They tend also to have

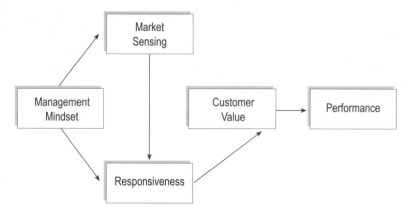

Figure 5.3: *The critical role of the management mindset*

a healthy respect for hierarchy but not to the extent that it dominates individual empowerment and willingness to respond. Such teams rely on respect for individuals' ideas and interpretations rather then decision-making rules. This enhances the speed and quality of information flow. Understanding about marketplace dynamics is openly shared and debated on an ongoing basis. One of the ways they do this is to adopt a non-threatening, apolitical perspective that seeks to promote trust between individual team members. The prevailing mindset is, therefore, that information about the realities of their own value-creating potential should be shared widely, challenged regularly and enhanced throughout the process of creating value.

CASE STUDIES: CREATING CUSTOMER VALUE: EASYJET AND THE 'BIG FIVE' PROFESSIONAL SERVICE FIRMS

Two examples from quite different industries at different stages in their development, Easyjet and the 'big five' professional service firms, demonstrate that meaningful alignment with the market is a reflection of management mindset.

One very startling example of this is the case of Easyjet, a UK budget airline competing with the likes of GO (a subsidiary company of British Airways), Ryanair, and of course the major scheduled airlines, ferries and bus companies. Easyjet's founders have sought from day one to minimize bureaucracy and hierarchy as much as possible. One way that they do this is to make virtually all information in the company, except payroll details, openly available. All mail, memos, business plans, sales data are scanned and are accessible to the whole organization. Easyjet's marketing director, Tony Anderson, has a direct telephone line (and no secretary to field calls), achieving the dual benefits of cost reduction and being in constant, direct touch with customers, suppliers and employees, all offering suggestions as to how to make a good service even better. Southwest, the US airline that successfully pioneered the idea of a no-frills airline loved by employees and customers alike, is clearly a role model for Easyjet, but even Southwest has not taken such an open approach to its handling of information.

Perhaps the best example of alignment reflecting a culture dedicated to customer value creation is the 'big five' (Meehan and Barwise, 1998). These are the professional services firms whose antecedents are in the provision of auditing and accounting services. They have built on their strong relationships with executives to become large-scale systems integrators, strategy houses, corporate finance advisors and law practices. Although we tend not to think of firms of accountants as customer-focused, a higher proportion of their employees spend more time in customer contact situations than almost any other business. I have estimated that of their available man days, 75% are spent in actually working with or selling to actual or potential customers.

Incentive systems (financial rewards and, perhaps more importantly, progression prospects) are defined absolutely in terms of one's record of customer value creation. The key factor is time-billed to the client at or above standard rates. This encourages long-term relationship building thus ensuring that the client perceives value in the continuing relationship - and demonstrates this by paying fees. This focus is built into the system from the moment a graduate is recruited, and is supported by heavy investments in information systems. A walk down the corridors of any of these firms confirms quickly that the preoccupation of all employees is their clients, particularly developments in their clients' marketplaces, research and knowledge creation of interest to the clients and, significantly, their competitors. Reliance on informal market sensing is critical, and organizational memory is persistently augmented by weak signals that have been quickly validated.

SUMMARY

Leveraging market sensing to create competitive advantage

Market sensing involves more than market research; it is defined as *all actions, formal and informal, systematic and random, active and passive, engaged in by all members of an organization, which determine and refine individual or collective perceptions of the marketplace and its dynamics.* Market sensing therefore goes well beyond market research, and at its core is a determination to derive unique insights into the needs of customers and the opportunities within markets.

However, the results of market sensing need to be actively applied - or leveraged - in order to provide competitive advantage. This requires *responsiveness* to market intelligence and *creative market sensing,* so that customer-sensitive action by employees is actively encouraged and reinforced. This can be promoted by:

- Emphasizing informal rewards (e.g. peer group recognition).
- Co-ordinating the work of different departments and having a shared understanding of marketplace dynamics.
- Influencing the management mindset: the beliefs, values and overall approach of managers in the organization.
- Fostering a healthy disregard for industry norms and encouraging a passion for experimentation and learning. This can mean blending hierarchy with empowerment and respecting individuals' ideas and interpretations. Creative solutions based on market sensing are one of the keys to competitive advantage and this creativity can be stimulated through a dialogue with the market.
- Promoting trust and openness between individuals so that information and ideas are openly shared and discussed in an apolitical manner.

BEST PRACTICE

Releasing the power of market sensing to create competitive advantage

Six steps are critical to realizing the full potential of market sensing:

1. **Make good use of market research.**   Review your current practices in this area. Does most research simply seem to validate the proposed approach to a launch or entry decision? If so, it is likely that research is being used to satisfy political agendas rather than to create insight about the market. Ensure your management team employs research to good effect, refining and updating their mental models of what drives key customer groups.

2. **Think creatively about how to engage respondents so that insights are likely to be unique (i.e. competitors are unlikely to have gained the same level of insight using traditional sources and methods).** Ask the question: could a stranger conducting research in this market learn this from their research? If the answer is yes, then you are not using all your accumulated knowledge to enrich your investigation.

3. **Institute customer contact programs.**   Without bringing top management into front-line contact with customers involved in real transactions, it is hard to convey to them the difficulties and indeed the importance of resource and organizational realignment. Many firms today

are instituting programmes to encourage senior personnel in non-customer contact roles (back office) to spend time experiencing customer contact. One company has coupled this approach with the hiring of a senior (board level) executive to be the voice of the customer. His business card announces his job title as 'customer' and his brief is to remind the board of the customer implications of any policies or changes that are being considered.

4. **Incorporate competitor analysis into the development and refining of your mental model of the marketplace – and develop foresight.** It is crucial to move beyond developing profiles (in the absence of anything else, these can be a valuable starting point) into the realm of developing *foresight* – specifically engaging your team in thinking about future scenarios and likely competitor actions and reactions.

   Foresight is vital for market sensing of customers and competitors. This can be best achieved by encouraging informal and continuous contributions to the firm's mental model of the marketplace. To do this, you must find ways to articulate consistently your understanding of that model, and then make it clear that the production of any evidence that further refines and validates it, or indeed invalidates it, is encouraged. Recently, intranet systems under the stewardship of business intelligence functions, but reporting to the head of strategy, have been designed making it easy for a broadly defined group to access knowledge and intelligence on competitors, key market segments and environmental trends. The key is to really make these resources of competitive significance so that people are actively using them and contributing to them. Here is the critical place where informal and formal systems meet, and it is the crunch point for whether the organization will leverage market sensing to create competitive advantage.

5. **Move to a process- or project-based organizational structure, so that functional barriers to creating customer value are minimized.** This is achieved in two ways:

   - First, by ensuring that the entire organization is focused on the customer and that everyone understands how they can contribute to customer value creation.
   - Second, managers can now be identified and valued by their collection of experiences, rather than their positional or formal status.

   This has the effect of making each person's understanding and augmentation of the mental model of the marketplace hugely valuable, focusing attention as a result.

6. **Ensure that information systems provide an understanding of business activity at the customer level.** It is remarkable how many companies' systems do not support such reporting, even to the extent that some very large (global) businesses cannot easily determine who their 20 largest clients are, measured simply on sales, never mind profitability. That situation is completely unsatisfactory in today's environment.

In the end, senior management really does have to decide how much creating customer value really matters. Their job is complex and the resources competing for time and attention are many, so they need a guiding light and vision. In the case of the leading software company Intuit, everyone is guided by 'do right by the customer'. This genuinely matters and thus it is likely that the organization will have the right mindset, and will do what is necessary to align itself to create customer value. It will then routinely ensure that investments in market sensing produce an appropriate return.

References

Riley, D. and Meehan, S. (1998) *Daewoo Motor Company UK (A)*, IMD Case M527, May 15, 12 pages and *Daewoo Motor Company UK (B)*, IMD Case M528, May 15, 12 pages. IMD – International Institute for Management Development, Lausanne, Switzerland.

Duckworth, Finn, Grubb, Waters (1996) *Advertising that builds strong customer relationships? That'll be the Daewoo.* Advertising Works 9 IPA Advertising Effectiveness Awards 1996 edited by Gary Duckworth.

ESOMAR (1997) *Annual Study on the Market Research Industry*. European Society for Opinion and Marketing Research.

Meehan, S. and Barwise, P. (1998) Professional Service Firms: unsung masters of marketing. *Financial Times*, Mastering Marketing series, part 8. November 2, pp. 2–3.

6

Decisions at the Speed of Light – the Impact of Information Technology

Information technology is helping businesses to profit from an ever-increasing knowledge of their customers, enabling them to rediscover and routinely apply high standards of customer service. In this chapter, **John Walsh** highlights current and potential advantages of technology for marketers' understanding of their customers.

CASE STUDY: RITZ CARLTON AND THE DRIVE FOR MASS CUSTOMIZATION

By applying information technology effectively and by training all of its staff to use information effectively, the Ritz Carlton hotel chain has, over the last ten years, developed into one of the most successful luxury hotel chains, providing customers with a highly personalized service. The Ritz strategy is quite simple and not at all uncommon: to differentiate itself from its competitors by offering distinctive service and customer value at a competitive price.

The approach that Ritz adopted from the late 1980s – which won the company a prestigious Baldridge Award for total quality – succeeded by emphasizing several key principles, all of which were underpinned by a blend of effective leadership and the successful management and application of technology. First, a vision of an efficient, personalized service was formed, and the individual commitment of employees to realizing this vision and providing a quality service was then developed. IT systems were standardized throughout the business, and an organizational culture was developed that emphasized the need to capture and disseminate useful information about each individual customer, as well as re-using information and knowledge gained about internal processes as well as customers' wants. This highlighted the general need to listen to the market, as well as the specific requirement to swiftly reconfigure people, information and processes whenever necessary in order to deliver the benefits of a highly customized and attentive service.

The current challenges for the business are to operate its hotels so that they are error-free, and also to retain all of their customers through a precision marketing strategy. To achieve this, Ritz Carlton have spent years accumulating in-depth knowledge about its work processes and have assiduously combined technology with individual skills and innovation. In practice, this means Ritz Carlton tracks individual customer preferences using several types of information systems to collect, store and disseminate information only when it is needed. For instance, at each hotel employees observe guests, record their preferences and store the data on a company-wide information network. This enables other employees to re-use the information and provide the most personalized service available, leveraging their contact with the customer to shut out competitors. When customers check in they receive the room and location they prefer, and throughout their stay Ritz Carlton supervisors scrutinize relevant details for each customer so that they can personalize their hotel's service, providing extra pillows, favourite beverages, preferred newspapers and so on.

The Ritz Carlton approach is a stunning example of the power of mass customization – *the ability to deliver rapidly, efficiently and profitably a range of products and services satisfying individual customers.*

Overview

In previous chapters we have examined the value of information – whether it is used to bond with customers and build loyalty, to improve the customer's knowledge of our products and services, or to leverage market sensing. However, as well as providing a foundation for these methods of achieving competitive advantage, information technology also offers a range of other potential advantages that can be exploited in order to delight customers, both now and for the foreseeable future. Chief among these is the ability to open up new relationships with customers, and this theme is explored in this chapter.

Knowing what the customer wants has been a precondition of a successful enterprise since commerce began. Early vendors won a customer's patronage by forming a relationship with them, knowing their likes and dislikes and thereby making transactions easier and more pleasant. Not only did the customer benefit from the personal attention, but the vendor could improve profits by charging different prices based on their knowledge of a customer's ability or willingness to pay. In the latter part of the twentieth century the corner stores that still offered this level of service have died off in the face of competition from large hypermarkets and shopping malls. These less intimate affairs know their customers too, albeit at a far less detailed level – they guessed correctly that most customers faced with a choice between very low prices and attentive service would opt for the former.

However, today's technology is helping firms rediscover the level of service and customer intimacy of long ago. Gigabytes of hard disks containing large databases have replaced the shopkeeper's memory as a repository of a customer's preferences.

> **"The application of technology to store, analyse and disseminate information is not only providing swifter and more effective methods for decision-making – it is also opening up new opportunities for building better and more distinctive relationships with customers"**

Technology is also helping firms to profit from this knowledge. For example, advanced statistical tools are computing the impact on profitability of customer loyalty programs, where lower prices reward frequent purchasing. Furthermore, information about customers' preferences and behaviours are being captured as businesses utilize technology in their day-to-day business activity. Retail stores, having introduced scanner technology to make transactions much quicker and more reliable, have found themselves with enormous databases of transactions that have proven very useful in decision-making. As many transactions migrate to the World Wide Web it is possible to capture not only purchase data, but also the information that the customer requested prior to making a choice. As companies accumulate this data, successful firms will differentiate themselves from less successful ones by understanding and utilizing the data to make a more profitable enterprise.

This chapter examines current trends in applying information technology for competitive advantage, and in this chapter we will:

- Highlight how technology can provide a decisive impact on marketers' understanding of customers and the marketing decisions that result.
- Consider the current and potential role of the World Wide Web in improving marketing effectiveness.

The benefits and applications of technology

Nowadays it is difficult to make a purchase without a beam of light being pointed at a series of lines of different widths located on the product. The scanner and the barcode that it reads have changed the way we buy products and the way companies operate and make decisions. After a slow diffusion process, scanners have become an integral part of the way that retailers do business. They have created efficiencies and reduced costs: as it is no longer necessary to stick a price label on individual products, training cashiers has become easier and pricing mistakes are less common. In addition, they have captured an ocean of data on customers' purchase behaviour that has helped marketing managers set prices, determine the nature and extent of promotions, and select new products for introduction and old ones for exit.

Product profitability analysis

Companies such as AC Nielsen and Information Resources collect scanner purchase data from retailers and report sales and market share data to manufacturers. Assistant brand managers become brand managers or abruptly change careers based on this data. However, the real value of the data is seen only when it is combined with the retailers' information of the in-store environment, such as promotional activity or end-of-aisle displays. Relationships between decisions and outcomes can then be observed, analysed and modelled. For example, the optimum level of price cut that maximizes the return from a promotion can be discovered.

Of course the data is collected at the individual store level, facilitating a between-store analysis. In a recent study, Montgomery (1997) showed that adjusting marketing activities on a store-by-store basis – or micro-marketing – can increase a supermarket's bottom line substantially. Working with Dominick's Finer Foods, a Chicago-based supermarket chain, he analysed purchase data and found that operating profit margins could be increased by *one third* to 83% if products were priced differently across stores, reflecting customers' different preferences and price elasticities.

Quaker Oats Company, the US-based breakfast cereal manufacturer, studied the redemption rate of coupons using individual-level scanner data. The heaviest purchasers of their product were (perhaps unsurprisingly) also the heaviest redeemers of coupons. So, instead of the intended effect of attracting new customers, coupons merely made the product cheaper for current customers (Bucklin and Gupta, 1998). Individual-level data enabled Quaker to identify the previous purchasing patterns of coupon users; an aggregate analysis of purchase data would not have uncovered this.

Hoch and Lodish (1998) used store-level data to study sales of retailers' private label products. Retailers generally make a higher profit margin on these products and have therefore focused on getting customers to switch from well-known, national brands, often offering large price discounts. By using the store-level scanner data, the researchers were able to show that the profit to the retailer from the product category (i.e. the sum of profits of private label and national brands) was highest when there was a small, rather than a large, gap in prices. Essentially, the private label products were being sold below their profit-maximizing price.

The suppliers of this data have created models to maximize the retailer's profit within a product category using store-level data. Both Information Resources and AC Nielsen offer retailers assistance with *category management* (the selection of brands within a product category to be carried by the retailer) and *shelf space management* (how much shelf space should be allocated to each brand). The retailer can identify those products that are of little value in the entire product portfolio and discontinue them. If consumers will readily purchase product X instead of product Y, then the retailer can keep unit sales constant and lower handling and inventory costs by not carrying product Y. For example, Kahn and McAlister (1997) describe a retailer reducing the number of cat-box filler products carried from 26 to 16 and increasing profits by 87% because of cost savings.

For estimates of market share and sales, brand managers are most comfortable with data collected at the store level. All purchases in the store are captured and market research companies that collect this data do a good job of covering most stores in a country. (Of course, the US has the highest coverage.) However, to study certain issues, store-level data offers too little information – one must look at individual household behaviour over time. Although all households cannot be tracked, large samples of volunteers are chosen. Market research companies have created panels of customers comprizing as many as 50 000 households, whose personal data (such as family size, income, head-of-household occupation) is combined with their shopping data collected from store scanners. Manufacturers who study the data from these panels can estimate the effect of marketing campaigns on brand switching, for example to see if promotions attract customers who usually buy a competitive product or merely give away money to loyal customers.

Analysis of customer data resulting from loyalty schemes and special offer promotions

In Chapter 3, Jacques Horovitz outlined the value of loyalty schemes for enhancing customer bonding, and recently a growing number of retailers have formed customer clubs. These have been promoted heavily by supermarkets such as Tesco and Sainsbury in the UK and Migros in Switzerland. Similar to frequent flyer programs offered by airlines, members of these programs are rewarded with discounts and special offers for joining and presenting their membership card at every purchase occasion. Not only does the retailer benefit by increasing the consumers' loyalty, but they also collect individual-level purchase data, similar to the market research companies' panels described above. The value of this data to the retailer can be significant. For example, the retailer can calculate which customers account for the lion's share of profit. So, rather than supporting manufacturers who account for most *sales*, retailers can focus on those manufacturers whose products are purchased by the relatively small percentage of loyal, high-volume customers. For example, the Piggly Wiggly chain of supermarkets operated by Sav-O Stores in Sheboygan, Wisconsin, USA found that 25–30% of its customers account for 70% of their purchases. As a result of this information they have now refocused their marketing on these heavy purchasers, even going so far as to have managers hand-write Christmas cards to the top 100 customers in each store. Initial results of these marketing efforts have shown them to be successful – those shoppers who were already spending over $600 per month increased their spending by 5–20%, mainly by increasing their transactions per visit (Yovovich, 1998).

Manufacturers pay close attention to individual-level data when they have recently introduced a new product. This individual-level data can be vitally important to profitability when introducing a new product, as the example of Quaker Oats mentioned above highlights. While aggregate sales figures tell whether the product is a success at the moment, the *trial rates* (percentage of customers who have bought the product once) and *repeat rates* (percentage of customers who have bought the product at least a second time) that are available only from individual-level data reveal the long-term prospects for the product.

Figures 6.1a and 6.1b show the same sales figures over time for a new product. However, the future looks much brighter for the product in Figure 6.1a. Although relatively few sales are coming from trial, many more are coming from people who have bought it before, indicating that the product will have a stable base of customers in the coming years. On the other hand, the product in Figure 6.1b is getting many of its current sales from people trying it for the first time, with very few of those then choosing to buy a second time. As a result, a sales dip (or slump) looms in the future as the number of customers who have not tried the product is exhausted.

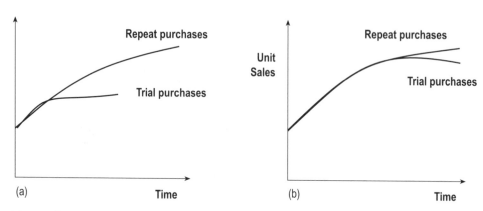

Figure 6.1: *Special offer promotions – repeat and trial purchases*

Estimates of trial and repeat rates are often used in deciding whether to introduce a product at all. By combining individual-level scanner data with responses to surveys, BASES, a research approach from AC Nielsen, estimates rates of product trial and repeat rates quite accurately: predictions of sales are within 20% of the actual (post-introduction) value, 90% of the time. Here, scanner data helps to refine the model prediction as post-introduction sales are tracked against the prediction, with the discrepancy used to refine the model for subsequent applications.

Measuring and refining advertising effectiveness

John Wanamaker, the early Philadelphian retailer, is famously quoted as saying: "I know half my advertising works, I just don't know which half." Market research companies have been trying to come to grips with this for quite some time. Information Resources offers a service called BehaviorScan that attempts to address this issue. Multiple small towns across the USA, from Pittsfield, Massachusetts to Visalia, California, have a panel of households equipped with split-cable TV. This technology allows experimental TV advertisements to be inserted into regular TV programs, resulting in neighbours viewing different ads. Since all purchases of these households are captured by scanners placed in local stores and traced back to them using technology similar to customer loyalty cards, the effectiveness of new and current advertisements can be measured. These towns frequently serve as experimental test markets for new products prior to a national launch, facilitating the refinement of the marketing campaign or dropping the introduction of the product altogether.

Looking at 389 different advertising tests in BehaviorScan markets, Lodish et al. (1995) found that for 61% of the time increased advertising expenditure is unwarranted – consumers do not purchase more of the product if it is advertised more frequently.

However, the split-cable technology is being surpassed rapidly by developments on the Internet. Because TV signals are broadcast it is difficult to customize advertisements very much, other than allocating participants to two or three experimental groups. The World Wide Web, on the other hand, has many more possibilities, and some entrepreneurial companies have been quite successful at using technology to leverage the data available there so as to learn more about their customers and deliver a better service.

The Web

Transactions taking place on the Web are effortlessly, economically and automatically recorded as an electronic collection of bits and bytes. The anonymity of cash-based transactions has not made its way on to the Web (although since the Web's not-too-distant birth the concept of *e-cash* has been discussed – and even e-cash may not retain the anonymity of notes and coins). To make a purchase on the Web requires giving personal information. Typically, the minimum is credit card details and a postal address, although you may also be asked or required to fill out a short questionnaire. Even where no purchase is made, some information may be asked of you. For example, newspaper websites such as the Financial Times and The New York Times, which are free, ask that you use the same username and password when you visit. This information can subsequently be used to analyse reading patterns. How many people read only the headlines, but do so every day? How many read each and every article, but visit the site infrequently? The anonymity of browsing through periodicals at a news stand does not exist on the Web, and the information that is recorded can be used by managers to great effect.

CASE STUDY: A GLIMPSE INTO THE FUTURE – PEAPOD.COM

For a glimpse into the future, visit Peapod.com, an online supermarket and one of the more sophisticated recorders and users of their customers' personal data and shopping behaviour. With over 100 000 customers in eight US cities, Peapod's website sells groceries that are subsequently delivered to customers' homes. A list of previous purchases (including brand, pack size, quantity purchased) is kept on the site, so a customer can make some minor changes from week to week, saving time and effort. Peapod creates a database on each shopper that includes their purchase history (what they bought), online shopping patterns (how they bought it), online attitudinal questionnaires (what they are thinking) and demographic data which it purchases from third parties. A shopper's profile is used by Peapod to determine which advertisement to show and which promotions/electronic coupons to offer. Demographically identical neighbours are thus treated differently based on what Peapod has learned about their unique preferences and behaviours over time. Shoppers seem to like this high-tech relationship marketing, with 94% of all sales coming from repeat customers. Manufacturers like it too. The more detailed customer information enables them to target promotions at customers who have repeatedly bought another brand, thereby not giving away promotion dollars to their own loyal customers.

Expect to see many more supermarkets in a variety of countries offering a similar service. Peapod has recently divested its software division, appropriately named Split-Pea, and its goal is to license the technology within the supermarket industry and in other industries with a similar structure. They have already signed a deal with Cole Myers of Australia.

Developing an effective and relevant website

Given the potential advantages to consumer and vendor alike, the manager's challenge is twofold:

- To develop a website that collects the relevant data in an unobtrusive way to which customers won't object.
- To determine how to analyse the vast quantity of data that will be collected and integrate it into decision-making.

So how do websites collect this valuable data? First, people who visit a site for the first time are asked to register, which typically involves giving a name, physical address, e-mail address and perhaps some other demographic data (such as age or income). From the customer's perspective this is all that needs to be done. They don't have to answer any more questions. When they come to the site in the future, they either type their chosen username and password or, more commonly these days, if

> **"For companies with a mass production mindset, achieving the full potential of the Internet may prove difficult. The key to marketing success on the web is *personalizing* – the concept of mass customization"**

using the same computer, the website recognizes the customer using a *cookie*, a small file that uniquely identifies the computer. In either case, we can associate each subsequent visit with the answers the customer gave on their registration form.

From the manager's perspective, the work is just beginning – the website has to be personalized for the user. How? From the initial survey, we may have learned that the user is male, young and British. If we are running a news site, we can provide information that typically appeals to this demographic profile. If we are selling clothes, we can feature items that are usually bought by people fitting this profile. As the user repeatedly visits our site, we learn more about him as we record his series of 'clicks', the information he requests using his mouse. An individual's sequence of clicks, called *clickstreams*, are at the core of personalizing websites. Clickstreams reveal what he is really interested in. Perhaps on news sites he always goes to the sports section first and immediately reads about Manchester United's latest soccer game. Advertisements for United's most recent merchandize could be shown to him with some effect.

Clickstreams allow the website to add behavioural information to the answers given at registration. They are at the heart of Amazon.com's famous personalized book suggestions. CDNow, the successful online vendor of music compact disks, is convinced of the richness of clickstream data. It analyses instances where shoppers look at information about a CD but choose not to buy: it is not only purchases that reveal what a person is interested in. The web page that customers see at BMG's Music Service website is actually dependent on their music preferences and purchase history. While the customization improves the relationship with the customer, the constant monitoring of the website enables BMG's marketers to move more quickly to change promotions that are performing poorly (Bresnahan, 1998).

In terms of volume, clickstream data dwarfs data gathered from in-store, barcode scanners. On the Internet, purchase data is a tiny fraction of the total clickstream data we have access to. Clickstream data is analogous to having data that follows a shopper's eye movements in a store as they consider one brand and, on looking at the price, reject it in favour of the lower-priced generic offer. Perhaps some other brands are never looked at. Mere purchase data does not reveal the *process* consumers use to buy a product, it simply yields the outcome. Companies that use clickstream data to understand the consumer decision-making process will be the market leaders of the future.

> "Using clickstream data, an efficient website can reveal the process that customers follow when purchasing a product or service, and this understanding can be used to improve marketing effectiveness throughout the business"

A consequence of clickstream data is that many marketing functions have to be automated. Rule-based criteria will determine what information each customer sees. The days when marketing analysts perform this function will soon be in the distant past. There need be no human input into the selection of, and communication to, customers. Computers can run profitability analysis to determine who should be targeted. Clickstream data can be analysed to determine customers' past decisions and, therefore, the communication message.

Understanding the implications of personalized marketing via the Web

The implications of personalization for consumers

Do consumers mind being asked to part with information in order to receive personalized goods and services? Most early research would suggest not, so long as they perceive a benefit. Reading a newspaper for free or saving time qualifies. However, it is worth keeping in mind the experience of one business that endeavoured to leverage new technology to personalize its service. Because of caller ID, a technology that allows one to know the phone number of the person calling, the firm was able to answer the phone with a personalized hello. Consumers reacted negatively, offended by what they considered an invasion of privacy. The benefit of not having to state one's name and address was apparently not enough.

In a recent study by Jupiter Communications, 35% of Internet executives surveyed said personalization capabilities is the most important determinant of who they use to develop their website. Clearly this is an issue that is capturing their attention. But has the collection and analysis of clickstream data and the subsequent website personalization that it facilitates been worth it? Have companies made more money from it or is it all hype? The addition of personalization capabilities can add up to $3 million to the cost of a website. Yet, Business Week reports that personalization pays for itself within a year. It does so by increasing the loyalty of users to a site. When people recognize that an offering is targeted to them, or moreover when they have a hand in its creation, they are more likely to return again and again. Stopping short of personalizing a website, one can buy a system that will automate Internet marketing (via e-mail) for $100 000 to $250 000. While such an up-front fee might seem high to many companies, the cost of reaching a customer by e-mail is only a few cents, compared with $2–3 using direct mail and over $10 using the telephone. In the long run, the Internet-based option will not only be quicker and more accurate, it will be cheaper too.

The implications of personalization for businesses

Companies selling information rather than products over the Internet have been able to charge advertisers more as their advertising becomes more targeted. Internet advertising has exploded in size, mostly because of the growth of the Internet itself, but also because advertisers can get their advertisements viewed by a more specific, targeted group of people. Unusual manifestations of this phenomenon have occurred recently, where various companies have offered free computers to people who would agree to have their online behaviour recorded and advertisements beamed at them.

How will business be affected by personalization? Treating customers as individuals will become more prevalent, and since we are talking about the Internet here it is likely to happen soon. Essentially, it will become just another cost of doing business. How will it be implemented? Silicon Valley is home to many companies that act as the outsourcing agent for companies wanting to use the Internet for marketing and developing customer relationships. These companies, rather than in-house divisions, will be at the forefront of integrating e-commerce functions with other databases within corporations.

The personalization we see developing on the Internet will have knock-on effects in the 'real' world as consumers' expectations are influenced by their online experiences. Safeway, the UK supermarket chain, is developing a system where a consumer's buying habits are analysed and a suggested shopping list is tailormade based on this past purchase information. Suggestions of new products and recipes can then be delivered on paper or to a hand-held electronic device such as a Palm Pilot (Hollinger, 1998). One-to-one marketing is here, regardless of the medium.

 # BENCHMARKING

Assessing your organization's success in applying technology to build new relationships with customers

The applications of technology for understanding, serving and delighting customers are not only many and varied, but are also constantly evolving with new developments in technological capability. The trend, however, is clear: customers in many markets now seek products and services that not only offer quality, but also provide precisely what they want at little or no additional cost. Achieving this is the concept of *mass customization*.

To assess your organization's effectiveness in applying information technology to marketing it is useful to consider the following general areas:

➡ pricing and profitability analysis;
➡ analysing and refining the effectiveness of marketing programmes (including market sensing as well as gaining maximum value from customer loyalty programmes);
➡ the success of the organization's Internet activities.

Product pricing and profitability analysis

Using data relating to sales volumes combined with an analysis of pricing can help to sharpen pricing strategies and enhance profitability, as the studies mentioned previously have highlighted. Using IT to study sales volumes and trends is also vital to maintaining the right level of inventory, in the right place at the right time. Key questions to consider include whether sufficient data is collected at the point of purchase, whether it is adequately analysed and used as a basis for future decisions, and whether it could be improved to deliver greater profitability. The example of Dell Computers outlined in Chapter 3 highlights the power of information for more effective and *profitable* marketing.

Analysing and refining the effectiveness of marketing programmes

As Sean Meehan outlined in Chapter 5, technology has an increasingly important role in market sensing and market research. It is useful to consider the extent to which technology is used to monitor competitors and refine mental models of the marketplace. Because IT can easily handle and manipulate large amounts of data, its value in tracking customer preferences and accurately targeting marketing activities is enormous. Consider also the extent to which the information systems provide an understanding of business activity at the customer level: for example, who are the largest customers according to sales and profitability? How have these changed over time, and why?

Another question to ask is how effectively does your business capture and analyse data resulting from loyalty schemes and special offer promotions? The value of such activities is not only in the fact that they build customer loyalty but that they also provide valuable customer information. This includes details about what people want, how they buy, how the product can be improved and how best to market to each individual customer.

Developing a successful website

Many organizations have rushed into developing an Internet presence, concerned that they may become marginalized or appear outmoded if they do not. However, along with presence must come the other key to success on the Web – personalization. Some of the issues to consider, therefore, include whether the website is relevant, attractive and up-to-date. Does the site collect all of the data that it could, and does it do so in a way that reinforces rather than undermines the brand and does not dismay or upset the customer? What customer benefit does the website deliver (increasingly this is personalization or speed of service)? This means capturing not only purchase information but *clickstream* data as well, which can highlight those factors influencing a potential customer's decision to purchase or not. This also raises the question, how well integrated is the site into the organization in general, and the centres of marketing and decision-making in particular? Other issues to consider include how well is the site advertised? Could linking with other sites strengthen it? Could any elements of the website benefit from being outsourced?

The future of technology for marketers

How companies learn about customers has changed greatly and rapidly over the last two decades and this trend is set to continue well into the twenty-first century. New technology will change the way transactions are made and, as a result, the way customer information is collected. As more companies move from mass production to one-to-one marketing, cost reduction will be surpassed by a need to understand one's customers as the key to competitive advantage and success. Increasing amounts of computing power will be dedicated to understanding customers' preferences from past behaviour and decisions.

Managerial decision-making will be different in the future. With volumes of data being collected and analysed automatically, decision-makers will have a richer sense of how the marketplace behaves and responds. Simulations of the marketplace will be easier and cheaper to develop, allowing managers to see the simulated impact of potential actions. Airplane pilots spend many hours in simulators before taking to the air – managers will spend time in simulators before taking to the marketplace.

Armed with an understanding of their customers, companies will be more proactive in the future. Rather than placing products on shelves and hoping that they are bought, companies will target individual customers with products that are suitable for them. Having the right product at the right price will not be enough in the future – eliminating consumers' search and transaction costs (essentially reducing the time they must spend to acquire the product they want) will become a critical success factor. As economies develop and consumers become relatively more rich, there will be a greater emphasis on saving time. Successful companies will respond to this.

Does the information revolution signal the end of surveys and focus groups, traditionally the life blood of market research companies? I don't believe so. Talking to customers and finding out their attitudes and motivations may become even more important in a world where so much is known about their behaviour. Only when we know why consumers behave the way they do can we know how to influence their actions.

 # SUMMARY

THE IMPACT OF INFORMATION TECHNOLOGY

As technology continues to develop at a faster and faster pace, even relatively recent marketing systems and innovations such as websites start looking dated and obsolete, failing to deliver their full potential unless they are constantly updated. Yet at the same time technology is enabling businesses to rediscover levels of service and customer intimacy of a bygone age, and the most successful firms are the ones that can adapt and profit from this knowledge by harnessing technology.

The most significant advantages of IT for marketers are centred on the ability to open up new relationships with customers. These benefits include:

- Capturing, storing and disseminating information in unparalleled detail about customer preferences. This in turn supports swift and effective decision-making on everything from product development and pricing strategies, to stock levels and future marketing plans.
- Speeding up the rate at which transactions are made, as well as improving the reliability of these transactions, has both created efficiencies and reduced costs.
- Examining current and *potential* relationships between decisions and outcomes, effectively modelling different scenarios and greatly enhancing the speed and accuracy of decisions.
- Combining and manipulating a wide variety of different sources of information (such as the tacit knowledge of employees or market research data) to measure and refine marketing effectiveness and profitability, usually through improved targeting.
- Enabling special offer promotions to run, which are sophisticated and offer significant value. As well as facilitating the running of the promotion in the first place, IT also enables customer data resulting from loyalty schemes and special offer promotions to be thoroughly analysed, with the results used to inform future decisions.

The value of technology and its role for the marketer is highlighted by the growth of the Internet, offering almost boundless opportunities for greater growth, profitability and competitiveness – as well as significant pitfalls. However, for those used to using technology for mass production, realizing the full potential of the Internet will prove very difficult indeed. Personalizing, precision and mass customization are the hallmarks of successful Internet marketers, whether it is Dell Computer generating a reputed *$15 million per day* from their website, or the innovative Amazon.com that is helping to reshape the global book selling business. However the personalized approach that is so effective on the Internet can also be replicated in other marketing activities, as it underpins the three-stage process for customer bonding mentioned in Chapter 3: the need to conquer, satisfy and build the loyalty of current and potential customers.

References

Bresnahan, J. (1998) Improving the Odds. *CIO Enterprise Magazine*, November 15.
Bucklin, R.E. and Gupta, S. (1998) Commercial Adoption Of Advances In The Analysis Of Scanner Data. *Marketing Science Institute Working Paper No. 98-103*, March.

Hoch, S.J. and Lodish, L.M. (1998) Store Brands and Category Management. *Working Paper 98-012*, Wharton School, University of Pennsylvania, March.

Hollinger, P. (1998) IBM and Safeway in electronic shopping innovation. *Financial Times*, December 17.

Kahn, B.E. and McAlister, L. *Grocery Revolution: The New Focus On The Consumer.* Addison-Wesley 1997.

Lodish, L.E., Abraham, M., Kalmenson, S., Livelsberger, J., Lubetkin, B., Richardson, B. and Stevens, M.E. (1995) How TV Advertising Works: A Meta-Analysis of 389 Real World Split Cable TV Advertising Experiments. *Journal of Marketing Research*, **XXXII**, May, 125-39.

Montgomery, A.L. (1997) Creating Micro-Marketing Pricing Strategies Using Supermarket Scanner Data. *Marketing Science*, **16**(4), 315-37.

Yovovich, B.G. (1998) Scanners reshape grocery business. *Marketing News*, **32**(4), 1-2.

Section B

Creating New Reality

CHAPTER 7

From Information to Knowledge –
How Managers Learn

Whereas previous chapters have focused on using information to add value with customers, the following chapters are concerned with using information to create new businesses, innovation and sources of competitive advantage. In this chapter, **Xavier Gilbert** focuses on the four elements for proactive and rapid learning, helping managers rethink how they learn and use information to develop innovative business solutions.

CASE STUDY: THE LEARNING PROCESS THAT BROUGHT SUCCESS AT NOKIA

Nokia, the world-renowned mobile telephony company, was in the late 1980s a nearly defunct diversified conglomerate, known mostly for its rubber and tissue products. The decision, against all odds, to put all the energy and remaining resources behind a minuscule (by industry standards) telecommunications activity – more specifically an emerging mobile telephony sector – triggered an intensive learning culture that still characterizes the company.

By the end of 1996, Nokia Group was the global market leader in digital mobile phones and one of the two largest suppliers of GSM networks. In just a few years, this resilient Finnish business had learned enough to become the pace-setter in mobile phone design, making this high-tech-loaded device a lifestyle attribute under a brand that many fashion products could envy. On the mobile network side, Nokia was also setting the pace with solution-oriented customer services, thus raising the competitive threshold.

Most companies, having achieved this level of success in such a short time, could be expected to miss the next industry turn if there ever was one – and there was: the Internet and its technological paradigm shift. If the telecommunications universe is shifting to Internet Protocol (IP) technology, Nokia will prove that all this hype is not worth much without mobility: the mobile information society is what customers will ultimately go for. A lot of new stuff to learn? "What we have really learned over the past few years," Nokia management says, "is the very rare capability of putting together end-to-end customer solutions."

Commenting on Nokia's strategic thinking process, one of its senior executives noted: "Of course, we get masses of information, but what is important is that we discuss it a lot among ourselves, kicking it around, looking at it from different perspectives. It is a collective learning process and the key point is whom we should discuss a new piece of information with, to augment it and give it more meaning than it had originally. Then we make some choices, try them out, listen to the feedback and redirect as needed. With this collective learning process we are all on the same wavelength and we can act very fast when needed."

Nokia has certainly suffered its share of setbacks, but to successfully make a journey from near disaster to world domination in less than ten years shows a sustained flexibility and desire to learn at all levels. Clearly this is vital for a business in an industry as new and fast-moving as mobile telephony, but the Nokia approach – applied throughout a business – highlights the value of moving from information to knowledge.

Overview

In the information-intensive, competitive environment that currently dominates, companies that merely do more of the same, better and better, end up competing solely on costs, eventually falling behind their competitors. The winners, by contrast, keep setting the pace, reconfiguring the business system of their industry sector before it is obvious to anyone else that it has to be done. They renew themselves constantly, either before competitors or, quite often, before new entrants prove them obsolete.

Some companies seem to be more agile than others at renewing themselves. A good laboratory to observe this capability is provided by start-up companies, many of which go through several experimenting phases before settling on an activity often different from what the founder originally had in mind. Famous examples include the Swiss mouse producer, Logitech, which started with word-processing in mind; Dell Computer, whose initial activity consisted of disk optimization; Microsoft, which did not even have an operating system of its own when it sold its first one; and the Virgin Group, which started as a student magazine.

It is easy to understand how the initial steps of these companies were very learning-intensive. The eagerness to run one's own business meant spotting even weak market signals (the mouse was hardly a common device when Logitech committed to it). This was followed by envisioning how they could be addressed in an untried way, trying it out and starting again after it failed, until it did work, but not as expected. These companies renewed themselves several times during their early life, driven as they were by an urge to learn fast to survive.

Similar examples of corporate renewal can be observed in companies undergoing a life-saving turnaround, when very fast learning is simply a matter of survival, as was the case with Nokia. But interestingly, when their success is confirmed, companies

> **"Success is not a good school. It tends to filter out challenging information; it recommends more of the same as the most viable route ahead; it discourages experimenting"**

seem to provide no more signs of renewal, often preferring to optimize the same routines through repeated rationalization, and using their market power to mitigate any urge to reinvent themselves. Very few companies understand *why* they have been successful and *what is required* to remain successful; in fact, many companies tend to attribute their past successes to the wrong reasons. In this chapter, therefore, we will:

- Outline the four elements of rapid and proactive learning – the key principles underlying an effective learning organization.
- Provide practical guidance on applying the four elements, moving from information to knowledge using the learning cycle.
- Explain how to design a learning architecture, applying practical techniques for information management that will build an adaptive, innovative and competitive organization.

The four elements of rapid and proactive learning

The common feature of those companies that seem to be more capable of renewing themselves to stay ahead of the market, and as a result ahead of competition, is their ability to learn fast and to keep creating their own proprietary knowledge. The learning process followed by these companies relies quite systematically on four elements that can be allegorically represented as the wind, the forest, the fire and the mountain (*see* Figure 7.1).

> "An ability to learn fast and innovate constantly – creating their own intellectual property – are the hallmarks of successful, competitive businesses"

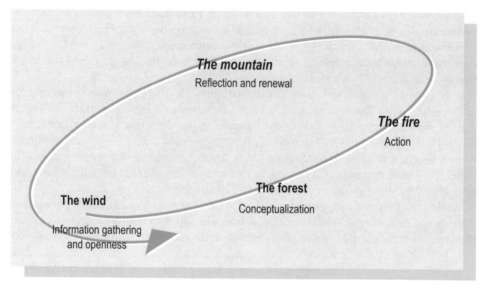

Figure 7.1: *The learning cycle*

The wind

The first characteristic of these companies is their eclecticism in information gathering. They make explicit efforts to remain open to many sources, as if they remembered that many of their critical decisions resulted from unexpected observations, often successfully distracting them from what they were really looking for. Curiosity, receptiveness, and having time for seemingly unrelated areas all seem to be part of their culture. They accept questioning of their current beliefs, challenging the opinions that are running the risk of becoming too solid, and confronting doubt. In these companies, information gathering is not necessarily a specialized task for senior management or planning departments. It is everyone's job, in every function and at every level of the organization. A metaphor for this step in the learning process is the wind, which is not avoided but is used, instead, as a source of energy.

The forest

A second characteristic of these companies is their efforts to keep their plans alive. First, they do have plans of their competitive landscape – conceptual frameworks of how their technologies, market expectations, aspirations and business systems all fit together. Senior management spends a considerable amount of time mapping these plans, discussing them and presenting them internally.

However, these plans are also continuously enriched with new information, redrawn to incorporate information that did not fit previously. They are seen as the necessary instrument giving meaning to information that would otherwise be left hanging, ignored and without being integrated into the business. They can be compared to a skipper's navigation plan that is continuously updated with changes in the wind, the currents, and the shape of the sea. Conceptualization capabilities thus play an important role in the learning process these companies follow to reinvent their future. A metaphor for this step in the learning process is the forest; indeed, we say of someone who lacks the overview of a complex problem that this person cannot see the forest because of the trees.

The fire

This leads to the third characteristic of these companies, which is their willingness to experiment, to nurture relatively small activities that could eventually change the market and from which they can learn and develop proprietary knowledge. For these companies, there is no learning without trying and experimenting. They know how to tackle these experiments in a controlled manner, and how to run several of them in parallel as learning opportunities. This means that in these companies certain things can be done without referring to the sacrosanct 'core competencies' and 'best practices', transgressing the established organization boundaries. A metaphor for this step in the learning process is the fire, with its virtues and risks. There has to be action – a spark becoming a flame – to create proprietary knowledge.

The mountain

However, action is not a good learning agent by itself if it is not also followed by debriefing and reflection. Taking the time for reflection is the fourth characteristic of those companies that are able to renew themselves. Without it, the learning path leads nowhere: no new, proprietary knowledge is created for use as unique information in future learning cycles. For these companies, drawing some lessons from what worked and what did not work is a must, to avoid both falling back all the time on the same routines and repeating the same mistakes. A metaphor for this step in the learning process is the mountain, from where we can stand to review the path that was followed and decide on the next course of action.

> **"Those businesses that constantly renew, revitalize and reinvigorate themselves are using the learning process in a systematic manner, with the approach taking deep root in their corporate culture"**

Learning implies going systematically through these four steps. None of them alone can support learning and lead to new knowledge. The accumulation of information by itself does not create knowledge; neither does conceptualization or action alone. It is the whole learning cycle moving from commodity information to conceptualization, action and debriefing, that creates new proprietary information for those who have gone through it. The companies that have the ability to renew themselves progress systematically through each of these steps, in a coherent manner. They leave enough organizational space for each of them. Each of them is embedded into their culture.

Moving from information to knowledge: enriching cognitive processes

There are good reasons why today these four steps have all become an integral part of the learning process, whereas some years ago information acquisition was a good enough substitute for knowledge acquisition. Information used to be disseminated slowly, in relatively limited quantities, to a limited audience. Within its target group, the interpretation of this information could be sufficiently homogeneous to point to a clear enough body of knowledge. Furthermore, as information was also durable, this body of knowledge, for all practical purposes, did not need frequent updating. The need for organizations to keep learning was not so critical. Good execution, resulting from careful advance planning based on accurate, and sometimes visionary forecasting, was enough. Corporate renewal was certainly an option, but, due to limited information volatility, there was little pressure for such a major strategic shift. Careful, adaptive, and even pre-emptive extrapolation would get you a long way.

The way that many executives cope with reality – their cognitive style – often remains shaped by this past information context. Executives often believe that they are expected to know, to have all the answers, and that it is natural for people to turn to them to get these. In many ways these executives are still rooted in the past where knowledge is power, ignorance is a weakness and learning is remedial.

Clearly the situation is no longer the same. A new piece of information is, today, available instantly to a wide and diverse audience. It is thus filtered through many different perspectives, subject to many different interpretations, and it leads to many different actions and applications. Forecasting and planning have become extremely precarious, which does not mean that they are unnecessary but that they have become part of an exploratory learning process. This massive information explosion is today's learning challenge.

Today's managers must realize that they only create their own view of reality. There are many other views of reality that are all trying to prove viable. This on-going creation of a viable reality is at the core of the learning process. Information is collected from a wide range of sources to enrich the manager's mental constructs that model their evolving perception of reality, and these models – or business ideas – are challenged by the rest of the world. Experimenting is therefore part of this learning process: it provides the feedback that will improve them further and gain the endorsement of the corporation's customers and stakeholders.

This on-going process of knowledge expansion is the engine of corporate renewal. Information acquisition is only a small part of it and, by itself, hardly leads to usable knowledge. Enriching one's model of reality – experimenting with it and making it more effective all the time – has become the most critical part of this learning process. Furthermore, this is where proprietary knowledge is created: by applying 'commodity' information into action to get unique feedback.

This impetus for learning requires from managers a richer cognitive approach, encompassing all four steps of the learning process: not only information acquisition, but also modelling a business idea, experimenting and implementing, debriefing and going back to the drawing board. Much of this learning will now result from collaborative work: multi-disciplinary teams working on the same project and organization members re-deploying their knowledge on new tasks. Many of the current efforts to establish knowledge repositories and make information flow across fragmented organization units seem to be inspired by an information-absorption view of learning and do not take into account the other steps in the learning process. Yet this cognitive approach that encompasses the full learning cycle is not new: it has been at the centre of every scientific discovery process, sometimes leading to the paradigm shifts described by Thomas Kuhn (1962) in *The Structure of Scientific Revolutions*. (The work of French mathematician Henri Poincaré, among many others, also analyses this scientific cognitive process.) In the current complexity resulting from the information explosion, managers must rise to this cognitive challenge.

> "Information is not power any more and, in fact, not knowing is the first step that points to deficiencies in the model, new questions and new knowledge to be developed. Learning is not remedial; it is like breathing"

Applying the learning cycle

In practice, even though the four steps of learning processes that we have described do make good intuitive sense, they rarely receive the necessary attention in corporations. The general view seems to be that learning can be taken for granted, as if it happened without requiring any particular attention. Much of this routine learning, however, merely amounts to confirming current beliefs and invalidating new ideas. It remains 'within the box' and cannot support the renewal capabilities we are looking for.

The extent to which managers are likely to spend time and energy on each of the four steps of the learning cycle can actually be measured. This measurement reveals a wide variety of learning styles within managerial ranks, and these styles are influenced by two forces. The first one is the manager's own inclination to spend time on certain preferred steps, rather than others. For instance, some are information hungry, some enjoy conceptualizing, some prefer action and others have a more reflective style. The second force is how the job and the organization emphasize certain steps and minimize others. In this portrait of the *learning manager*, we will exaggerate certain characteristics precisely because, if exaggerated in practice (and it happens), they do prevent learning and, ultimately, renewal.

Information gathering – the importance of information surfing

Within the managerial population the information-gathering step is likely to be quite focused. Searching for information is often perceived as a menial task that should be delegated to assistants. This reduces the possibility of hitting the odd piece of information that does not fit but could add, when placed on the map, a new perspective on a familiar landscape. It inhibits exploring information inductively, a cognitive process that also triggers new perspectives. Managers, when they search information themselves due to time and other pressures and view it as a chore, will also tend to be quite selective, filtering out whatever does not obviously fit. Reinforcement of current wisdom is likely to follow, rather than mind-opening new insights. In the information age, even though the information scope should be broader rather than narrower, and even though thinking that can make a difference can only start from *unexpected* ideas, surfing information is not yet a legitimate managerial activity.

Conceptualization – maintaining a dynamic overview and using it to set clear priorities

With information that is focused rather than open, conceptualization, the next step in the learning cycle, will necessarily be simplistic. Fit-all-sizes, two-by-two matrices tend to be extremely popular. Indeed little time is generally spent synthesizing the information, giving it some meaning that can enrich the map and ultimately improve or renew the competitive formula. Managers often have difficulty developing an overview, a *helicopter view* of their competitive situation and of the possible approaches to address it. They often have difficulty prioritizing issues and re-prioritizing them to incorporate new information. In the information age, simplistic strategic maps are likely to reflect commodity, me-too strategies that really make no difference.

It is interesting to observe how complex the strategic conceptual frameworks of the leaders of self-renewing organizations can be and their mental agility in enriching and reshaping them with new data. It is even more interesting to observe how they can synthesize this complexity into a few, clear priorities that they communicate to their organization. They are strong conceptualizers and effective model-builders, providing their organization with this simplification of a complex reality that allows its members to proceed in the right direction, doing the 'right things'. However, many managers have difficulty with this step in the learning cycle. Synthesized capabilities are essentially neglected by intensive mass-education systems, and professional life, with its compartmentalized organization systems and processes, further deteriorates them.

Action – controlling the fire

Contrary to the first two steps in the learning cycle, information openness and conceptualization, the third step, action, is at the centre of the manager's preoccupations. This is clearly revealed by assessments of managers' learning styles. They generally prefer those activities where things get done, where tangible results can be shown, where there is fire. This is corroborated by many studies of how managers spend their time and by the observation of certain managerial myths and role models.

However, action without information openness and conceptualization is likely to be either repetitive, sticking to the same routines time and again, or fire-fighting. In either case this is not the type of action, with a well-conceived dose of experimenting, that can lead to learning and ultimately renewal. Action by itself is not enough to provide 'action learning'; rather, the obsession with action alone will lead to a narrowing of focus and specialization, resulting in the same repetitive scenarios that run the risk of becoming totally irrelevant in a fast-changing context.

Reflection and renewal – maintaining momentum for renewal

The fourth step in the learning cycle, debriefing and reflection, is given little, if any, time and attention in most organizations. Yet in terms of organization processes, it would be relatively easy to support. Systematic, periodic debriefing meetings would go a long way to supporting the reflection step: it seems very much a question of discipline.

This lack of interest for debriefing has cultural reasons anchored in the cognitive styles inspired by the earlier, more stable information contexts, such as the unwillingness to face failures or the expectation that a senior manager must know everything. It is reinforced by performance assessment processes that provide neither tolerance for errors nor support for initiative.

Other reasons have to do with the fact that, interestingly, success tends to be even less debriefed and, as a result, less understood, than failure. It is more gratifying to attribute it to abstract forces such as the inborn wisdom of the chief, the dedication of the team, or even the strength of the brand, than to specific, well-co-ordinated and well-executed moves, relying on identifiable capabilities meeting the needs of a particular situation. As a result, we do not know exactly what can be replicated, when and where, and we start believing that this is the right way – full stop. For example, IBM is just beginning to understand that the global mobilization of its information technology services creates valuable, saleable know-how, in many cases more profitably than its computer manufacturing capabilities. A well-known chain of pharmacies realized only recently that its purchasing know-how, rather than its brand, could be leveraged globally. Apple never realized, nor drew the consequences of the fact, that its most valuable knowledge was in user-interface software, not in computer manufacturing. Without reflection and debriefing, there is no action learning; there is no creation of new, proprietary knowledge that can be re-deployed and combined with other knowledge streams to nurture strategic renewal.

Designing a learning architecture

Reinforcing certain attitudes and implementing specific actions within the organization can support each step in the learning cycle. Before investing in costly information and knowledge systems, a *learning organization architecture* must be in place. This architecture, like all architectures, pursues two goals. Its soft features should inspire attitude (as places of worship inspire meditation or contemplation). Its more solid features guide movement, like a high street, avenue or esplanade.

The soft features can usefully be regrouped into two categories: organization culture and leadership. The *organization culture* consists of underlying beliefs that are questioned only rarely. They often have regional cultural roots, like the importance of Finnish *sisu* – stubborn determination to continue and overcome in the moment of adversity; a combination of stamina, courage, and obstinacy held in reserve for hard times (Finland Page Website) – in Nokia's culture. The organization culture also relies on specific norms and values, such as Nokia's four values: customer satisfaction, achievement, respect for the individual, and continuous learning. *Leadership* is the role model provided by senior management, through their own behaviour, the questions they ask, the things they say, what they focus on, and their key messages.

The more solid features consist of processes and infrastructure. All *organization processes* can have an impact on learning, but most important here are people-related processes such as recruitment, development, career management, objective setting, performance assessment, and reward. The *infrastructure* covers of course the organization structure: the definition of responsibility areas, the hierarchical system, and the cross-organization interfaces. Also of great importance is the information infrastructure and the use of information technology.

Every corporation has its own architecture; some of its features have been explicitly developed. Others have emerged spontaneously over time, inadvertently shaped by organization members. Designing, creating and maintaining a *learning* architecture is the job of the CEO. And it is not a matter of a few big systems; it relies on a lot of small details that require continuous attention.

Thinking about the learning architecture, it is critical to remember the evidence that learning is an individual commitment, supported by individual attitudes and capabilities. The organization's architectural features are only second-order learning agents, supporting or not individual commitment. So, for each step in the learning cycle, we will review:

- which attitudes and capabilities need to be reinforced; and
- which architectural features need to be implemented to support the corresponding attitudes and capabilities.

Building information openness using divergence agents

Information openness requires *divergence agents*, factors contributing to distinctiveness in the organization's architecture, in order to encourage heightened awareness of:

- new signals providing a different perspective;
- information that does not fit and questions current beliefs; and
- new fields from which meaningful inferences can be drawn.

Individual attitudes and capabilities are divergence agents when they allow such unsettling information to flow:

- *Curiosity* – admitting that there is more to learn from others and outside.
- *Openness* – the willingness to receive unsettling and challenging information.
- *Access* – the willingness to reach out for this information.
- *Transparency* – being non-protective and non-defensive with what one knows and does not know.
- *Exchange* – volunteering information.

The organizational culture must support these attitudes and capabilities, promoting information-sharing inside the business and making information openness both feasible and legitimate. At 3M, for example, the norm is that 'technologies belong to the company', not to a department and even less to an individual. The organizational culture must also support outside co-operation in alliances, and with suppliers or customers, as a means of gathering new information and learning.

The leadership must promote these attitudes and capabilities by admitting that they do not have all the answers, by asking many questions that broaden the scope of people, by asking for feedback from their subordinates, and by telling the truth. During an encounter with high-potential young managers, the newly appointed senior manager of a large European company in need of a sharp turn-around was asked what his priorities were. His answer was "What do you think they should be?". The young managers started telling him which business units they believed should be divested and his comment was "Well, this is exactly it! And you gave me all the right reasons." Needless to say, the young managers were all on board, particularly those from the units in question who knew that they were not getting the necessary resources to develop.

The processes must support these attitudes and capabilities by providing divergence opportunities. People management, for example, can ensure that recruitment is eclectic, avoiding one single educational background, one single nationality, or one single language, and that career paths provide an exposure to different technologies, functions, markets and competitive contexts. The tendency of large French companies, for example, to fill their top management teams with graduates from the same two *Grandes Ecoles*, Ecole Polytechnique and Ecole Nationale d'Administration, has been mentioned as the reason for the lack of questioning that has ultimately led to some well-publicized disasters.

The infrastructure will also contribute to information openness. Flat organizations with limited hierarchy are known to facilitate the circulation of information. Direct interpersonal contacts, rather than hierarchical channels, also ensure the wide availability of relevant information. Richard Branson, the founder of Virgin, explains that by talking directly with front-line employees about their problems, he can learn about potential crises before they develop.

The information infrastructure must provide wide information access with few restrictions as possible, and should also support information sharing across organization boundaries. Systems such as ABB's Abacus, for example, have done a great deal to stimulate fast learning at all organization levels.

The architectural layout of buildings can also make an important contribution to this attitude of open communication. Hewlett-Packard's European headquarters in Geneva or Nokia's new headquarters in Espoo, near Helsinki, are good examples of buildings designed to facilitate communication openness.

Supporting conceptualization: the key role of convergence agents

The conceptualization step in the learning cycle requires *convergence agents* in the organizational architecture, focusing everyone's attention on an overall direction, as well as a few key priorities and guidelines. In effect, these convergence agents shelter the organization from some of the complexity of the world.

They should inspire and reinforce attitudes and capabilities of synthesis, of reconciling conflicting demands, of dealing with tensions. Managers often have difficulty accepting the fact that this has become a critical dimension of their job: ensuring that the necessary co-ordination is present so that these tensions yield positive energy. Their job is no longer smooth, linear implementation, as used to be the case. Such capabilities need to be complemented with interactive, communication and negotiation capabilities:

- *Seeing different perspectives* – the ability to put oneself in different functional, regional, product 'shoes'.
- *Overview* – the ability to take the helicopter view, to see how the pieces fit together.
- *Synthesis initiative* – the ability to cascade the overview and to see how a part fits with, and contributes to, the whole.
- *Providing focus* – the ability to prioritize and simplify the world for others.
- *Enriching the map* – the ability to reshape the map, taking into account new information.

The organizational culture should contain convergence agents that encourage and support interaction and co-operation through which individuals, representing different perspectives and business requirements, co-ordinate with each other. In many organizations, this co-ordination is difficult without going all the way to the top, which prevents the formation at intermediary and front-line levels of the syntheses necessary to act, and deprives these levels of important learning opportunities. In some companies, like 3M, this co-ordination seems almost instinctive. New projects will naturally establish their interface with existing ones without resorting to top-management arbitration.

The leadership obviously plays a very critical part in providing focus, priorities, frameworks for action and a sense of direction. Some senior managers always seem to carry in their briefcase the half-dozen slides that explain how they see their industry shaping, what the implications are for the company, and where they see it three to five years down the road. This same message, repeated time and again, clearly provides people with a map they can use to give meaning to the new information that keeps coming to them.

The processes, like people management, need to develop a co-ordination mindset through work experience and career opportunities. Siemens has had for years a process for rotating high-potential young managers through functions, products and regions, thus creating a cadre of managers who could quickly grasp the key dimensions of a new business. Co-ordination processes, such as steering committees and co-ordinating committees, are critically important to provide timely focus at the front-line level, where most of the relevant knowledge is available. ABB has been known for its large number of such co-ordination mechanisms to balance local–global tensions.

The infrastructure must also support the convergence needed here. Still in many corporations, for example, large chunks of the information infrastructure cannot connect to each other. Many information technology-based tools, meant to help virtual teams exchange views and converge, organize inputs in ways that cannot support synthesis, for example chronologically. Instead, co-operative tools allowing co-ordinated, progressive and coherent models for action to be developed will prove to be an important innovation for the future.

The physical facilities, for example by bringing units together, will also contribute to providing focus. Descarpentries, the CEO who turned Carnaud around before it was merged into Carnaud MetalBox and then acquired by Crown, Cork & Seal, had located sales at the plants to ensure a service focus – an approach that had actually been enforced by John Connally at CC&S in the sixties.

Applying action learning

Contrary to common wisdom, the action phase in the learning cycle requires divergence agents. Without the willingness to experiment, there will be no action learning, and experimenting implies deviating from the mainstream. Coherent implementation that is totally effective may sound extremely attractive, but not only is it not feasible, it would also be the best way to march orderly, better and better, in one single direction that will inevitably become outmoded and irrelevant at some future point. The reality is that action will never be totally coherent because situations change and evolve; these necessary divergences must, however, be executed in a way that produces learning rather than maverick intentions.

Some of these divergence agents exist in attitudes and capabilities of taking responsibility for what ever needs to be done. Many managers would be quite happy just to be told what to do, and in fact many organizations expect no more from their managers; but if organizations could really operate in that manner, they would probably not need managers at all. However, in the reality of an information-intensive environment, where knowledge must be expanded all the time, this attitude no longer works. The attitudes and capabilities that provide the controlled divergence necessary to learn from action emphasize initiative:

- *Action orientation* – the urge to make things work – which is more learning-oriented than the urge to get things done.
- *Initiative* – the view that one can do it, without necessarily being told; the view that it is up to oneself, not to the rest of the world.
- *Taking responsibility* – taking it upon oneself to make things work and feeling accountable for it.
- *Trying things out* – the willingness to get off the beaten path, and to take some personal risk.
- *Action learning* – the view that learning has to be one of the outcomes, and the related ability to set up learning parameters and to control risk, for example when experimenting.

The organizational culture should support the controlled divergence attitudes and capabilities necessary for action learning. In some organizations, it is 'someone else's job'. The newly appointed senior manager of a large company was referring to his single biggest disappointment since he had started on this job as a situation when a part was needed urgently by the assembly department. This part was promptly requested from, and made by, the manufacturing unit, but never reached the assembly department in the required time. Transporting the part between the two departments had been someone else's job. It will be difficult for this organization to imagine and develop, for example, value-adding services to its customers.

An organizational culture that supports experimenting is also an obvious requirement for learning – lectures on the fact that someone else did it are not good enough. Intel's practice of taking options on several technological paths concurrently until a standard would emerge was a substantial source of learning – particularly from the path that had apparently led nowhere: the knowledge accumulated there always resurfaced later in another project.

The leadership is also essential in supporting action-learning. In many cases, senior

> **"The best thing is to do the right thing; the second best is to do the wrong thing and learn; and not taking action is the only unacceptable behaviour." Percy Barnevik, former CEO, ABB**

managers are just too happy to be asked to intervene as decision-makers or referees in situations that should be resolved at lower levels, not only for effectiveness reasons, but so that the learning takes place where it can make a difference in the future. Pushing back decisions to front-line levels is critical to developing initiative and ensuring action-learning. A famous case on ABB's relays business (Bartlett, 1998) depicts the head of one of the 60 business areas pushing back three times in a row, to the *ad hoc* cross-organization team in charge, the decision on how to allocate products among four, newly merged plants, until the team would finally reach a unanimous decision. The first time the team came back with no decision; the second time it came back with a split decision; only at the third attempt were the team able to sort it out among themselves: huge learning on which criteria ought to be used for such recurring decisions.

The processes, such as decision-marking, allow decisions to be made at the level where learning will be mostly applicable, which is normally closer to the front line than to the top. Other organization features ensure the necessary transparency to manage the risk of experimenting, such as explicit experimenting methodologies, attention to 'due process' and not only to results, proper documentation of experiences, and 'best practice communities' from which experience and advice can be tapped. Among these, attention to the process is probably absent most frequently, due to the insistence on results. However, it is the *process* that is the source of learning, not the results.

The infrastructure makes room for initiatives by hosting them where support knowledge will be available. 3M, for example, is able to place new ventures under the wing of existing units that master a related technology, or have manufacturing know-how, or can provide channel and market access. The information infrastructure can also provide the necessary transparency by publicizing new initiatives and allowing the whole organization to learn from it.

Fostering reflection and renewal

Reflection again requires convergence agents to draw from explicit action learning points and feed renewal. As discussed before, these agents are generally missing in organizations. Numerous studies, including our experiences at IMD, have shown that managers have their best ideas away from work. This not only confirms the need for distracting information in a learning process, but also underlines the lack of the necessary convergence agents in organizations. Managerial mindsets, organization cultures and systems, and even physical layouts, seem not to leave room for reflection.

Reflection agents first exist in attitudes of self-development, of pushing one's limits beyond the safe replication of what seems to have worked before, and of venturing into new, still partly unproven models of how the future could be changed:

- *Debriefing orientation* – the inclination and capability to revisit what has been completed to draw learning points.
- *Non-defensiveness* – the ability to give and take constructive criticism.
- *Thinking* – the ability to review one's own behaviour, and to draw personal behaviour and process lessons from experience; the ability to think through the next steps as a result.
- *Learning* – the willingness to learn and to take personal responsibility for it.
- *Improving* – the ability to point at improvements rather than at culprits and the belief that 'good can be done better'.

The organizational culture that supports these convergent attitudes and capabilities is more a question of everyday discipline than of high-level values. "It's like saying graces," stated an executive. "At the beginning of a project phase, you restate the objective, and at the end you revisit the process." Necessarily, such a culture will also value self-development.

The leadership will promote forward-looking attitudes that assume that individuals will develop further, away from their comfort zones, if provided with the necessary context. Part of this context is the mental, organizational and physical space for reflection. The mental space, in particular, is created by asking questions, rather than by giving the answers. Managers need capabilities of the good 'case teachers' whose value is to help learners be bright and find the answers, rather than demonstrate how bright they are themselves. Their questions often have to do with the 'how' – the process from which we can learn and improve - rather than with the 'what' – the results, which are what they are.

The processes have to do with the debriefing discipline promoted by the culture. These are rituals providing a framework, a checklist of points to look at when debriefing, of questions to ask, and of dimensions to draw lessons on. Such processes must be found, in particular, in objective-setting and performance-assessment systems, and in career management processes which should rely on explicit learning red threads that are clear to all parties.

The infrastructure leaves a large role to information systems and technology and to documentation technology. Collecting the accumulated knowledge, organizing it and making it easily retrievable prove to be complex tasks. An aggravating difficulty is the fact that the piece of knowledge that can make a difference is often not the obvious one, but the one that was hit inadvertently – a challenge for 'smart' browsers.

The thinking and reflection infrastructure also includes physical layouts: the body composure of a reflecting person (even without going to Rodin's extreme metaphor) is not necessarily for public display. Who wants to be caught thinking? Some layout features help, such as areas where it is acceptable to sit back, where there is a landscape to gaze at, where you can 'think aloud'. The sixteenth century French philosopher Montaigne was known to have, at his mansion, a long corridor where he could walk up and down to reflect. The Japanese after-work socialization is a form of debriefing where a lot of feedback is sought and given in a lower-risk context. Some companies provide time off that can be used, for example, to attend more reflective learning events, to perform studies of specific interest for other business units, or to contribute to community or charity projects. All these features provide space for reflecting, as dreams do during sleep; it is then up to the organization to make good use of the knowledge that develops in the brains when this is allowed.

CASE STUDY: THE LEARNING ARCHITECTURE OF ABB

Matrix organizations are associated with horror stories: many have failed; most end up being dominated by one of the dimensions of the matrix; front-line managers generally end up paralysed by the conflicting expectations of their various bosses. Yet many would agree that the brand of matrix organization adopted by ABB in the late 1980s has had a decisive impact on the company's growth. What people often fail to realize is that this was the case because this organization was in fact supported by a complete 'learning architecture'.

The organization culture fosters entrepreneurship, front-line initiative, information transparency, and face-to-face resolution of issues (current CEO, Lindahl, has outlawed the use of e-mail to vent criticism). This has helped the front-line managers – of newly acquired companies, for example – identify growth opportunities that had always been out of their reach under previous management. It helps front-line managers understand the perspectives of other business dimensions and take them into account. It provides a fertile soil for many initiatives from which to learn across the company. Finally front-line managers, not being confined to their silos, know which other front-line managers to go to to get hold of best practice.

Leadership typically sees its role as making learning opportunities inescapable, by creating stretch opportunities, challenges, and questioning assumptions, opinions and approaches – like good case teachers. Leaders ask what-if questions; they push back the resolution of cross-organization tensions at the front-line level, refusing to act as referees; they don't allow the upward delegation of tough issues; they do not have all the answers on issues where the front-line managers are paid to be the experts.

Numerous processes have been developed to support and ensure co-ordination at the most appropriate front-line level: business-area boards comprizing representatives of other dimensions of the matrix; steering committees that bring around the same table all those who have a stake in a conflicting issue; functional councils to ensure functional co-ordination across countries . . . Such processes are meant to broaden everyone's scope outside their immediate areas of accountability, to facilitate the development of a common sense of direction, support implementation and share experience.

The infrastructure similarly supports organization learning. Front-line managers run a real business, with the ability to control the necessary resources – and single-handed accountability for their results. Abacus, the company-wide performance-assessment system, allows them to benchmark, to learn from, each other.

BENCHMARKING

Assessing the four elements of rapid and proactive learning within your organization

For each of the four stages of the learning cycle, there are key attributes to recognize, foster and encourage, as well as behaviours to avoid, in order to build a dynamic learning organization that emphasizes corporate renewal.

Harnessing the wind – information-gathering expertise

Gathering information is like harnessing the wind: it can provide a refreshing and powerful source of energy, or it can be ignored or even resented.

⯈ *Curiosity – are managers hungry for information and inquisitive?* Are people interested in what others in the organization know? Do senior managers ask a lot of questions from the employees they meet? Are critical external trends systematically scanned? Are subscriptions to online information sources widely available?

⯈ *Openness – are people open-minded and receptive to new ideas?* Are good ideas well accepted, where ever they may come from? Do senior managers ask for feedback on their areas of responsibility? Are recruitment processes sufficiently eclectic? Are there many processes to bring non-routine issues to people's attention?

⯈ *Access – is information-gathering part of everyone's job?* Is it all right to go and get the information where it is, irrespective of hierarchies and organization boundaries? Do senior managers spend a lot of time gathering information from customers, suppliers and other outside sources? Are there processes to gain as much information as possible from customers, suppliers and other outside sources? Is internet access considered a normal working tool?

⯈ *Transparency – are people open about the information they have and the information they need?* Is it all right to admit that you do not know, even to subordinates or to bosses? Do senior managers seek diverse opinions on critical issues? Are there many formal processes allowing organization units to share information? Is the organization culture relatively flat?

⯈ *Exchange – are people volunteering information?* Do people share information openly? Do senior managers share willingly what they know? Do objective-setting and performance-assessment processes take into account information-sharing attitudes? Is information technology used to capture and disseminate information across the organization?

Mapping the forest – conceptualization

The second stage is like mapping a forest: it is impossible (and probably useless) to put every new tree we see on the map. But it is critical to have a sufficient overview of how the forest might look – a model of the forest – to interpret whether a new tree observed has some significance, to decide which way to go next, and to decide whether the map needs rethinking.

➤ *Seeing different perspectives – are people able to look at issues from different perspectives?* Is it natural to get out of one's functional, or product, or country perspective? Is management able to integrate many different perspectives? Are co-ordination taskforces used widely to bring together different perspectives? Are the facilities equipped to facilitate cross-organization encounters?

➤ *Overview capabilities – do people have a good understanding of the essentials of the business?* Do people have a good sense of the most critical business issues? Is management able to communicate clear strategic frameworks? Are careers managed to provide early co-ordination responsibilities? Are the facilities equipped with convenient meeting rooms?

➤ *Synthesis initiative – are all managerial levels involved in shaping the overview picture?* Are people expected to reconcile conflicting issues at their level? Does management involve different people in discussing the significance of new information? Do decision processes ensure that decisions are made close to action? Is there technology to facilitate collective decision-making?

➤ *Providing focus – do people share the same map?* Do people have clear action priorities? Is management able to simplify complex issues into actionable priorities? Are the processes providing a coherent sense of direction? Is the information infrastructure allowing a coherent sense of direction?

➤ *Enriching the map – can the map be rethought to take into account new meaningful information?* Can people relate their new decisions to the overall direction? Can management integrate new business trends into their strategic maps? Are careers managed in a way that helps shape an overall understanding of strategic issues? Are practical techniques available to bring discussions and meetings to a closure?

Mastering the fire – action

The third stage in a learning voyage is action; like fire it can create energy and embers can be reused; or it can consume resources and go out.

▥▶ *Action orientation – do people have an urge to make things work?* Do people focus on what can be done, rather than on what cannot be done? Are people expected to take well-calculated risks when necessary? Are there implementation follow-up processes? Is progress information transparent?

▥▶ *Initiative – is there enough decentralization? Do people feel empowered?* Do people feel that there is no need to check with everyone before starting anything? Do managers refrain from involving themselves in decisions they have delegated? Do objective-setting and performance-assessment processes support initiative? Can new initiatives be decided at relatively low levels?

▥▶ *Responsibility taking – do people take it upon themselves to make things work?* Do people tend to fix things rather than to look for culprits? Do managers throw the ball back at their subordinates who try to 'delegate upwards'? Do career management processes emphasize early front-line responsibilities? Can front-line people make the necessary decisions themselves?

▥▶ *Trying things out – can people experiment?* Are people encouraged to get out of the beaten path? Are people encouraged to question the way things are done? Do management-development processes emphasize action learning? Does the organization allow experimenting across units?

▥▶ *Action learning – is learning seen as an important outcome of action?* Are failures seen as opportunities to learn? Does management challenge people beyond their comfort zone? Do career management processes take into account the learning opportunities of a new job? Are knowledge synergies taken into account in organization design?

Conquering the mountain – reflection and renewal

The fourth stage in a learning cycle ensures that there can be many more to come; having climbed a summit, our eye is already on how to get to the next one: what has been achieved? how was it achieved? how will that get us to the next peak? Reflection and debriefing – often neglected as part of the process – are vital here.

▥▶ *Debriefing – what worked and what did not work? How should we do it the next time?* Is regular debriefing part of the culture? Do managers regularly ask for key take-away lessons? Are there formal processes to support debriefing? Is the outcome of debriefing sessions well documented?

▥▶ *Non-defensiveness – is debriefing conducted in a constructive spirit?* Is constructive criticism generally accepted? Do managers admit that they may not have the answer? Are there processes to analyse past projects? Are the lessons from past projects systematically disseminated?

▥▶ *Thinking – is setting aside time to think a legitimate managerial activity?* Are people expected to be able to reflect on their own actions and behaviours? Do managers ask questions that make people think? Do objective-setting and performance-assessment processes take into account a person's ability to draw lessons from action? Are the physical facilities designed to support more reflective types of activities?

- *Learning - is learning considered a priority activity?* Are people expected to invest into their own development? Do managers insist on giving high priority to learning initiatives? Are there processes to assess the company's knowledge base? Is the company knowledge easily accessible?
- *Improving - is there an expectation that there is always room for improvement?* Do people naturally look for possible improvements in everything they do? Do managers frequently ask questions on how to improve even what seems to be well under control? Do career management processes take into account knowledge-transfer opportunities? Are improvements systematically documented and publicised?

SUMMARY

How managers learn

Learning is vital to an organization's sustained competitiveness. In fact the value of learning has risen steadily as a result of the speed of change: as situations constantly shift and alter, managers are foolish if they believe they have all the answers. What matters now is not how much people know, but *how they react to what they do not know*. Rapid and proactive learning leads to knowledge expansion, and this in turn is the engine for corporate renewal. Learning provides the ability to adapt, innovate and compete.

Four elements form the basis of the learning organization, and each element can be approached in sequence through the learning. The four stages are:

1. *Information gathering and openness (the wind)* - this is an important task that should be given priority (its full value is rarely recognized by managers), and managers should be open to as many sources of information as possible. The value of this information openness is in how it challenges existing views and triggers new perspectives.
2. *Conceptualization (the forest)* - information openness is useless without the next stage of conceptualization. This part of the learning cycle requires careful synthesis of the information, using it to enrich and enhance existing plans, tactics and strategies. The need here is to improve the map of the forest whilst also taking the right path through the trees.

3. *Action (the fire)* – energy is vital to ensuring that actions are effectively executed and followed up. Managers are most often preoccupied with this stage of the process, usually at the expense of the others; however, action by itself at best perpetuates the status quo, preserving the danger that the organization will become out of touch and out of date.
4. *Reflection and renewal (the mountain)* – the final part of the cycle that links back to information openness, is the stage of debriefing and reflection. Many organizational features can help and support reflection and these in turn lead to steady improvement, new ideas and approaches – a change from existing patterns of behaviour to ones that are progressive, taking account of current realities.

 **BEST PRACTICE**

Building a learning organization

Creating the right conditions, changing and influencing attitudes, and taking specific actions will all help to support each step in the learning cycle. Building the right architecture to support the learning organization is clearly important, and there are four areas where each part of the cycle can be actively enhanced:

1. the organization's *culture*;
2. the organization's *leadership*;
3. the organization's *processes* and the way that information is used;
4. the organization's *infrastructure*, including the use of information technology.

Actions needed to support each stage of the learning cycle are summarized in Table 7.1.

Table 7.1: *Examples of learning architecture best practice*

	Culture	Leadership	Processes	Infrastructure
Building information openness				
Curiosity	People are interested in what others know	Senior managers ask a lot of questions	Critical external trends are systematically scanned	Subscriptions to online information are available
Openness	Good new ideas are well accepted	Senior managers ask for feedback	Recruitment processes are eclectic	'Push' information is used for non-routine issues
Access	Getting the information where it is	Senior managers gather a lot of outside information	There are processes to scan suppliers, customers, etc.	Internet access is a normal working tool
Transparency	Admitting that you do not know	Managers seek diverse opinions on key issues	Organization units regularly share information	The organization structure is flat
Exchange	People share information openly	Senior managers share what they know	Performance includes information-sharing attitudes	Information technology is on every desktop
Supporting conceptualization				
Flexibility of perspectives	Looking outside functional boundaries is natural	Management builds on many perspectives	Co-ordination taskforces are used very frequently	There are areas for cross-organization encounters
Overview capabilities	People have a good sense of the most critical issues	Management constantly communicates the strategy	Career management ensures a good overview	There are convenient and effective meeting rooms
Synthesis initiative	People have to resolve conflicts at their level	Different people are involved to discuss new information	Decisions are made where information is available	Technology facilitates involvement in decision
Providing focus	People are able to keep clear priorities	Management simplifies complex issues	Processes ensure a coherent sense of direction	There is one common information infrastructure
Enriching the map	New decisions refer to the overall direction	Management can interpret new business trends	Career paths take people through many perspectives	Techniques are available to bring discussions to closure

Applying action learning	Action orientation	We focus on what can be done	Management encourages well-calculated risks	There are processes to support new initiatives	IT is used to advertise the new initiatives
	Initiative	Checking with everyone before acting is discouraged	Management takes delegation seriously	Performance emphasizes initiative	Initiative can be decided at low levels
	Responsibility taking	People take responsibility for fixing problems	Managers generally throw the ball back	Career paths include early front-line responsibilities	The infrastructure ensures frontline decision making
	Trying things out	People are expected to get out of the beaten path	Management encourages people to question things	Management-development emphasizes action-learning	Units can take initiatives outside of their boundaries
	Action Learning	People look at failures as opportunities to learn	Management provides people with challenges	Career paths look at learning opportunities	Initiatives are hosted where the knowledge is
Fostering reflection	Debriefing	Meetings are always debriefed	Management insists on key learning points	Debriefing meetings are a normal practice in projects	IT is used to document and disseminate learning
	Non-defensiveness	Constructive criticism is well accepted	Managers admit it when they do not have the answer	Sources of poor performance are analysed	IT is used to collect and disseminate best practice
	Thinking	Reflecting on one's own behaviour is important	Managers typically ask for feedback from their team	Performance includes learning from experience	Areas for more reflective activities are available
	Learning	People must invest in their own development	Managers are responsible for their team's learning	The company's knowledge base is reviewed regularly	There are internal 'yellow pages' on who knows what
	Improving	Reflecting on improvements is part of the culture	Management typically focuses on what to do next	Career paths facilitate knowledge transfer	IT is used to document and publicize new projects

References

Bartlett, C.A. (1998) *ABB's Relays Business: Building and Managing A Global Matrix*, HBS Case 9-394-016, Harvard Business School Publishing, Boston, USA.

Finland Page. http://www.csc.fi/tiko/finland.html.

Kuhn, T. (1962) *The Structure of Scientific Revolutions*. The University of Chicago Press.

CHAPTER 8

From Information and Knowledge to Innovation

Information for innovation is more externally focused and forward looking than information for operations, and it can be viewed as a clear business process with a top-down and bottom-up dimension. In this chapter, **Jean-Philippe Deschamps** outlines the innovation process and describes how information can be used to support innovation.

CASE STUDY: INNOVATION IN FINANCIAL SERVICES — THE DEVELOPMENT OF THE CREDIT CARD

The word innovation conjures up the image of a process that is spontaneous and unpredictable – and hence unmanageable. The innovation literature abounds in stories of serendipitous discoveries; in most of these cases, independent-minded champions doggedly pursue an idea until they hit the jackpot. Often – as the stories don't fail to stress – the inventors have to persist in the secret of their labs against the knowledge and will of management. The archetypes of such innovators are Art Fry and Spence Silver, the legendary 3M chemists who turned a poorly sticking adhesive into a billion dollar blockbuster: Post-It Notes. In most of these stories, innovation proceeds in a bottom-up fashion. Ideas and the drive to see them through originate from the labs or marketing outposts, not from the top of the organization. The role of management – as former 3M CEO, Lewis Lehr, stated – is to create a "spirit of adventure and challenge" in order to encourage entrepreneurship.

However, the role of senior managers in proactively developing innovation is often more significant and direct, and it relies for success on the support and active use of information and knowledge. The commercial development of the credit card is an example. In 1958 a research group called the Customer Services Research Department at the Bank of America, with the remit to develop potential new products, created the first credit card. This development was augmented later by seven bankers at Citibank who added the key features of credit cards, including merchant discounts, credit limits, and terms and conditions.

This development did not occur in response to a market need: it emerged because people within the banking business used their tacit knowledge and information. This included using their market sensing abilities; understanding of customers, information and forecasts about economic and social trends; experience with similar product ideas (such as instalment loans); and knowledge about new developments in technology to devise a popular and practical service. It can be argued that this start heralded the beginning of major innovation within the financial services industry, with a lineage that can be traced for more than 40 years and includes ATM machines and now the growth of Internet banking.

There are a number of important points to note about this innovation which distinguish it from the more famous bottom-up (and often serendipitous) innovations such as the Post-It Note. First, senior management support was essential: they set up the unit, helped to develop its features (largely using their experience) and gave it the support needed to take root and grow. Indeed, in 1977 Citibank innovated in this sector again, this time in their marketing drive to increase their share of the lucrative market for credit cards in the USA. With a single 26 million-strong mailshot, they became, virtually overnight, the largest issuer of Visa and Mastercards in the world. This was a platform from which they could strengthen all of their activities, eventually becoming the world market leader in banking. Clearly this level of innovation required top-level support. Second, the senior management role was particularly significant early on in the process, creating the right conditions and providing support and momentum. Third, information was at the heart of top-down innovation. Management and harnessing of information and tacit knowledge is an essential part of ensuring that the innovation process starts, continues and delivers success.

Overview

The need to foster greater internal growth is inducing an increasing number of companies to look proactively for innovation. Nestlé's entry into functional foods, and Daimler-Chrysler's commitment to fuel cells, exemplify this second type of innovation. It is driven by the ambition of management to create a new business territory, and it is fuelled by a compelling vision of new opportunities. For this reason, it is sometimes referred to as 'top-down'. Unlike bottom-up innovation, which proceeds in a somewhat erratic fashion, top-down innovation generally results from an organized, but non-linear, process.

Whatever its origin, bottom-up or top-down, innovation is a business process, and like all business processes, it is highly dependent on information. But the information needed to feed and support innovation is of a very different nature from that required to run and optimize operational processes. In short, it is much broader in scope and considerably *softer* in nature. Indeed, innovation is driven more by intelligence, foresight, insights and market after-thoughts, than by hard facts and data. These soft and creative types of information are needed in order to:

- Scan the market, competitive and technological environment for opportunities, sensing potential leads.
- Generate ideas and evaluate alternative methods for implementing the most promising of these leads.
- Identify the new competencies that need to be developed to exploit these opportunities.
- Manage the technical and commercial development process and the risks linked with building and introducing something new.

In this chapter we will:

- Outline the role of information in generating innovation.
- Explain the innovation process and practical techniques for using information to drive innovation.

Information and the innovation process

Figure 8.1 highlights the point that even within the realm of innovation there are major differences in the type of information generated under the two types of processes: bottom-up and top-down.

Information pattern	Bottom-up innovation process	Top-down innovation process
Scope (breadth and depth) of the information gathered	Limited	Extensive
Mode and process of acquisition of that information	*Ad hoc*	Systematic
Number of people involved in information acquisition/ exploitation	Few	Many

Figure 8.1: *Information patterns – bottom-up and top-down innovation*

To simplify, information is an important element of bottom-up innovation, but it is not its main driver. The idea or insight generally comes first, often by chance, and information is searched mostly to validate, challenge or enrich the initial idea. In top-down innovation, on the other hand, information is at the root of the process.

> **"Information – for example on trends and disruptions that will create opportunities – is generally what triggers management insights and starts ideas flowing"**

The importance of information for top-down innovation

When management decides to pioneer a new business territory it is generally in reaction to streams of information which all point to an opportunity. The pursuit of these opportunities generally involves starting a series of interlocking activities and projects – we will call them processes – geared to satisfy two main objectives:

1. Generating, validating and selecting the best possible ideas to address those unfulfilled or unarticulated customer problems, needs or desires, which managers sense lie at the root of the opportunity.
2. Developing, launching, marketing and exploiting the best possible solutions to these customer problems, needs or wants, in terms of attractive and economical new products or services.

The numerous and diverse activities geared to meet the first objective can be called the *upstream processes* in innovation. They establish the context and prepare for the actual development and launch of the new product or service, which are the *downstream processes*. The type of information required for each of these two types of processes will generally be quite different.

CASE STUDIES: THE ROLE OF INFORMATION IN TOP-DOWN INNOVATION

*To illustrate the diversity of activities and decisions which stem from a top-down innovation drive – and the corresponding information requirements and flows – let us examine what lies behind **DaimlerChrysler**'s or **Ford**'s recent moves to pioneer the use of fuel cells in cars. If successful, and we will not know this before well into the 2000s, this undertaking will probably be one of the most dramatic examples of top-down innovation. The sums involved in terms of research and development or investments clearly precluded this type of innovation from occurring spontaneously in a bottom-up fashion.*

Over the years both DaimlerChrysler and Ford, in common with all other car manufacturers, gathered an enormous amount of information and intelligence on:

- *the likely trends in environmental legislation, and the impact of increasingly restrictive 'clean-air' rules on car sales and consumer behaviour;*
- *competitors' current developments of alternative power sources, views of technology and likely responses to the environmental challenge; and*
- *the state of the art regarding alternative, 'clean' propulsion technologies and their pros and cons.*

One can assume that the information collected must have been similar across the industry. But the interpretation which companies made of that information, particularly regarding the outlook of competing technologies, was different. Several manufacturers probably judged more severely the technological and cost obstacles that fuel cells would have to surmount before they displace current engines. They saw more immediate benefits in focusing their efforts on developing cleaner versions of current engines, and adopting a follower, 'wait-and-see' attitude on fuel cells. This seems to be the case, among others, for Mitsubishi, the champion of gasoline direct injection (GDI), or PSA (the Peugeot group) for advanced diesel systems. This leads us to a basic but often forgotten first observation: the innovation process is fuelled, upstream, by an insightful interpretation of market, competitor and technology intelligence.

The amount of intelligence DaimlerChrysler and Ford collected probably reinforced their managements' hunch that it would be a matter of years before the sales of internal combustion engines would be curtailed. It also reinforced their perceptions of the limits of existing technology alternatives – like battery-powered cars – and highlighted the promising future of fuel cells. But most importantly perhaps, management probably saw the benefits they would derive from being the first to offer this new revolutionary, environmentally friendly technology. This triggered their ambition to be the first mass-producers of automotive fuel cells. This leads us to a second observation: when it feeds a management ambition, intelligence is often at the roots of a new vision.

Once a vision has been formulated, such as at DaimlerChrysler or Ford, additional intelligence is needed to:

1. *Generate, evaluate, validate and rank the best possible ideas, product concepts and technological routes to exploit the opportunities identified. The 'ideation' process is not just a matter of creativity: robust ideas are rooted in insightful information, and lots of it.*

2. *Build the necessary technological resources for product and process development, and to determine which should be developed internally or through alliances. Knowing they didn't have the necessary chemical engineering expertise to develop fuel cells, DaimlerChrysler and Ford had to find a partner, and this is why they teamed up with the Canadian technology pioneer, Ballard Systems.*
3. *Develop mutually reinforcing product and technology strategies and plans to implement the vision over time. For DaimlerChrysler and Ford, this means determining:*

   - *what types of cars ought to be developed to test and introduce the new technology;*
   - *when, at what price level, and how they should be introduced in the market; and*
   - *which R&D and product development projects need to be programmed to get to that stage in the most time- and cost-effective manner.*

   Given the early stage of development of the technology, both companies are probably still struggling with these types of decisions, and generating a considerable amount of information and knowledge.

Owing to their soft, uncertain and often chaotic pattern, the complex set of activities and decisions – such as those faced by DaimlerChrysler and Ford – are sometimes referred to as innovation's 'fuzzy front-end'. The downstream processes, on the other hand, are more tangible although not devoid of uncertainty. They deal with:

- conceiving, developing and implementing the development projects that have been programmed;
- launching and commercializing the first products or services resulting from that innovation effort; and
- nursing them over their early years to extract the maximum business benefits while sustaining a leadership position.

All of these processes, upstream and downstream, are dynamic and interlocked through information exchanges (*see* Figure 8.2). The information generated through one process will typically serve as input to the next process in the chain. It will also feed back to the process that preceded it in a continuously enriching loop. These processes are also proceeding in parallel. New intelligence, ideas and competencies are constantly generated to enrich the innovation stream.

There is a difference, however, between the type of information needed to manage upstream and downstream processes. The upstream processes deal with broad and diverse types and sources of information, and should typically be viewed as 'on-going', or at least recurring at regular intervals. For the process to succeed the following steps need to be taken:

- *Intelligence on markets, competitors and technologies should be collected on a permanent basis,* to feed the 'ideation' process. But intelligence will also help validate and refine ideas and projects as they are being implemented.
- *New ideas should be generated and collected continuously,* and reviewed at regular intervals to feed the project portfolio. They will also be needed to

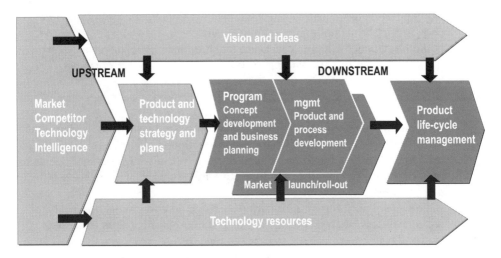

Figure 8.2: *The innovation process*

enhance the attractiveness of the new product or service and solve problems.

- *Product and R&D portfolios should be reviewed and challenged at regular intervals* to ensure the company's offering remains competitive and to review product development priorities in light of change in market and competitive environment.
- *Technological resources should also be scrutinized regularly* for missing, underdeveloped or redundant competencies, or simply for opportunities to outsource to, or partner with, more advanced or effective suppliers.

The downstream processes, on the other hand, deal with increasingly specific information. They are concrete, *ad hoc* processes, with a clear beginning (the decision to start a project) and an end (the post-mortem project review and feedback session, well after the market launch).

BENCHMARKING

Ten questions to assess your use of information for innovation

1. Do you make a distinction between the information needed to optimize operations and that needed to enhance innovation?

2. Do you have a systematic and formal process to collect customer, market, competitor and technological intelligence?
3. Is the intelligence you are collecting looking forward beyond your normal planning horizon? Is it covering at least the duration of two product lifecycles?
4. Is this intelligence combining hard aspects (data-based facts and trends) with softer ones (early signals, insights, predictions)?
5. Are you tapping all parts of the organization (functions, business units and geographical markets) to collect that information?
6. Do you have a process to cross-fertilize these various forms of intelligence to enrich their perspective and identify robust opportunities at their intersection?
7. Have you set up internal information-sharing and communication tools to collect, discuss, analyse and disseminate the intelligence thus collected?
8. Do you organize regular sessions (exchange forums, management workshops) to make sense of that information and exploit it?
9. Have you entrusted someone (or several entities) with the responsibility to orchestrate and exploit information for innovation and new business creation?
10. Have you set up a system to recognize and reward people for information and insights leading to innovation?

Using information to drive the innovation process

New types of information are necessary in order to feed the innovation process. Companies are generally well organized to generate the information necessary to feed their innovation projects (the downstream processes), but less so to generate, evaluate and disseminate information from which *future projects* will emerge. This probably explains why upstream processes are still perceived as incomplete and unco-ordinated in the best of cases – hence the reference to the 'fuzzy front-end' – and sometimes plainly deficient.

This discrepancy comes from the fact that the two types of information are quite different, as highlighted in Figure 8.3.

Deficiencies in collecting information relevant to innovation upstream are caused by an inadequacy, or sometimes even a complete absence, of process and organizational mechanisms to carry it through. In many companies, the process of intelligence collection tends to be:

*   Functional, rather than cross-functional. Market intelligence is seen as the domain of market research, a specific department within marketing, not as a cross-functional process that should build on inputs from throughout the organization.
*   Driven by the need to support short-term decisions and operations, rather than set up to enable the building of a long-term vision or identification of new business opportunities.

Information pattern	Upstream innovation processes	Downstream innovation processes
Focus and nature	• Very broad scope • Predominantly qualitative • Uncertain and exploratory	• More focused scope • Qualitative *and* quantitative • More precise and reliable
Purpose	• Build foresight/insight • Identify options • Select course of action	• Reduce risk/build confidence • Narrow the option funnel • Make investment decisions

Figure 8.3: *Information pattern – upstream and downstream processes*

As a consequence, the information challenge in the management of innovation is threefold:

1. Define the type of intelligence that will feed the innovation process.
2. Mobilize the whole organization to be alert and search for that intelligence.
3. Set up mechanisms to support that search and exploit its output.

Defining intelligence for innovation

Whether it deals with *market, competitors* or *technologies*, intelligence combines three elements, as one goes from 'hard' to 'soft', and from generic to specific:

1. *Intelligence starts with hard facts, data and trends about the current situation and changes in the environment.* These facts, which may consist of many small bits of information, need to be collected, aggregated, disseminated for interpretation, and filtered for relevance. Data then needs to be consolidated at the right level of resolution for the big picture to appear, prior to being 'mined' in a creative, exploratory fashion. This process typically requires:

   • a very broad network of diverse people from all parts of the organization, as well as from outside (for information collection);
   • effective network information management systems (typically intranet-based) for dissemination, cross-examination and interpretation; and
   • a small group of dedicated and talented analysts for consolidation and formatting.

2. *Facts, data and trends become 'intelligence' only after they have been 'unbundled', enriched through cross-fertilization, interpreted and screened for the detection of weak signals.* These preliminary insights typically focus on opportunity-creating changes. This process of information enrichment is best achieved through a cross-examination by dedicated people from different functions or disciplines, because creative sparks usually occur at the interface of different perspectives. In most cases, this will not happen spontaneously. It needs to be organized and managed as any other process.

> **"Creativity and new ideas are usually achieved at the interface of different functions and disciplines, as different perspectives are brought to bear"**

3. *The robustness of these insights to change assumptions should be tested before significant investments are made. This can typically be done through the formulation and exploration of alternative scenarios.* It is a good management practice to look at alternative futures before venturing into predictions and choosing a course of action. Once again, this will not happen unless it is organized and managed professionally in a cross-disciplinary environment, again by a small group of dedicated people including representatives from top management.

The quality and effectiveness of the intelligence process is often unequal for the three types of intelligence mentioned earlier. It is generally best for technology intelligence, average for competitor intelligence, and relatively poor for market intelligence. A member of the executive committee of Dutch consumer electronics giant, Philips, emphasized these discrepancies when he talked about the multimedia challenge. "The issue," he declared, "is not about the technology. All information technology manufacturers have reasonably predictable technology road maps at their disposal, highlighting which technology will be available by when and at what price. The issue is about market applications and competitors' interpretation of customer preferences. What will customers want to do with multimedia? There lies the greatest uncertainty!"

Technology intelligence

Technology intelligence is, indeed, often available because chief technology officers (CTOs) typically see it as one of their first responsibilities to shed light on technological opportunities and risks. Many have mobilized the technical community in that direction and allocated, more or less formally, responsibilities for the four types of technology intelligence processes:

- *Technology scanning*, or gate keeping, done at regular intervals on a broad base but superficially.
- *Technology monitoring* on a continuous basis on fewer, more focused, critical areas.
- *Technology scouting* in an exploratory mode in selected emerging areas of interest for the company.
- *Technology forecasting* undertaken in a predictive mode for critical technologies, typically as a prelude to an investment decision.

The limiting factor is the fact that technology intelligence often remains within the confines of the technical departments. Feeling isolated and often misunderstood, many R&D managers still wonder how they can better inform and 'educate' their business colleagues about technological opportunities, thus ensuring better decisions.

Competitor intelligence

Competitor intelligence is generally available, sometimes in minute detail. The key issue, however, is twofold. Firstly, it is often fragmented among the various functions and departments, with each function collecting that information relevant to their activities, and with no-one being responsible for putting all the jigsaw puzzle pieces together. No-one feels responsible for turning facts and observations into realistic predictions of competitors' next moves. Secondly, and because of the above, the focus of competitor information is more on what competitors have done or are doing, than on how they *think* and are likely to react in the future.

Market intelligence

Market intelligence is the most difficult to collect, particularly the type of intelligence that will give management insights and foresight. For innovation purposes, market intelligence covers a very broad spectrum:

- Changes and breakpoints in the customer environment, triggered by technological, societal, commercial, regulatory or other forces, creating market opportunities or threats.
- Changes in customers' perceptions of what constitutes value, and as a result changes in the hierarchy of preferred attributes, not just for direct customers, but for customers' customers and on through the value chain to end-users and recyclers.
- Unarticulated customer needs and wants, whether these are semi-conscious, partially but poorly fulfilled, latent but unmet, or truly unconscious.

Market intelligence and insight will typically come from a combination of sources. They will also include a variety of exercises, from the most structured to the most spontaneous, as illustrated in Figure 8.4. To be effective, these exercises need to involve a broad cross-section of the organisation and representatives from diverse functions, not just marketing staff. Intelligence 'nuggets' often emerge at the intersection of diverse perspectives and complementary interpretation of market signals. Even if they listen to the same customer, a marketer and a technical developer will tend to filter out or hear different signals. Insights lie in the creative combination of perspectives when questioning market signals or customer evidence. Creative intelligence comes from asking not just *what*, but *what if*? Not only *who*, but *who else*? Not simply *why*, but *why not*?

Mobilizing and alerting the whole organization to search for intelligence

Management often underestimates the huge potential for intelligence and insight that lies untapped within its own organizational boundaries. Many see intelligence-gathering as a game for specialists, involving sophisticated market research techniques and external service providers, database firms and consultants. In reality, there is a high likelihood that a significant part of the critical intelligence required lies some-

Sources of intelligence	Examples of structured intelligence-building exercises	Examples of *ad hoc* sources of intelligence
Desk research	• Structured trends reviewing exercises • Monitoring of key trend-setting indicators	• Exploratory, unguided literature scanning • Review of trends in other relevant industries
Field research	• Exploratory market immersion by 'sniffers' • Focus groups and 'lead customer' interviews/clinics	• Tapping of the company's field management insights • Unguided customer watching and contacts
Others	• 'Delphi' trends forecasting studies • Formal scenario planning exercises	• Intranet-based chat-rooms on market news and gossip • Contacts with industry specialists and watchers

Figure 8.4: *Sources and types of market intelligence*

where in the company. This may either be in a readily usable form, for example through the observations of field managers or service staff in permanent contact with customers, or more likely in the form of dispersed but convergent insights built by different people, each owning a piece of the final puzzle.

Facing the challenges of finding information for innovation

The challenge for management is therefore twofold:

1.   How to build a process that will enable the company to discover (or realize the implications of) what it knows already and make it known widely, internally.
2.   How to mobilize the most inquisitive of its staff into intelligence-gathering networks, to search for what the company does not yet know.

The first challenge is probably the most difficult, particularly in large multinational companies with marketing offices and service staff scattered around the world. It was almost an impossible task until very recently. The increasing attention on knowledge management and the emergence of intranets and groupware is putting the spotlight on these untapped opportunities. Today, on-screen information exchange forums have started to spread in companies, allowing management to tap the first-hand knowledge, observations and insights of its most remote employees, and to initiate online debates as to their implications for the company. This, however, will not occur spontaneously. It needs to be organized, sustained and channelled to ensure that intelligence is generated in areas that matter, and that it is put immediately to good use. This will typically require setting up a dedicated steering and support function in corporate management, and networks of intelligence animators as exemplified below.

Relying only on spontaneously collected intelligence, however, will not suffice even if it is sustained, because its results are likely to come randomly. If one does not know what to search then there is little chance of finding something significant, or of recognizing meaningful signals. The second challenge is to search for intelligence proactively in certain areas – typically unusual customer attributes or market segments that are suspected of offering untapped opportunities. This can be done by dedicating certain individuals, selected on the basis of their personal curiosity, drive and interests, and mobilizing them into organized intelligence networks. This applies to market intelligence, but also to competitive and technological intelligence.

Setting up search teams to collect insights

To search effectively for information for innovation, three complementary types of networks should be set up covering the three types of intelligence: market 'sniffers', competitor scouts and technology gate-keepers.

Market 'sniffer' networks are useful to generate market and customer intelligence in specific areas of particular interest to the company, be it a specific customer or consumer group that has previously been ignored, or on a specific issue worth investigating. (The full potential value of this type of network is outlined in greater detail by Sean Meehan in Chapter 5.) A beer company, for example, might want to broaden the target group of its marketing research – typically males aged between 18 and 65 – to investigate opportunities from other important segments. It might do so by setting up consumer intelligence networks to monitor and better understand the behaviour and perceptions of lower-consumption groups, e.g. women, or critically important prescriptors like bar tenders. Similarly, a dialysis machine manufacturer may broaden the scope of its attention from traditional target groups – medical doctors and hospital purchasers – to currently ignored user groups down the chain, such as nurses, maintenance personnel and patients. Market sniffer networks will not replace traditional marketing research tools like focus groups, but will complement them by generating lots of insights worth investigating further through such tools.

Competitor 'scout' networks may be an effective way to mobilize staff from different functional areas or regions to unearth complementary competitive intelligence on a particular competitor. As for market sniffers, the objective is to tap the knowledge of those very people who, because of their experience and function, have the broadest exposure to the topic under investigation, in this case competitor behaviour and plans. Each network member can contribute their own piece of the overall jigsaw puzzle and cross-examine information provided by others, until a pattern emerges.

Technology gate-keeper networks are essential to monitor the ever-increasing field of relevant technologies for opportunities or threats. By allocating specific technologies to specific people – usually the most knowledgeable people in a given discipline – management ensures that it remains abreast of the latest developments and technology sources. Unlike the other two networks, which rarely exist in a structured way, technology gate-keeper networks are common. But they need to be better integrated into the overall intelligence effort.

Establishing mechanisms to support the intelligence process and exploit its output

Correcting deficiencies in market and competitive intelligence is usually the first priority. It is therefore in those areas that new mechanisms have to be put in place. Indeed, the marketing department is often ill-equipped to launch and support a major corporate-wide intelligence effort mobilizing all functions, not just its own forces. In many companies, the marketing function suffers from two limitations. First, marketing is often established with most of its resources at the business unit level – yet many new business or innovation opportunities typically occur either at the interface between business units, or entirely outside the scope of current businesses. Second, most marketing research departments at business unit or corporate level tend to be heavily loaded with short- or medium-term research geared to support operations or new product introductions. They are usually less available, and probably ill-prepared to launch longer-term exploratory investigations – even less so to set up, organize and manage intelligence networks.

Therefore, in addition to current marketing functions, management ought to consider setting up two types of management mechanisms:

- Intelligence network champions or 'animators'.
- Dedicated innovation intelligence support functions – *advanced marketing*.

Deploying network champions

Individual network champions or 'animators' need to be identified and empowered to set up, motivate and keep vibrant the networks that will monitor or scout specific market segments, industry issues or competitors. Intelligence networks will not form spontaneously in the organization. Management needs to support their creation by empowering specific individuals, the animators, who will act as central network nodes. Four conditions are essential to make the concept work:

1. *Network animators should be assigned an intelligence mission on a voluntary basis, as an additional (part-time) job.* It is a mission given to someone *in addition* to their job, provided the latter can be scaled down to some extent to cope with the assignment. The responsibility should be seen as an ideal testing ground for promising new managers, whatever their function and location within the corporation. It is a unique opportunity to demonstrate initiative and leadership across organizational boundaries. As such, it should obviously be part of the management development tool-kit, and included in the company's career tracking and performance evaluation and reward systems.
2. *Network animators should be selected on the basis of their background, but also their personality.* The job of network animator requires a number of specific personal traits and skills which should be recognized from the start:
   - curiosity and open mindedness to track and pursue weak signals;
   - enthusiasm and *drive*, to keep a high level of energy within the network;

- social skills to attract, mobilize and keep 'sniffers' or 'scouts' motivated;
- the ability to consolidate, synthesize and document intelligence results;
- organizational skills to fulfil this mission while pursuing their other job.

Network animators should be selected from people whose age, gender, current job and personal interests predispose them to such a function. In our previous example of the beer company, the mission to set up and animate a network to monitor female consumers (or non-consumers) could be allocated, say, to a younger female executive in the marketing department. The animator of a competitor scouting network will typically be entrusted to someone who has had a broad exposure with that particular competitor, possibly having been employed by that competitor.

3. *Network animators should be supported strongly by management and particularly by their direct line managers.* The latter should:

- approve their nomination and mission;
- give them the time and (limited) budget allowance to perform their mission;
- support them in case of conflicts with their other job, and provide advice; and
- ensure they get proper recognition and reward.

The last three points are essential if management wants to avoid the risk of seeing the enthusiasm of network animators wear-down as a result of unmanageable conflicts of priorities or, worse, lack of interest by management.

4. *Network animators should be clear as to the tasks entrusted to them.* Whether these animators are asked to monitor a certain market or customer segment, a specific issue or a given competitor, their task will be similar:

- Identify and enlist the most qualified and motivated 'sniffers' or 'scouts' from the most relevant parts of the organization, and set up sub-networks if the number of members becomes unmanageable.
- Set up and manage the network communication and exchange system, facilitating the access of each member to the group and to each other, and building a database of findings.
- Synthesize and disseminate the outcome of the intelligence exercise at regular intervals in a newsletter or intranet chat-page, flagging the most interesting opportunities (or threats) to management.
- Keep the network motivated and working by organizing intelligence debriefing workshops in the presence of management, and ensuring that exceptional efforts by network members or valuable insights are recognized and rewarded.

Building an advanced marketing capability

In addition to these activities a *dedicated innovation intelligence support function* needs to be set up at corporate level to organize the intelligence gathering effort, mine the data collected to look for relevant insights, and exploit its results. Indeed, given the important role they will be playing, these network animators need to be selected, supported and managed carefully. Because the networks should cut across business unit lines, they should be managed at corporate or divisional level, ideally by the chief marketing officer.

To distinguish this long-term oriented task of intelligence-gathering and exploitation from more operationally oriented marketing responsibilities, management could establish an *advanced marketing group* at corporate level. Advanced marketing should do in the marketing area what advanced development or advanced engineering do in the technical area. Their focus should be on longer-term innovation opportunities. This group does not need a big staff since most of the intelligence network members and animators will be drawn from existing functions. Even in large multi-business corporations, a few dedicated and energetic people will suffice. A typical advanced marketing group would include three people: a department head, a market intelligence specialist, and a competitor intelligence specialist. As they will have to mobilize and rely on people from the rest of the organization, they should be well established and respected within the company.

In the absence of a corporate marketing officer, the advanced marketing group could report to the executive in charge of new business development. If none of these functions exist at corporate level, other alternatives can be envisaged:

- Setting up an advanced marketing group within central R&D function, focusing on new business creation (as opposed to supporting existing businesses).
- Establishing it, not as a dedicated group, but rather as a team of divisional or business unit marketing managers, sharing the intelligence mission collectively.

Besides setting up, supporting and managing the work of intelligence networks and their animators, advanced marketing will typically contribute to the company's innovation and new business creation efforts in several ways:

- By providing *ad hoc* marketing research expertise (and contracting out specific research) to explore the attractiveness and feasibility of new ideas and concepts that do not fit in any of the current business units.
- By supporting the activities of the new venture teams that will be appointed at the end of the ideation process to follow up specific opportunities judged particularly promising.
- By evaluating and arraying the various opportunities in the pipeline in the form of portfolios, thus helping management to select the most attractive new product projects.

SUMMARY

Information fuels innovation

Management can stimulate innovation in two ways:

- bottom-up, by fostering a 'can-do' climate, encouraging the entrepreneurial behaviour of champions, and supporting promising new ideas, from wherever they come;
- top-down, by launching a proactive search of new business opportunities and implementing them.

Whether it is driven from the top or follows a bottom-up process, information is what triggers insights on new business opportunities and starts ideas flowing. More than that, it is essential to validate and refine new ideas, approaches and products, contributing to their successful implementation

The type of information that will drive innovation is quite different from that which managers generate and use to run operations. It is broader in scope, softer in content, and exploratory in its acquisition process. The bad news is that most of the management mechanisms that have been put in place to generate information in support of the business – like marketing research departments – are ill-prepared to generate innovation-relevant information. This is because they tend to focus on the past and present to predict the future. They focus on *facts*, whereas innovation requires *insights* and *foresight*. The good news, however, is that most of the information management needed to drive innovation probably lies somewhere in the organization, or can be obtained if managers search for it with an exploratory mindset.

The information challenge for management is therefore twofold:

- How can they mobilize their staff and tap their knowledge and ideas? How can they discover what they know already but were never asked, that could point to interesting new opportunities?
- How can they deploy teams of people to 'sniff' around to bring market, competitor and technology intelligence? How can they discover what the company doesn't know but needs to know to pioneer new markets?

New challenges require new responses, in this case, new organizational mechanisms – we will call them *innovation networks*. These mechanisms are fundamentally different from most existing functions or departments. They are groupings of people that management empowers to search for new opportunities. They will typically share a common interest, be it in monitoring new market developments, discovering unarticulated customer needs, tracking competitors' moves or unearthing promising new technological developments. Whether they are called *market sniffers*, *competitors' scouts*, or *technology gate-keepers*, the members of these networks will be selected on the basis of their passion for the external world outside the company, their insatiable curiosity, and their dedication to sharing their discoveries.

Such networks will not emerge spontaneously. They must be fostered by management, steered towards the most promising new areas to be explored, and encouraged to break new ground. In turn, this will require establishing a light coaching infrastructure, as well as mechanisms to exploit and follow up on the information thus generated. Management will have to learn to:

- instigate and foster these networks without commanding them;
- guide them without over-managing them;
- encourage their professionalism without stifling them with bureaucratic demands.

Again, such network coaching mechanisms do not exist in most companies. *Network champions* or *coaches* will have to be appointed and deployed to guide these networks, and an *advanced marketing* group set up at corporate level to provide guidance, support and follow-up.

 **BEST PRACTICE**

Fostering an intelligence culture to support innovation

The collection of intelligence is an essential first step in the top-down innovation process. High quality and timely intelligence constitutes the foundation on which senior management can build a vision of future opportunities and chart an exciting course for the company. When it is adequately disseminated, it also constitutes a fertile soil for the generation of attractive, targeted ideas.

Many of the measures recommended earlier to organize and exploit intelligence are common sense: tapping the observation potential and brains of one's own field staff seems the obvious thing to do to find out about markets and competitors. This is, however, more complex to implement than it looks, mainly because of the classic obstacles to a networking organization, i.e. short-term tunnel vision and functional turf defence on one hand, and the famous *not invented here syndrome* on the other. Overcoming these obstacles is necessary to foster a true intelligence culture, and as with most culture changes it requires several reinforcing factors to achieve success.

First, a visible commitment and example from top management is needed. Not surprisingly, companies that have developed an intelligence culture like Rubbermaid, Procter & Gamble and 3M, also seem to be the most obsessed with innovation and new products. In these companies, management seems to be more externally-oriented, more curious, and more open to new ideas than in conservative ones.

Secondly, it requires adequate incentives. Innovative companies typically measure the performance of their managers in terms of innovation output. 3M's and Hewlett Packard's legendary indicator of "30% or 35% of sales from new products introduced in the past three years" is a strong indirect incentive to foster an intelligence culture. Managers in these companies are so used to being measured and rewarded on that basis that they cannot afford to be complacent or to adopt negative attitudes. They know that they have to promote a culture of absolute openness, customer intimacy and continuous market exploration within their organisation if they want to meet their target.

Thirdly, and this is specific to the intelligence challenge, it may require adopting practices that will make the 'voice of the market' heard and felt – physically and emotionally – throughout the organization, particularly by those who are not in daily contact with customers or competitors. To make its staff feel the heat of the market, some companies, e.g. Rubbermaid, bring customers (in their case retail chain management teams) on a weekly basis to their headquarters in Wooster, Ohio. These visits are generally planned to explore opportunities for improved service, but many provide the company with invaluable insights into the market and competitors. More importantly, these visits contribute to create a climate of market insecurity and constant reassessment.

Other companies achieve the same result with other means, for example by insisting that all their managers mix with their customers to sense first-hand the product experience. Harley Davidson's CEO, Richard Terlinck, insists that the permanent 'customer immersion' climate that he has encouraged, where all managers are expected to visit dealers wherever they go and ride with their customers, is what contributed greatly to his company's success. This approach has allowed the company to combat the three enemies of continuous performance and, we would add, innovation: arrogance, complacency and greed.

Section C

Reducing Costs

9

Co-configuration: Efficient Personalization through Information and IT

One of the main challenges facing companies is to drive success by providing personalized products and services whilst simultaneously reducing costs. In this chapter, **Andrew Boynton** and **Bart Victor** outline the concept of co-configuration to achieve a dynamic strategy that raises customer value while implementing efficient cost control.

CASE STUDY: MOVING BEYOND MASS CUSTOMIZATION – USING NEW TECHNOLOGIES AND INFORMATION TO PROVIDE INDIVIDUALIZED PRODUCTS AND SERVICES

Supplying a product that is customized to each individual's needs is an established requirement in the provision of hearing aids. Lars Kolind, the CEO of the Danish company Oticon, revolutionized the industry's approach to customization by questioning existing norms and linking 'the expertise of scientists, physicians, hearing care professionals and users'. This 'human link' has been at the forefront of developing competitive advantage.

Oticon, established in 1904, has long enjoyed a reputation of being a leading provider of high-quality hearing instruments. They led the transition from pocket instruments to behind-the-ear aids in the 1960s. Customized in-the-ear instruments followed in the 1980s. Given the degree to which this industry now benefits from individualized products – each user's needs vary with their degree of deafness, specific sound sensitivity and ear shape – Oticon found themselves asking what is beyond mass customization?

The company had gathered a great deal of information from various sources. Having customized millions of hearing aids, they leveraged this configuration knowledge to reassess customers' changing needs. They found that despite customizing the hearing aid, the existing analogue technology required the user to adjust the aid physically to suit different sound environments. Oticon realized that a product that could automatically adjust sound amplification and signal processing would enhance customer value. A new digital hearing aid, Digifocus, was developed, which not only benefits from being physically customized and professionally tuned, but is also able to 'learn' and respond to each individual's lifestyle, incorporating their various sound environments. Digifocus uses Pentium-processing capability to differentiate 100 sound parameters on seven channels in real time. This ground-breaking achievement was the result of co-configuration.

Utilizing the knowledge they had accumulated, Oticon had established a rewarding partnership between their customers, their distributors and themselves. Co-configuration demands building and sustaining a completely integrated system that senses, responds and adapts to the experiences of each individual. In essence, it is this co-configuration partnership – the product network – that adds value, rather than simply the company. The company had improved the interaction between the product and the customer, creating an intelligent product that received both the 1997 European Information Technology Grand Prize and the European Design Prize.

Overview

As the need to drive competitive advantage narrows the distinctions between companies offering similar personalized products, companies need to innovate and challenge the accepted norms in order to emerge as the industry leader. Increasingly, it is no longer enough to offer one-off, limited customization. Leveraging all the information, expertise and new technology available, companies must tailor products that adapt to a customer's changing requirements or that evolve in line with the latest technological advances.

Products that are tailored to individual preferences and that are also capable of adapting continuously to changing needs may seem the stuff of science fiction but, as the development of digital hearing aids by Oticon showed, they are a powerful source of competitive advantage. What value would a customer place on such potential: a car that is capable of upgrading its level of comfort and performance without the need for visiting a garage; a radio alarm clock that 'learns' which music you enjoy, and not to wake you at the weekend . . .

These products customize themselves in response to your needs and preferences as they change. This *customer-intelligent value* has moved considerably beyond the precision customer value of current mass customization. Whereas precision customization meets the needs of a customer at a given time, *customer intelligence* enhances greatly the value of the product by customizing continuously over time.

> "Adding customer-intelligent value to products and services will be a major new source of competitive advantage in the twenty-first century"

Thus the product is neatly and intelligently responsive to the customer's changing needs. Clearly this is no small order; to achieve such efficient personalization, companies need to build the potential to respond to changing needs and new technologies into the product or service.

In this chapter we will outline the competitive advantages of co-configuration, and explain how following the *right path* can ensure success.

The advantages of co-configuration

Increasingly matching customers' individual needs and wants with use over time

Co-configuration offers potentially powerful competitive advantages. First among these is the capability to build a product or service that, with use and over time, more and more matches the customer's individual needs and wants. From the innovative craftsman's first efforts to create a new product or service, through the rigour, problem-solving, and modularization that lead to mass customization, firms like Oticon work and learn to satisfy customer's needs and wants. Customer-intelligent products take this quest to a new level. The company and customer collaborate to co-configure the product or service to provide more and more of what the customer wants. Oticon, for example, wants its hearing instrument to become an integral part of the customer's life, a *real* part.

Directly including the customer in value creation (staying close to the customer)

A second significant advantage created by co-configuration is the inclusion of the customer in the ongoing value creation system for the company. For many years a common call of management guru's, and perhaps the most common dictum for business success, has been 'stay as close to the customer as possible'. Co-configuration offers the best opportunity yet to integrate the customer into the firm's business system.

> **"With the organization of work under co-configuration, the customer becomes, in a sense, a real partner with the producer, and that partnership can endure as long as the product or service platform can continue to grow and adapt to the customer's needs"**

In following mass customization, many firms have built strong relationships with their individual customers. These relationships are beginning to extend beyond the specific exchanges required to customize the product. Involving the customer in the design and realization of the product creates value. This trend signifies the fact that only by involving the customers more and more deeply can the company learn and respond effectively. This happens when the involvement is at the very general level required for process improvement, or the more individual level required for mass customization and co-configuration.

Creating sales opportunities that are genuinely valued by the customer

Mass producers often use a product strategy that includes *planned obsolescence* – products are designed intentionally to become outdated. For example, the automobile industry plans on a three-year replacement cycle for new cars. By periodically introducing new styles, features and technology that make the older, but still functional, cars obsolete, the companies stimulate demand for new cars. In contrast, co-configuration can create products that can be upgraded, enhanced and even fundamentally altered without replacing the product itself. Oticon designs its Digifocus hearing aid to take the user through the several stages of increased hearing improvement, without changing the instrument itself. Hearing professionals can simply reprogramme the software in the hearing aid using capacities built into the original design.

Using information so precisely that little money, energy, time or other resources are wasted

Increasingly, companies are facing the dual challenge of being the low-cost operator in their industries and also the most customer-responsive. Moving beyond mass customization, where products are partly standardized (80–90%) and partly customized (10–20%) to meet the differentiated needs of customers on a one-to-one basis, requires that companies sense, respond and adapt their products to the individual experience of each customer.

> **"Co-configuration is not just an ability to provide new value to customers. It is a new way of working by continuously linking the customer, the product and the company to achieve maximum customer value and cost efficiencies at the same time"**

The right path to co-configuration

Meeting the individual needs of customers is certainly not a new concept. Mass personalization has long been the mainstay of marketing departments. Moreover, a product or service that interacts with the customer to adapt to their shifting desires or varying circumstances over time may seem fantastic and beyond the scope of current companies capabilities. Yet such customer-intelligent products are already beginning to define the state of competition within some industries. To maintain competitive advantage, firms will no longer be able to rely on traditional concepts: they will need to embrace this new trend and take the path to co-configuration.

The increasing importance of exploiting new technologies to supply adaptive products and services is evident from recent developments in two industries: the provision of medical devices and computer software systems. In these two areas, the

> "Supplying a customer-intelligent product requires a company to interact with customers to reconfigure that product continuously. The product has to be constantly remade to reflect changes as both the customer and the company 'learn'. The work of co-configuration never ends"

match between what the individual customer wants and what the product actually delivers needs to be precise. Medical devices have to be fitted specifically to each individual and they must also be adaptive to the individual's body. Today's computer software industry is highly competitive; the Holy Grail of seeking customer value is determined increasingly by usability for individual customers. Moreover, telecommunications companies aim to provide more individual and high-quality services – such as call-forwarding, improved quality transmissions and extra bandwidth – that incorporates often rapid technological advances, prevalent and evolving market forces, and dynamic customer needs.

Clearly, mass production, process enhancement and mass customization do not meet the full capability requirements of customer intelligence: a precise, dynamic and adaptive fit between customer and product. Customer-focused industries which benefit from, and even drive, technological advances, are leading the way in co-configuration and stealing the initiative from their competitors. As Oticon's approach has shown, it is apparent that industries pursuing the *right path* towards co-configuration focus on *organizational learning*. The task of achieving co-configuration is undoubtedly challenging; the stages on the path are outlined in Figure 9.1.

The challenge to transform your firm's capabilities, thus allowing your company to succeed, is an ongoing process, not simply one-off re-engineering. A dynamic, ongoing approach has to be built into your company, and to achieve co-configuration this approach requires four transformations along the right path.

The logic of learning along the right path to mass customization and beyond to co-configuration, is increasingly a source of competitive advantage for many firms. Each of the types of work is based on capabilities along the right path (shown in Figure 9.1) and has its own strengths in creating market value. In terms of organizing a firm's

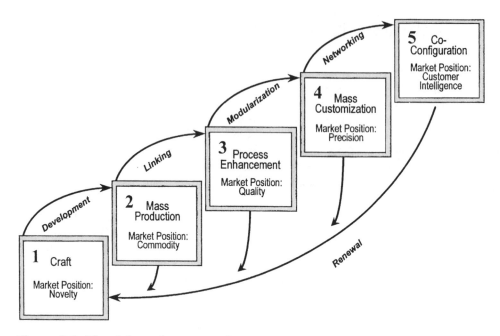

Figure 9.1: *The right path to co-configuration*

work, each capability and its associated market value form a strategic *destination*. Think of each destination as a capability to be acquired in order to compete more effectively in a particular market at a particular time (*see* Table 9.1).

- Craft is strong in inventing and creating high-priced *novel products* that make strong, unique impressions on customers.
- Mass production is strong in discipline and in achieving value through predictable, standard, 'no-surprise', low-price *commodities.*
- Process enhancement is strong in thinking and doing, and wins by creating products that customers perceive as having superior *quality.*
- Mass customization is strong in modular configuration and can dominate a market with *precision*, providing made-to-order, affordable, tailored products and services.

Most importantly, each type of work is related to the others in a specific and pre-determined way. It is a learning system. Mass production cannot be reached except through some form of craft work; process enhancement is impossible without the company's first having made some effort at learning from mass production; mass customization is not feasible without the learning from process enhancement. We think of the four work capabilities as four destinations on a map, because there is a single path of learning between them; that's why we call it the *right path*.

Craft and tacit knowledge

The right path begins, most naturally, with *craft*. For all firms, craft work is the well-spring of invention and renewal, the first step to vitality and viability for products and

Table 9.1: *Each market position requires a distinct set of capabilities*

Market positioning	Capabilities positioning	Market advantage
Novelty	Craft	Customers are willing to pay premium prices for the products' and services' perceived value.
Commodity	Mass production	Products and services are marketed and purchased primarily on price.
Quality	Process enhancement	Customers express a preference, and are willing to pay premium prices for the perceived value of its products and services.
Precision	Mass customization	Despite product quality, which may rival other competitors, the firm does not require a premium price to remain competitive.
Customer intelligence	Co-configuration	A perception of partnership links the customer, company and product in an ongoing developmental relationship.

processes. It typically takes place in small groups, organized like the gun shops of the fifteenth century, the professional teams of consulting, engineering, advertising, or any other service firms of the year 2001. Craft workers augment their personally held skills and expertise with general-purpose tools: whether the smithy's anvil and hammer of 1450, or the consultant's spreadsheet, presentation software, and Internet search engine. What craft workers know about products and processes rests in their personal intuition and experience about the customer, the product, the process, and the use of their tools.

When craft workers invent solutions, they create *tacit knowledge.* Tacit knowledge is held personally by the craft worker and is coupled tightly with experience, technique and tools. The specifics of how the work is done can't be described, yet tacit knowledge is the foundation for excellence in craft. Craft workers generating more solutions create even more tacit knowledge. Workers become smarter and smarter, but at this point the organization does not. The knowledge is in the heads of the workers, and there it remains under craft.

Information technology and craft

Along with organizational innovations, new technological tools are emerging that make craft an increasingly powerful, competitive capability. Under craft, new intelligent information technologies do not take the place of human ingenuity, but they can certainly make the craft worker more effective than ever before.

IT plays a pivotal role in increasing a firm's ability to structure craft work and manage tacit knowledge. Chosen wisely, IT can provide a firm with the means to capture, store and disseminate knowledge across a community of practice. Using an appropriate IT system, a firm can count on improved co-ordination, greater collaboration, increased knowledge exchange, and a more cohesive social network for workers. These benefits translate into more knowledge re-use and replication, and therefore into greater market advantage.

IT is the craft worker's most vital tool. Craft workers have historically used tools – the weaver's loom, the blacksmith's anvil, the surgeon's scalpel – to carry out their work. Today, computers have become perhaps the most all-purpose craft tools ever devised, ones that can work differently in different jobs. However, it is also abundantly clear that computer tools improve the very practice of craft work itself. In the world of manufacturing, numerically controlled machines and flexible manufacturing technologies don't just automate and replace workers, but augment the rich tacit knowledge of experienced workers. IT in these settings is the thread in the fabric of the crafts people's work, part of their own idiosyncratic approach to work.

In almost every corporation, professionals are crafts people who now use their workstations to carve out unique information environments. These environments support their personally held work experiences, insights, judgement-creating schedules and agendas, e-mail, database access patterns and filing systems, and elaborate Internet push–pull configurations. Computer workstations are the new craft worker's tool, mirroring each worker's particular style, job demands, and professional desires. These tools provide the professional with a personal information context that is largely self-designed. As firms and their employees use more and more information, they will rely increasingly on the information management tools that build links inside and outside the company.

Although firms can meet the IT challenge by providing craft workers with the most robust tools available, they should not fall into the trap of providing what's best for each worker, without considering what's best for the company's management of knowledge. Wherever possible, they should standardize. This is a strategic issue because without standardizing the tools of the community of professional crafts people in the firm (be they managers, engineers, consultants, or salespeople), the ability to create a community of practice and to leverage knowledge through information-sharing is severely limited. Selecting similar tools speeds up the creation of new knowledge, while also providing a means to institutionalize knowledge sharing.

> **"It is always important to remember that individual craft is a tremendous capability for market response, but that the firm's objective should be to move beyond smart craft, to smart communities of practice that benefit from the power of the individual, as well as the power of sharing knowledge across a smarter organization"**

The key here is to strike a balance: invest in IT tools that allow individual craft workers to do their jobs in a precise and skilful manner, but refrain from purchasing tools that are so individually tailored that information cannot be shared. With IT tools, firms can capture craft workers' experiences as 'hard' information. They can also codify such knowledge in a firm's computer network, allowing it to be catalogued and improved.

The concept is a critical one: as information technologies encourage the sharing of knowledge within communities of practice, these technologies also allow knowledge to be allocated, controlled, re-used, even priced – all elements critical to business improvement. At its simplest level, e-mail is an information technology that allows both the sharing of information and its selection, storage and re-use at some later date. E-mail also saves time and money, and generally increases a firm's effectiveness.

To create a repository of IT knowledge, firms face a dual challenge. One is to build the kind of technical infrastructure that allows the knowledge gained through craft to be captured, stored, and later accessed and disseminated in a manner consistent with the firm's changing needs. A firm benefits little from an IT tool that does such tasks at too high a price in time, money or effort. A firm must choose an IT architecture that helps it manage knowledge with ease.

The second challenge is even more difficult. A firm must select an IT architecture that provides the means for building a valuable core of tacit knowledge. Many companies believe that once they have captured vast quantities of information, they have succeeded in leveraging tacit knowledge. Nothing could be further from the truth. These firms end up burdened with information, little of it valuable. Firms must think carefully about what information they want to capture and who will have access to it. IT provides the means to capture tacit knowledge, but management has to figure out what is valuable.

Despite the many advantages of craft work, history shows that sooner or later a product comes along that has mass market appeal. At that point, large demand looms on the horizon. In these instances, management decides to produce that product, over and over, the same way every time. It is then made available to consumers everywhere, at one low price. At this point, work other than craft is called for, so craft takes a back seat. Craft work also disappears when, sooner or later, a firm doing craft finds a single best way to carry out a process or activity. For example, rather then rely on the expertise of each consultant (crafts person), a consulting firm might decide to create a template for industry analysis and do it one way for every client. Here, too, craft takes a back seat to another form of work as the firm prepares to take its first step along the right path.

Mass production and articulated knowledge

Progress from craft to mass production is possible because craft generates another important type of knowledge, one that lays the foundation for mass production. As crafts people learn more and more about their work, they understand more clearly the best way to structure the routines, organize the processes, and use their tools. With the experience they have gained, they are ultimately in a position to *describe* the details of how they do the work. This description provides the steps, the processes, and the 'how to' of how the products are made or the services are delivered under craft. We call this *articulated knowledge.* The organization can ignore this knowledge, let it go untapped if it remains in craft, or leverage the articulated knowledge to create new value in the market. Here management learns to identify and codify the articulated knowledge from craft work, or incorporate engineers' know-how into machines or procedures, and transfers it rapidly to all workers to be used repeatedly.

As firms capture and codify the by-product of articulated knowledge generated under craft, the story of the right path unfolds. We call the activities underlying the codification of articulated knowledge the *development* transformation, and it leads to mass *production* work. Through development, a firm gleans, then begins to re-use, the best ways to do the work. In short, development is a transformation that mines the rich veins of articulated knowledge and builds a machine-like organization that mass-produces.

Using tools such as time and motion studies, process engineering and automation, development captures the best approaches discovered in craft and applies them across the company. Development instils discipline through processes, procedures or automation so that work can be replicated anywhere, at any time, in any amount. Mass production is characterized by repeatable tasks, hierarchical control systems, functional structures, standardized routines and processes, automation, and division of labour.

For many firms, the right path through development ends in mass production. For as long as the market will bear, mass producers keep filling demand. Fixed costs allocated to each unit of service or production sink with every additional unit produced. Occasionally, process R&D (craft) engineers tinkering with better ways to do the work may find a better sequence of steps or use of technology. When this occurs, firms go through the craft–development–mass-production cycle – but not too frequently! The end of a product's life in mass production signals the moment to reach back to craft to develop a new product and new processes. The lifecycles repeat, with a predictable rhythm – every year, cosmetic changes; every decade, a fresh new product.

However, some firms never venture into mass production, but build and nurture the skills of experts and continue to manage craft work. Their strategy is to fill the niches of demand too small to warrant the investment required of fully fledged mass production. Niche markets include those for the superlative automobile offered by Rolls Royce, the specialized financial advice provided by Swiss investment bankers, and the expert consulting advice offered by Bain or McKinsey. These firms, dominated by craft work, play a very different game to those in mass production. They attract the customers with special needs and charge a premium price.

Information technology and mass production

For craft, technology is a tool that extends or enhances the skill of the worker. Under mass production, technology serves a different purpose. Technology for mass production either replaces or directly controls the work. The power of an automated process is that it works without human intervention. Programmed with the right instructions, and maintained and supplied with the right raw materials and energy, the machines do the work. They manufacture, serve, deliver, collect, move, store, refer and even thank the customer.

New advances in IT are revolutionizing machines, making it possible to automate more effectively under more diverse conditions and at a lower cost. With mass production, IT issues revolve around two sets of concerns that at times compete.

1.   First, a firm must decide when and how to capitalize on possible scale advantages.

2. Second, a firm must be clear about the ways it will apply the new technology and who will control it.

Given today's competitive challenges and the changing technological landscape, firms need to be paying more attention to the management of IT, especially when applied to mass production.

IT is currently one of a firm's largest expenses and offers clear benefits. For a mass production firm, the key benefit, obviously, is knowledge, re-use and replication to gain scale advantage. Since the mid-1990s, modern computing technology – its mainframe applications, database systems, and programming languages – have offered all the necessary ingredients to reflect mass production's strategic interests. IT, therefore, is a critical investment for any mass production firm. If a firm wants to exercise extreme control over the application of production knowledge and achieve scale advantage, it will need an advanced IT system.

Under mass production, the *structure and control* of IT refers not so much to the physical location of the technology, but rather to its application and the control of the information it contains. In other words, *structure and control* refers to where the information is and who can use it. In addition, under mass production the lower unit costs of IT (whether for acquisition, maintenance or use) and its faster, cheaper applications have changed the rationale behind managing and applying the technology within a firm. The implications for IT under mass production are changing. Under pressure from scale economies and distributed information-and-application control, companies are finding that skill specialization and application, which drove the need for a centralized, single-site structure, is a thing of the past. As IT has developed, firms have favoured movement over stasis.

Today, mass production firms are facing the challenge of keeping scale advantages in focus, while still benefiting from new IT systems. They have to use capabilities inherent in new distributed technology, especially for global control, but they have to stay free of the trend toward decentralized control and localised applications.

CASE STUDY: MASS PRODUCTION THAT WORKS

In short, despite any new technological trend that might divert their attention, mass production managers must keep their eyes on the ball. In applying IT to mass production, nothing beats knowledge re-use and replication, along with scale and control – perhaps for the first time over a globally extended enterprise. We have even seen firms such as SAP AG, with headquarters in Germany, reap huge benefits due to the control it offers today's enterprise. SAP has created software that can manage a firm's entire supply chain, from the price of raw materials, through manufacturing, to the delivery of the product to the customer. Rather than figure out what their supply chain should look like, many firms simply go to SAP and say "We'll take one". They buy the SAP solution because, frankly, it works, and many of their own attempts to run a global, pan-European or regional supply chain fail and fall by the wayside. As a result of offering mass production that works, SAP has been one of the fastest-growing firms in the world over the past five years.

Quality and process enhancement – the importance of practical knowledge

Is there anything beyond craft and mass production, as both synergistic and competing forms of work? At first, only a few visionaries believed there was. The most well known of these, W. Edwards Deming, sought in vain to convince the mass production masters of his time – the American automobile makers – that there was indeed a next step along a path to provide higher quality to consumers: the automobile that doesn't break down every 10 000 miles; the credit card with faster, friendlier customer service and clear, informative reports each month. To create the value offered by quality, mass production firms have to take another step along the right path.

> **"Quality emerges as customers come to understand the attributes that seem especially important and attractive to them – more reliable or efficient, quieter, safer, cleaner, friendlier, tastier or faster"**

Just as in the progress from craft to mass production, progress beyond mass production is created by learning. Mass production workers follow instructions absolutely, without modification, but they also learn about work through observation, sensing and feeling the operations. They learn where the instructions are effective and where they are not. This learning leads to a new type of knowledge, *practical knowledge*, which bursts forth from doing a job over and over again. However, this practical knowledge that a firm gains through workers' following instructions and doing the work over and over can dissipate into thin air and add no value if the firm stays in mass production. After all, under mass production no-one ever asks the workers what they know.

Linking is therefore the transformation that bridges mass production by leveraging practical knowledge and creates the work that we call *process enhancement*. The tools used in linking include process documentation and mapping, team building, customer-satisfaction measurement systems, process-improvement tools, and techniques such as Quality Function Deployment (QFD) and brainstorming. Linking involves setting up a team system in which members focus on process improvement, which promotes the sharing of ideas within the team, and which fosters collaboration across teams and functions.

Like the shift from craft to mass production, the transformation to process enhancement is a move to a very different kind of work and organization, one that combines thinking and doing. Workers add to their commitment to getting the work done, and come up with ideas about how to do the work better. Managers play a key role as coaches who make connections between the firm's processes and encourage their teams to communicate, interact and improve their work.

Information technology for process enhancement

Integrating production and innovation is an extension of the integration of doing and thinking, but is crucial to process enhancement at an organizational level. Teams integrate production and innovation to attack problems as they arise. In addition, the composition of research teams changes as different parts of projects reach conclusion. Systematic overlap of production and research from the very inception of a new product idea guarantees that innovations quickly become part of new processes and products. The tight integration of production and innovation is a major reason why, for example, Japanese firms can move products so quickly from research to production.

Integrating production and innovation is also critical to adopting information technologies into the fabric of work. This is perhaps most evident in the comparative abilities (measured in degrees of responsiveness) of Japanese and US companies to adopt flexible manufacturing technologies. Mass production firms, predominantly in the USA, use flexible information technologies not to promote the flexibility of the work environment, but to produce a relatively small set of *standardized* parts and operations. Under process enhancement, especially in Japan, firms integrate flexible information technologies into work environments and combine them with workers' knowledge, skills and assets. Thus information technologies in process-enhancement environments effectively increase process flexibility, while maintaining a focus on the execution and thinking so critical to increased market value.

> **"For managers attempting to achieve process enhancement, the watchword is *integrate* production and innovation"**

The essential point here is that the organization builds new knowledge over time. Only if that knowledge is recognized and leveraged can firms proceed along the right path. Process enhancement cannot occur until practical knowledge, generated by the 'learning by doing' typical of mass production, has accumulated. This brings us to the next episode in our story of the right path, with changing market demand once again playing a pivotal role.

Mass customization and architectural knowledge

Many markets are moving beyond quality and toward customers seeking products or services that offer not only quality, but also precisely what they want at little or no additional cost. To meet this market demand, which we call *precision*, firms turn away from process enhancement and work toward *mass customization*, along the transformation path we call *modularization*.

New knowledge is generated by undertaking process enhancement work. Again, this knowledge can be leveraged and put into action as the company transforms its process enhancement work to mass customization. This transformation is based on a new and deeper understanding of work gained in process enhancement, which we call *architectural knowledge*, the understanding of work required to make the transformation to mass customization.

During this transformation, the tightly linked process steps developed under process enhancement are now exploded, not into isolated parts, but into a dynamic web of interconnected modular units. Rather than the sequential assembly lines of mass production and continuous improvement, work is now organized as a complex, reconfigurable product and service *system*.

Modularization breaks up the work into units that are interchangeable on demand from the market or customer. And everything has to happen *fast* on demand from the customer. The units vary from firm to firm, ranging from telephone service representatives, consultants, software, factories, participants in a supply chain, to sets of distinct organizations. Modularization transforms work by creating a dynamic, robust network of units. Within some of these units (such as elements of manufacturing or customer service) there may still be active craft, mass production or process enhancement work taking place, but all the possible interfaces among modules must be designed carefully so that they can rapidly, efficiently and seamlessly regroup to meet customer needs.

Our experience demonstrates that going to market with mass customization is best attempted by those firms that have learned to mass customize along the right path. The path of learning to mass customization can be accelerated if it is well understood – but no shortcuts! Taking the wrong path leads to failure, frustration and missed market opportunities. Firms must know the product and the processes inside and out. Without a deep understanding of the product, a firm cannot know which variations create value for the customer, and which are simply a source of expense and difficulty. Without a deep understanding, beyond just the steps in the production process and the interactions between those steps, the firm cannot control the enormous challenge of variation needed to customize.

Even after they reach mass customization, companies eventually discover that some customer needs cannot be met. Even with quick response and nearly infinite product variety, they run up against a simple fact: no universal formula can meet all customer demands for precision. Firms that fail to develop new capabilities that better address customer requirements will run into trouble. Companies that reach this point can choose to follow the process we call *renewal*. Their stories cycle back to craft, collecting information that has come to light under mass customization and using it in a process of invention in which process and product engineers leverage their personal knowledge to create new opportunities for the firm. Thus change begins again. Managers who understand the process of change can accelerate it, but they never successfully redesign it, ignore it, or otherwise avoid it.

Information technology for mass customization

To meet the new century's competition with mass customization, firms are building all kinds of new capabilities that rely on advanced information systems. If a mass customizer depends on a network of global capabilities, it must also depend on information it can control through a hub-and-web structure that links its modules of capabilities with its marketplace. In this context, IT – more specifically the Internet – is an important but untested resource that may have profound effects on firms' ability to mass customize. Mass customization is driven by information and the supporting technologies. The two go hand-in-hand and create a sustainable advantage for many firms who take the path to get here.

With the Internet, firms can reach customers and exact precise customer specifications over barriers of time and distance. The Internet can help isolate and identify customer needs. Our belief is that although the Internet will be a boon to all firms' customization efforts, their work will still have to become a powerful dynamic network of reconfigurable modules. If firms use the Internet to achieve a precision market strategy, they will have to back it up with solid mass customization service, manufacturing and supply chain capabilities.

Co-configuration and knowledge

As we explained at the outset, the right path does not always end with renewal. If we look further into the twenty-first century in some of today's leading-edge firms, we can see beyond mass customization. Mass customization generates yet another type of knowledge that leads us *beyond* mass customization. Working the challenges of mass customization yields to truly systemic understandings of the dynamic interactions between the product, the customer and the firm. We call this knowledge *configuration knowledge*; it is the basis for moving beyond mass customization, to what we call *co-configuration*. Co-configuration work occurs at the interface of the firm, the customer and the products or services. It requires constant interaction among the firm, the customer, and the product. The result is that the product adjusts continuously to what the customer wants. Co-configuration creates *customer-intelligent* value in products or services, where the lines between product and customer knowledge become blurred and interwoven. Beyond mass customization is the future, and it represents an exciting opportunity for those who are positioned to go there.

An ongoing process

Co-configuration not only has the potential to offer a product that learns and adapts; it also promotes an invaluable, ongoing relationship between a consumer–product pairing and a company. Co-configuration goes beyond mass customization to the next level, enriching customer-focused competitive advantage. Although co-configuration is a continuous process, the added value of an adaptive, intelligent product to customer bonding and loyalty cuts through the competition.

In the case of Oticon, developing an intelligent, digital hearing aid is not the end of the story. As more customer information is gathered with each individual hearing aid adapting to, and therefore betraying, individual needs and circumstances, the firm will use this new information to add further value to its products. For example, using infrared signals Oticon can reprogramme digital hearing aids with upgrades.

The network

As already mentioned, co-configuration never ends; rather, a continually evolving *network* develops between customer, product and company – the human link. Mass customization generates a great deal of information. It is essential to gather information about how the product needs to vary in step with customers' changing needs or desires. This is known as *configuration knowledge*.

Configuration knowledge can be used to design products and services that sense, respond and adapt as needs change. Such a process can not be contemplated without a network – it is the natural outcome of a closely knit relationship between the customer, product and company. The network lies at the heart of dynamic co-configuration methods. In order to leverage configuration knowledge, companies need to apply the accumulated information and then develop customer-intelligent products and services. The network is a living, growing entity – not simply a means of adding value but, inevitably, a new way of working.

Changing company attitudes

Co-configuration is no longer a vision of the future; it is upon us. The unique integration of customer, product and company that co-configuration allows is setting the standard for industry leaders. Tomorrow's successful companies will see customers becoming 'real' partners through co-configuration networks, to provide products and services that will dominate demand.

In a world of customer intelligence, the automobile manufacturer works to improve the latest four-door sedan while the customer uses it, as all customers use it, and as everyone involved changes and learns. Telecommunications companies work to improve their telephone services for every customer, by creating and enhancing a system of services by adding new features like call-forwarding, extra bandwidth, or higher-quality transmission. And the telecommunications companies do this in a way that fully incorporate the dynamic needs of each customer and the constant technological and market forces that drive the industry.

The central marketing idea to personalize and customize products is not new. Many firms have long been trying to meet the individual needs of customers. However, to interact continuously with the customer to meet changing wants and needs is something beyond the scope of what many firms contemplate, much less can achieve today. Looking back, we see that several hundred years ago even the most skilled craftsmanship could never design, build, and continuously adapt a product for every customer. Even mass production, process enhancement and mass customization fall short of the capability requirements of customer intelligence. Why? Because the need for reliability ties in tightly to the need for a precise, dynamic fit between customer needs and product characteristics. So it is no surprise that customer-intelligent products would first emerge in industries like these. From the perspective of the right path, it is also no surprise that the most successful firms in these industries focus obsessively on organizational learning.

CASE STUDY: ORGANIZATIONAL LEARNING AND THE RIGHT PATH AT OTICON

In the last ten years, Lars Kolind, CEO of Oticon, has dismantled the company's bureaucracy to reinvigorate the creativity of his organization. Kolind and Oticon revitalized Oticon's capabilities, moving the company to an industry-leading capability to mass customize their hearing aids. Customization of hearing aids is critical because no two ears are identical. Everyone has his or her own unique 'soundmap'. Hearing varies not only in the degree of deafness, but also in the specific loss of sensitivity to different sound qualities. As a result, the market for individually fitted and tuned hearing aids is very strong. In response, Oticon, like its competitors, tailors each hearing instrument precisely to each user. Hearing care specialists physically mould the instrument to the ear and tune the amplifier to each person's needs and preferences. The competitive

*requirement to deliver such a product at a competitive price has made mass cus-
tomization the basis of competition in the industry.*

*However, even with mass customization, Oticon would still not settle. Not only are
every customer's hearing needs different, they also vary from situation to situation
over time. Their response was to develop a new generation of customer-intelligent
hearing aids, called Digifocus, that actually learns with use. (For their Digifocus line
of hearing aids, Oticon received the both the 1997 European Information Technology
Grand Prize and the European Design Prize.)*

*Oticon gained the configuration knowledge necessary to know what parameters
needed to be adjusted, how to adjust them, and how to put all this into Digifocus while
they were doing mass customization. The company leveraged what it learned from customizing millions of hearing aids, to make the Digifocus automatically adjustable.
Oticon accumulated knowledge about how individual hearing needs vary over time
and from sound environment to sound environment. This knowledge enabled the
company to assess hearing requirements, and automatically make adjustments in
sound amplification and signal processing.*

*With the knowledge they accumulated, Oticon created not just an intelligent product,
but a partnership between their customers, their distributors, and the company. It is
this partnership or network that delivers the value, not just the company. The hearing
instrument 'learns' how to adapt its performance to the changing needs of the customer;
the customer learns to 'teach' the hearing instrument about his/her needs; and the
company learns how to improve the interaction between the customer and the product.*

SUMMARY

Co-configuration: efficient personalization through information and IT

The work of co-configuration involves building and sustaining a fully integrated system
that can sense, respond and adapt to the individual experience of the customer. When
a firm does co-configuration work, it creates a product that can learn and adapt, but
it also builds an ongoing relationship between each customer–product pairing and
the company. Following mass customization requires designing a product at least once
for each customer. This design process requires the company to sense and respond
to the individual customer's needs. Co-configuration work takes this relationship to
the next level. Adding to the relationship, co-configuration brings the value of an
intelligent and adapting product. The company then continues to work with this
customer–product pair to make the product more responsive to each individual user.
In this way, the customization work becomes continuous.

Unlike previous work, co-configuration never results in a 'finished' product. Instead, a living, growing network develops between the customer, the product and the company. Oticon's Digifocus hearing aid is initially fitted to the user, but the work hardly ends there. As the user's hearing needs change, so too does the hearing aid. It adjusts automatically to different hearing environments. Hearing care professionals can reconfigure it to allow the user to 'step up' to greater and greater levels of sound as they become accustomed to the new sensations. Using infrared signals, the company can also reprogram it with upgrades.

How can a company learn to create customer intelligent products and services? What do they have to do to get there? We believe that they simply have to continue along the right path. By doing the work of mass customization, the organization generates a new kind of understanding, a new kind of knowledge by-product. That knowledge is how the product or service, in its essential elements or modules, must vary as the customer's needs and wants vary. We call this *configuration knowledge*.

With *configuration* knowledge, the organization can create products and services that dynamically and continuously respond to the needs of the customer, without the customer or the organisation having to intervene. The application of configuration intelligence to the product creates a system of customer, product or service, and company. The complex of interactions among all three, the way a product or service adapts and responds to the changing needs of the customer, is the underlying, dynamic source of value. Having this configuration knowledge available as a by-product of mass customization is not sufficient if the destination is co-configuration. To leverage configuration knowledge, organizations have to go beyond mass customization and transform work to achieve co-configuration.

10

Using Information for Strategic Cost Reduction

In the previous chapter, the emphasis on cost reduction was the need for businesses to use information so precisely that customers are satisfied in a way that wastes little money and other resources. In this chapter, **Bob Howell** focuses on systematic techniques for achieving cost reductions in a way that can actually *create business value,* rather than reducing the company's competitiveness.

Overview

Strategic cost reduction to create economic value is a relatively new business activity, not performed well by many companies, and is dependent in many respects on the availability of useful information. It is likely that you consider the previous sentence preposterous. Cost reduction efforts have been around for years. What were Frederick Winslow Taylor and his efficiency contemporaries doing in factory after factory, studying detailed labour operations to make them more productive, almost a century ago? Most companies utilize standard cost accounting systems and responsibility-centre accounting to budget product and organizational costs, measuring actual costs against the budgets and analysing thoroughly the variances. Is it not the case that the generic strategic concept of low-cost position and its elements of high-volume output, economies of scale, product and process simplification, and the lessons of the learning and experience curves, all emphasized the importance of cost minimization?

All of the above statements are true. There have been a number of broad conceptual ideas and specific practices aimed at reducing costs over the years. However, in an industry where all of the participants are relatively cost-inefficient, that participant which is most efficient, as a result of higher volume or real cost advantage, will have the lowest cost position, even though this cost position might not be as low as it could be. One only has to consider the US steel and automotive industries over the past 50 years to see the point. If budgets are set loosely, performing better than budget may not represent good cost performance. The time and motion study of detailed labour operations may reduce costs at this very specific cost-element level. Whether it has a positive impact on total costs or is the most important place to put emphasis is questionable, given the shift in cost structures such that productive labour is a relatively small element of costs.

Until the last ten years or so, a real urgency to significantly reduce costs was not present in a number of businesses and industries. If costs increased due to

> **"Firms and industries have begun to recognize that in an increasingly competitive environment, where prices are more likely to fall than to rise, systemic cost reduction is a critical element for long-term business success"**

increasing input costs, inefficiencies, or poor decisions, the normal reaction was to raise prices to sustain profit margins, rather than address the rising costs. As the competitive landscape has changed dramatically, the ability to raise prices as costs rise has been altered. No longer is it automatic. If prices cannot be raised in the context of rising costs, a firm finds itself in a classic price cost squeeze. When the profit margin erosion becomes severe enough, many companies have reacted by initiating across-the-board cost reduction initiatives – and such initiatives frequently do not stick. If prices continue to drop and costs continue to rise, the cycle repeats itself: another significant cost reduction initiative is introduced.

For many years, information to enable good cost and other decisions was not readily available due to the limitations of IT. However, over the years competitive forces have heightened product and market changes as well as increased emphasis on quality, speed and cost. Fortunately, IT and management constructs and applications have developed as well. But even today there are a number of cost reduction practices that many companies have failed to develop.

This chapter develops a set of cost reduction initiatives that constitute a comprehensive cost reduction programme. These initiatives are:

1. Cost and profitability analysis.
2. Waste elimination and lean operations.
3. Flat, focused organizations.
4. Product cost planning (target costing).
5. Supplier management, value chain analysis and outsourcing.
6. Kaizen costing.
7. Asset economics.

Although the order is important – especially for firms at very early stages of truly systematically reducing costs – it is certainly possible for firms that are either further along or believe they have particularly critical cost reduction opportunities to start and proceed in their own order. To realize the full potential of these measures requires the development of new approaches to information collection and presentation. This is not always an easy thing to accomplish, but the potential benefits are huge.

Cost and profitability analysis

Product cost and profitability analysis

The proliferation of products emanating from an increasingly competitive business environment, coupled with simple, historically-based cost assignment methods will inevitably result in inaccurate product cost and product profitability information, leading to poor understanding and decisions.

For example, assume that we have two products, one that we might call *easy to make* and the second that we might call *hard to make*. Assume that it is possible to trace both the material and productive labour costs directly to these products, such that we feel reasonably confident in assigning their costs. However, also assume that the manufacturing overhead is spread evenly across the two products based on the relative amount of direct labour in each. If 'easy to make' means there are significant competitors, that might suggest competitive pressures on pricing. As a result, it might appear as though the easy-to-make product is under some profit squeeze. On the other hand, the hard-to-make product, with fewer competitors, may have stronger pricing and appear to be more profitable. If the descriptors 'easy to make' and 'hard to make' are intended to suggest that the amount of manufacturing costs that should be assigned to the products might, in fact, be low for the easy-to-make product and high for the hard-to-make product, then it could very well be that the real profit margin of easy-to-make is higher than assumed, and the real profit margin for hard-to-make lower than assumed.

There are innumerable examples of product cost analyses that have demonstrated that classical, simple overhead cost assignments can be very misleading. In the past decade, a number of companies have undertaken *activity-based costing* (ABC) initiatives intended to better assign manufacturing overhead costs to products to better ascertain relative product cost and profit performance. Such a process yields several major benefits.

Understanding costs

The first benefit is a better understanding of just what drives costs in a business. Characteristics such as product complexity, number of outside vendors, numbers of purchase orders, the nature of production processes, the number of production set-ups, and special customer requirements, for example, are principal drivers of product costs. Knowing this, a management is in the position to make the appropriate changes so as to influence the drivers and resultant costs.

Understanding profitability

The second major benefit from such product cost and profit analyses is a richer understanding of which products actually make more money and which ones make less or, in fact, actually lose money. For example, an industrial tyre manufacturer produced more than 140 varieties of lawn mower, ride-on tractor, snow blower and similar application tyres. Upon analysis, it was determined that the price, volume and cost structure of these resulted in them being unprofitable. To assure that these models were never sold again, the production department actually cut up the tools to prevent any chance that they could be manufactured.

Similarly, a large corn syrup and starch producer undertook a similar analysis. Again, a number of specifications were determined to be unprofitable, because of weak prices, inadequate volume and high costs. These products, too, were eliminated from the company's offerings. After dropping the losing products from the product line, overall profitability actually is improved.

Avoiding the pitfalls of overhead cost assignment

When competition increases, product lines proliferate, product lifecycles shorten, and product development costs go up; similarly, market channels multiply and marketing expenses increase. To the extent that engineering and marketing costs are product-line- or product-related, vary across product lines and products, and are not adequately identified with the product lines, major errors of cost assignment also result.

Furthermore, most product cost systems virtually ignore the cost of carrying inventory. Some of the carrying costs such as warehouse space, material handling, and insurance costs may be included in the overhead cost structure and get related to products generally – but not to the right products. The financial costs of carrying inventory are ignored in the product cost calculation process. If some products move through the production process quickly and other products move through more slowly, resulting in higher inventories and costs, when these differences are not identified, picked up and considered in product costing, an additional deficiency in the accuracy of product costing results.

Information requirements for product cost and profitability analysis

The information requirements and systems implications of product cost and profitability analysis are significant. If the information regarding manufacturing overheads is pooled in such a way that it is difficult to assign to particular products, the ability to determine products costs and profitabilities – and to make rational business decisions – is compromised. If certain costs such as research, engineering, development, distribution and sales are driven by product characteristic differences, but are not captured in the products' costs, decisions may also be misdirected.

Customer cost and profitability analysis

Knowing what a customer pays for a particular purchase is straightforward: it is detailed on the invoice. However in many large, diversified companies, knowing *how much* a particular customer buys is a problem, if that customer buys products from more than one operating unit. Were Wal-Mart to buy paper products, toiletries, health-care items and babies' nappies from Procter & Gamble, unless P&G had the ability to aggregate all Wal-Mart's purchases across P&G's various businesses, Wal-Mart might know how much it buys from P&G, *but not the other way around*. This is a problem for many diversified companies that collect financial information along internal unit dimensions, rather than by external customer.

There are a number of other costs in addition to product costs in a business, referred to as operating expenses or period costs. These are not captured in the product cost definition and are, in fact, probably more related to market, channel, and individual customer distinctions than to product lines and products. To really understand customer profitability, these costs have to be attached to individual customers. Different commission rates, discounts and other allowances, advertising and promotion expenses, field support and customer service may be driven by customer characteristics rather than product. If there are differences in a customer's demands on an organization, then the cost implications need to be understood and captured.

It is clearly important for managers' strategies to prioritize and focus their approach to customer groups depending on the turnover they generate and the profitability they provide. High-volume, highly profitable customers are the ones that need to be maintained. They provide a firm with much of its overall profitability. Those customers who fall in the low-volume, highly profitable category need to be developed such that their volume increases. This may be accomplished through additional effort or some price/volume tradeoffs. The high-volume, low-profit customers need to be managed in a different way. It needs to be understood why they fall in that category. Is it because of the nature of the mix of products that they buy? Is it because of the pressure that the customer applies for price concessions? Or is it a result of the additional demands that the customer places on the firm for support services? This kind of information permits the management of these three customer groups.

The low-volume, low-profit (or even unprofitable) group of customers also needs to be analysed to determine whether there are any opportunities to move these customers. Many companies have a number of customers to whom they sell low-volume, poor-margin products and provide additional services, such that these customers are unprofitable. Just as unprofitable products need to be eliminated, so do unprofitable customers for whom there is little opportunity to turn around. Dropping these customers can reduce costs and improve overall profitability and value creation.

Information requirements for customer cost and profitability analysis

Many businesses do not know which customers are most profitable, which need to be managed differently, and which ought to be dropped. This is because their existing information practices have not been oriented toward markets, channels and customers. Their process of aggregating cost and profit information has been product-, product-line- or business-unit-oriented. The distinctions between product costs and period costs are also a problem. Many of the period costs related to distribution, sales and service are driven by customers' locations, selling difficulty and service demands.

Database systems are available that can permit management to slice their data in a variety of ways, including customer sales, aggregate product costs and other costs that can be related to customers. As companies move in the direction of utilizing such data, they will be in a much stronger position to make better customer profitability decisions.

Waste elimination and lean operations

The objective of the product and customer cost and profitability analysis is to determine what it really costs to produce different products and serve different customers. The decision to eliminate certain unprofitable products and customers can reduce costs and, depending on the relative price-, variable-cost- and fixed-cost-structures, may improve profitability. In cases when no decisions are made to discontinue products or customers, activity-based costing will merely move costs around for better understanding and decision-making. However, activity-based thinking also provides the foundation for markedly reducing costs in other ways.

Waste elimination

For decades, leading Japanese companies have directed much of their cost management efforts toward what they call *muda* or waste elimination. As Western companies began to understand the 'Japanese Miracle' of the 1970s and 1980s, and the concepts of just in time (JIT) and waste elimination, terms such as *process analysis*, *process mapping* and even *re-engineering* became a part of the business lexicon. The idea of process analysis is to think of the activities of a business as a chain of events, perhaps from the beginning of the manufacturing process through to the end, and to break down the chain of activities into very discrete, yet identifiable, tasks. It is much more than a traditional manufacturing routing sheet that focuses only on those activities performed by direct or touch labour.

In most cases, direct touch labour constitutes a very small fraction of the total amount of time and number of activities involved in a process. In a business in which inventory turns over four times a year, the inventory is in process for an average of three months. Were one to accumulate all of the direct labour touch time associated with the production and completion of a given product, it might represent only a few days of accumulated time. The question, then, is raised: what consumes the rest of the time and why? It turns out on closer analysis that what frequently happens is that large batches of products are run together, such that while one unit is being worked on, the rest are waiting. When the batch is finished it may be moved some distance and returned to a stock-keeping area. When that particular category of part or sub-assembly requires further work, the batch is moved from the stock area back to another production location. Then the products wait again. Then they are moved back into storage or to another production area and so forth. The net result is that much of what is going on is a series of moves, storage, waiting, record-keeping and periodic quality checks. Having information about processes at this level of detail provides the opportunity to get at this waste and reduce or eliminate it. Without this kind of analysis the assumption is made that much of what constitutes waste really is necessary, or efforts to reduce waste do not fully comprehend their magnitude nor opportunity.

The idea of thinking about everything that goes on in a leading Japanese business, such as Toyota, in terms of processes (or a series of activities) and waste elimination, is absolutely fundamental. If one visits a Japanese factory one can actually see how processes have been laid out and can almost feel the continuing search for better ways to do things, while at the same focusing on eliminating waste.

CASE STUDIES: ELIMINATING WASTE – HARLEY DAVIDSON'S AND CATERPILLAR'S
ROUTES TO PROFITABILITY

Harley Davidson went through very hard times during the late 1970s. After the management buy-out in 1981, senior managers had the opportunity to visit Honda's Marysville, Ohio, motorcycle facility. The difference they saw between that facility and their own was dramatic in terms of layout, production flow, efficiency and inventory management. The management concluded that if Harley was going to be competitive with Honda and the other Japanese motorcycle manufacturers, they would have to effect a business-wide, just-in-time manufacturing initiative which they called MAN – materials as needed. Production operations were moved together, markedly reducing the amount of resources required for material handling. Harley was able to reduce the amount of inventories received too early, and produced too early, and reduce the amount of space required to manufacture their product. As it later turned out, they were creating space for additional production.

Caterpillar had a similar experience. During the 1980s Caterpillar concluded that their cost structure was significantly higher than their principal competitor, the Japanese firm Komatsu. Caterpillar concluded that whereas they continued to move their parts and partially finished products from one functional production area to another, Komatsu was using much more of a 'flow' process. Caterpillar undertook a significant plant re-arrangement initiative called PWAF – Plant With a Future – which led to their own flow process and a marked reduction in distances between operations, material handling expenses, inventory levels and cycle time to produce their products. In some cases, cycle time was reduced by as much as 80%.

Eliminating waste in non-manufacturing businesses

The application of process analysis thinking and practice can be equally applied to non-manufacturing activities. There are innumerable examples of improvements being realized by applying mapping to the new product development process, purchasing, distribution, sales and service and even such administrative areas as finance and accounting. Companies have taken traditionally paper-intensive areas as purchasing and have totally rearranged them, such that the work flows from one person to another in a quick, efficient fashion, rather than in batches from one function to another. Several finance organizations have applied the tools of process analysis to such activities as credit approval, accounts payables, payroll, collections and even their general ledger accounting and monthly closing activities.

Information requirements for waste elimination

Process mapping and analysis goes much further than classical cost assignment. It gets down into the details of just what activities exist, how many resources they consume, what that constitutes in terms of costs, and what really drives those costs. It is information such as this, coupled with an incessant drive to minimize waste, that results in major cost reduction accomplishments. General Electric has taken their inventory turnover from three times to close to ten times, or a two-thirds reduction in the level of inventories that they have to carry. Harley Davidson has been at it longer than GE and is turning their inventories 30 to 40 times a year. Companies such as Toyota turn their inventories 60 or 80 times a year. Dell computer is turning their inventories every three or four days. These are huge savings.

On an ongoing basis, being able to accumulate information such as throughput, cycle times, speed, inventory turnover and levels, material handling costs, scrap losses and yield rates, total cost implications of poor quality, and other indicators of waste and waste elimination, is important. Many companies' traditional cost and financial reporting systems are not well structured to do so.

What is needed is almost a complete change in thinking regarding the purpose of cost systems and information. Instead of focusing on inventory valuation and financial reporting the focus needs to shift to cost reduction and cost assignment for decision-making purposes. This is as much a management issue as it is an information issue.

Lean operations – the 'pull' philosophy

Some companies have begun to think in terms of 'lean' operations. The difference between the idea of 'lean' and waste elimination is the degree of emphasis placed on the customer's needs and expectations. In a highly competitive environment, one way that a supplier may differentiate itself is to be very responsive to the unique demands of individual customers. The supplier must be able to produce a variety of products and services quickly, at low cost. That requires the flexibility to respond, to produce small orders of great variety, quickly. The only way to do this is to be able to switch from one small order to another small order virtually instantaneously. Set-up times have to be reduced to practically zero for this kind of processing flexibility and response time to be achieved.

The waste elimination initiative is primarily generated and focused internally. It emanates from the conclusion that there is a lot of unnecessary activity in typical processes. This waste can be eliminated by structural changes such as rearranging facilities and eliminating unnecessary work and resources. However, the lean operations perspective starts with the view that everything a business does should be customer-driven and that virtually nothing should be done until customers demand it. If an activity is not wanted or needed by the customer, and the customer would not pay for it because it has no value, that activity should not be done. For those products, services and specific activities that are important to the customer, response has to be very quick. Lean companies think in terms of *pulling* products or services out of an organization, rather than *pushing* them through.

This 'pull' philosophy reinforces the need to think in terms of process flows as contrasted to functional operations. If a Harley Davidson customer wants a particular motorcycle model, that model has to be assembled. If the assembly line needs to produce that particular model, sub-assemblies need to be pulled out of their respective flow lines. Sub-assemblies, in turn, need to pull the individual parts that are required. The part requirements pull on the vendors. Some people have described the difference between pulling products or services through an organization and pushing them as equivalent to the difference between pulling on a string and pushing that string. A pulled string is straight and moves in one piece. A pushed string becomes curled. The end of the string away from the end being pushed may not make very much progress. That is the story of many businesses – lots of pushing going on to try to get things done, but not much really getting accomplished.

Developing flexibility and reducing set-up times

Once this pull thinking is in place and processes are lined up in order and close together to minimize the waste, it becomes important to build flexibility into the process such that the variety of customer demands may be met quickly and easily. This requires significant focus on reducing set-up time. Most companies have little appreciation for the implication of set-up times. Their information systems are totally non-responsive. The costs associated with set-ups, such as labour, equipment, maintenance and supplies, are scattered throughout a number of accounts and departments; the benefits of actually reducing set-up times and costs are frequently lost on most managers.

In a mass production environment, where large quantities of standard products are produced, set-up times have typically been accepted and utilized in analyses such as economic production quantity calculations to determine so-called economic productions runs. If set-up times are long and costs high, then the obvious reaction is to produce a large number of units before setting up for another product. This does, of course, result in large batch sizes, significant levels of inventory and explains, in large part, the three to four times average inventory turns which many traditional businesses consider normal.

The concept of economic production quantities is relatively straightforward. If one were to assume an average cost per set-up, then the more set-ups that are made, the more total set-up costs become. On the other hand, if a company has fewer, even one set-up, a year, then batches will be very large – up to a year's volume in the case of a single set-up and production run a year. The more set-ups that are made, the smaller the batches that can be run, and the lower the level of inventories and concomitant cost of financing, storing and other related expenses. The economic production quantity theorist would conclude that the number of set-ups that should be made is that number resulting in the lowest combined total set-up costs and inventory carrying costs.

Lean advocates understand that if set-up costs and inventory carrying costs can be reduced through process analysis, waste elimination and simplification, then more batches of smaller size may be run, and faster response and lower inventory levels and costs will result. If set-up costs can be reduced to practically zero then companies' can get pretty close to what has become known as 'one-piece flow'. This means that each time a customer orders, the final operation in the sequence gets the signal and passes it all the way back up the line to the beginning. The parts and components that need to be made for that order are then pulled through the system quickly to fulfil the customer's order.

Information regarding set-up times and cost is not a typical component of many companies' information systems. Set-up costs may include people, materials and equipment, which are scattered throughout the financial accounts. Without knowing what these costs are – and what drives them – one is unable to focus on this absolutely critical element of customer-focused, high-speed response capability.

The idea of set-up time reduction is equally applicable off the factory floor, and in non-manufacturing businesses as well as manufacturing. Order processing, credit approval, mortgage approval, accounts payable, capital appropriation, business planning and monthly reporting are all processes in which there are embedded fundamental set-up activities resulting in batch thinking and practice. Thinking in terms of lean, pull, one-piece flow and set-up reduction can have a marked impact on cost reduction.

Information requirements for lean operations

There are two major information implications of lean thinking and operations. First, much of the information normally utilized in a more traditional environment, such as forecasts of future expectations and the concomitant upstream requirements, become less necessary. If the various stages of a process are clearly and understandably linked, the demand on one stage triggers the appropriate demand on the previous stage, and so forth.

Second, new information may be very important. If set-up costs and inventory-carrying costs are critical aspects of a fast, flexible and responsive process, then knowing what costs are incurred during the set-up process or as a result of carrying inventory is essential. Most companies' information systems cannot provide such information quickly or easily. In the case of set-up costs, various types of costs from different organizations may be involved. If all of these costs are not gathered into one cost pool, it becomes very difficult to fully understand the cost of set-ups and the potential for cost reduction; this is also true for inventory-carrying costs. Order costs, receiving costs, inspection costs, moving costs, storage costs, insurance, damage, and obsolescence are just some of the costs of carrying inventory. Without knowing the aggregate of these costs, the ability to make cost trade-offs is lessened. Without knowing set-up costs and carrying costs, and the processes involved with each, it becomes very difficult to keep reducing these costs so that smaller lot sizes, faster response times and truly lean organizations can be achieved.

Flat, focused organizations

The 'lean' orientation is focused on customer needs and expectations rather than forecasts and internal expectations. This results in an alignment of processes geared to satisfy external customer requirements. In many businesses there are a number of supporting activities that are organized centrally, based on the economies of scale philosophy of mass production. These might include activities such as purchasing, scheduling, inventory control, plant engineering, maintenance, quality control and plant accounting. These activities are normally referred to as indirect costs, because they may not be traced easily to end products or services. Companies have procedures to assign these costs, first to various stages of the manufacturing process, and subsequently to individual products. This is what cost accounting is all about and what activity-based costing is intended to address. Activity-based costing attempts to determine what benefits activities provide and how the activities are utilized, such that the costs may be more accurately attributed to those products that use them.

Some companies have shifted from the economies of scale model such that these support activities are actually embedded into the lines of business. What this does is make indirect, difficult-to-trace costs directly identifiable to the lines and much more traceable. Some Japanese companies contend that 80–90% of their costs can be traceable directly and as a result their need for activity-based costing is relatively minor. One Japanese financial executive has been quoted as saying: "The need for activity-based costing is a symptom [of a host of other problems] rather than a solution." A very thoughtful statement.

Several initial reactions immediately arise to this idea of the desegregation of support costs into the lines of business. It conflicts with the economies of scale and knowledge sharing, which may be realized in a more centralized organization. The question of economies of scale versus focus and economies of scope is analogous to the set-up/economies of scale argument. Distributing support activities, such as purchasing, may result in the purchasing people knowing much more about customer needs and the characteristics of the flow process. The decisions that they make and the items that they purchase may contribute more to the bottom line than if they were buying in a more centralized model. If less than a full purchasing or scheduling person is required for a particular line of business, companies that have moved in this direction have consolidated job responsibilities, broadening their people's talents. Such mechanisms heightened the degree of cross-functional understanding.

Purchasing departments have been measured on their ability to buy cheap and beat standard costs. This has prompted large orders, excess inventory, additional storage facilities, insurance, and the risk of product damage and obsolescence. Beating price frequently comes with a cost, one of which might be lower quantity. This may result in production problems, re-work costs and delivery delays. Putting purchasing right into the business and making it an integral part of the business team results in an entirely different attitude, buying what is needed, when it is needed to meet end customer needs and expectations, rather than some self-serving objective. The information that purchasing needs to make decisions, and the measures and controls applied to motivate, are entirely different.

> **"With many support activities, leading Japanese companies have put responsibility for preventative maintenance and the assurance of quality right into the hands and minds of line workers rather than making housekeeping, preventative maintenance and product quality separate and, at times, adversarial activities"**

As focused factories or operations are created and supporting activities are distributed so that self-contained, integrated teams are responding to customer needs and expectations, the requirements for additional levels of management are reduced. Businesses have been organized with a number of producing departments supported by centralized support activities, such as purchasing and maintenance to constitute a manufacturing plant. Above the plant organization level, there are higher levels of organization, such as divisions and groups, which ultimately get consolidated into the corporate office. Corporate offices have staffs, as do groups, divisions, plant managers and so forth. Information has typically flowed from the lowest level to the top, and directions have flowed from the top to the bottom. Concern and response to markets, channels and customers have been lost in this up and down hierarchy of information and direction.

Information requirements for flat organizations

Some companies have concluded that this vertical activity is misdirected and that:

- focus should be horizontal rather than vertical;
- information should flow from customers into the business; and
- timely response should flow from the business to customers.

This puts a totally different focus on information needs and organizational staffing. Major corporations, such as General Electric, have dramatically flattened their organizations, such that the corporate staffs, group, business unit and division staffs have been markedly reduced. Whole layers of organizations have been removed, and this flattening gets those near the top of the organization closer to where action is happening.

Activity and process analysis, emphasis on the customer, cleaning out waste, and emphasizing focus and flat structures, collectively represent huge cost savings opportunities. For most businesses, it is not unrealistic to think that 10–20% of all costs can be reduced. The impact on assets, principally inventories and space, may be even more significant. Most companies' information systems are unable to gather data along such dimensions. It becomes difficult to demonstrate the potential that exists in most organizations to markedly reduce the cost and asset structure of it.

Product cost planning (target costing)

Most businesses' costs are determined during the early product planning and development phase of a product's lifecycle. Yet most cost management, control and reduction efforts are applied late in the product's lifecycle, when materials are purchased, labour is utilized and products are actually *produced*. This is like locking the barn door after the horse has been stolen.

A complex product design will tend to drive product costs higher: product designs will influence the degree to which outside vendors will be utilized. The work intended to be completed by an internal manufacturing unit will influence the capital investment and other manufacturing and cost requirements. By the time product designs are frozen, material, labour and manufacturing overhead costs are virtually determined. Product design decisions may also strongly influence non-manufacturing costs such as distribution, sales and service. Complexity may necessitate special packaging, storage and handling. Sales personnel may require special training, or require more time and expense to complete a transaction. Field support and service costs may be driven higher by the decisions made earlier in the development process.

In many companies the product development process proceeds functionally.

Engineering designs, purchasing estimates, material input costs, plant engineering and manufacturing determine the capital investment requirements and manufacturing routings, and all of this, ultimately, is accumulated to arrive at a cost estimate. In a cost-based pricing model, costs determine prices; in a more competitive environment, it might only be at the end of the prototype phase that a company realizes that it has a margin problem. At that time, it can go back and try to take costs out of the product by cheapening the inputs or redesigning, which may delay the product launch and its success.

> "Companies such as Toyota, DaimlerChrysler and others utilize cross-functional design teams to shorten the product development process. This is achieved by reducing the amount of recycling that historically occurred in the sequential design model. Toyota has reached the point where it will not release a product to production unless it is fully convinced that its target cost objectives are achievable"

Alternatively, some companies are beginning to reverse the cost management process, such that market prices and predetermined profit margins are being used to drive allowable costs. As the product concept and design stages are occurring, representatives from engineering, purchasing, key suppliers, plant engineering, manufacturing, finance, marketing, sales and service get involved simultaneously to ensure that the product concept and design decisions are made in the broadest perspective. The intention is that the final result of the concept and design phases meets, or beats, the requirements in the market place, influencing favourably material input costs, capital investment requirements, business processes and overall costs, such that the targeted profit margin is realized.

Information requirements for target costing

The information requirements for target costing are significantly different than those for the more traditional 'inside-out' cost plus model. First, it is necessary for a company to have good information regarding its customers wants and needs in terms of functionality, price and comparable competitive product information. Many companies spend little or no time trying to truly understand customers' future wants and needs – what customers consider the most important attributes of the products or services they are considering – and *how much* customers are willing to pay for them. In a similar fashion, many companies have virtually no information regarding competitive products and services, what functions are offered, how they differ, and at what price they are offered. Without this kind of information, it is virtually impossible to establish the target price relative to the products and functions to be offered.

Second, many companies do not have a good framework for developing target margins for specific product or service offerings. They have aggregate historical margins, or even disaggregated product line or product margins, but these may suffer from the inadequacies of cost assignment simplicity described earlier. If a company's product costing system is such that many of the costs are averaged to products, then the product cost and profit information is flawed and misleading. Similarly, if different markets, channels and individual customers require different resources, and if these are neither fully understood nor incorporated into an understanding of customer profitability, then again it is difficult to establish appropriate target margins for segmented channels and products. If a company's business processes, organization structure and utilization of resources are replete with waste, then any historical profit margins serve little useful purpose as a benchmark for future target profit margins.

Increased competition, price pressures, and the necessity to manage costs relative to price and margin objectives require significantly richer information regarding customers, competitors and the company's own costs and performance. For many businesses this represents a major information management challenge.

Supplier management, value chain analysis and outsourcing

The importance of supplier management for cost reduction

The major element of cost that many businesses incur is the *aggregate purchases* from their many vendors. One approach that many companies have used in the past to control the cost of purchased materials has been to solicit quotations from a number of potential suppliers. When the quotations are received they either give all the business to the supplier with the lowest bid or spread the business around to several suppliers, such that there is no dependence on one supplier and the several suppliers keep each other honest. One way to beat the standards is to set loose standards. Another is to purchase in large quantities, creating leverage on one's suppliers to reduce prices to get the large volume of business.

> "To put into perspective the relative importance of purchased materials it is worth considering that for many businesses, particularly in the manufacturing industry, purchases from vendors may represent 50% or more of every dollar of revenue. It is interesting to contemplate how little attention executives place on this fact"

If purchases are where the costs are, this is where the greatest attention should be placed to achieve significant cost reductions. Many companies have virtually no information regarding the root causes of the costs and prices they experience from their vendors.

Controlling the drivers of high material costs

Standardizing specifications

There are a number of drivers of high material costs; many are generated internally. For example, going back to the discussion regarding product design and development, if every single product development effort starts from scratch and proceeds to produce a unique set of specifications when standardization could be possible, many unnecessary costs could have been avoided. One illustration of this is a consumer product company buying a large volume of packaging materials in a plethora of specifications, with virtually no attempt to think through common packaging concepts across multiple products and business lines. Once this was recognized and co-ordination achieved between the purchasing personnel, standardized specifications and major reductions in costs were realized.

Working closely with suppliers

The second internally generated driver of high purchased material costs is the decision to seek multiple bids and offer contract awards to the lowest bidder. The process of multiple bids and periodic re-bidding turns out to be expensive. Many businesses are concluding that the lowest purchase price may not, in fact, result in the lowest lifecycle cost. If a vendor is unreliable or delivers a product that is of lower quality than specified, such that downstream manufacturing, distribution, sales and field service costs are affected adversely, it can very well be that the 'lowest-cost supplier' turns out to be anything but the lowest cost. Sometimes it may turn out to be the highest.

When companies focus on their purchasing activities, they realize quickly that they have thousands of vendors. Many could get along with far fewer. The objective should be to identify those vendors who have the overall capabilities to provide high-quality inputs, when they are needed, on time, just in time, at the best lifecycle cost, taking into consideration input price, impact on inventories, manufacturing, distribution, customer satisfaction and field service implications.

> **"Xerox initiated a vendor reduction programme some years ago and moved from thousands of suppliers to a few hundred. Other companies have had similar experiences"**

Few companies know very much about, care about, or even work with, their vendors to do anything about their *vendors'* costs. The opportunities are as significant as in one's own business, perhaps even more. Once a company has identified a vendor with whom it plans to work, there should be the understanding that this is to be a long-term relationship and that the customer truly wants to help the vendor become as proficient as possible. The company should work closely with that vendor to do so, with the expectation that the two parties will share the cost improvements.

If vendors' costs can be reduced by 10–20%, the customer could be expected to share in half of that, and materials represent 50% or more of a customer's costs, then such a reduction can have a significant impact on the customer's cost and profit structure. Opportunities that can have long-term benefits for both parties include:

● The application of activity-based costing to determine product costs and cost drivers.
● The utilization of process analysis and mapping to identify and eliminate waste.
● The rearrangement of facilities.
● Set-up time reduction.
● The application of target costing at the vendor level.

Reducing the costs of the purchasing process

In addition to *specification standardization* and *vendor rationalization and support*, there is frequently the opportunity to take costs out of the procurement process itself. Traditionally, there has been multiple form paper associated with placing orders, expediting, receiving, storing, accounting, and paying vendors. Some companies have dramatically reduced and virtually eliminated such costs. E-commerce, blanket purchase orders, vendors actually on-site and payment on the basis of customer usage of vendor materials are some of the ways such administrative costs have been reduced.

Information requirements for supplier management

Information plays a critical role in this whole area of purchasing and vendor cost management and reduction. One needs to know what one buys, in what quantities, from what vendors. It is also vitally important to know common or potentially common purchases across businesses, as well as information regarding vendor performance. All of the underlying information described earlier can be invaluable in the drive to help one's vendors to become extraordinarily proficient.

Value chain analysis and outsourcing

Businesses may be thought of as a series of major processes, sub-processes and activities. At the *major processes level* one might think in terms of market assessment, new product development, outside procurement, inside operations, distribution, sales and service. Such a sequence has been referred to as the 'value chain'. The chain is obvious; the term 'value' is intended to indicate where along the chain value is created, or potentially dissipated. In the last few years the argument has been put forth that a firm should concentrate on its core competencies and capabilities, and that it should offload, or 'outsource', those processes that are not core to its own success and which may be performed by others more proficiently.

Some businesses actually think in terms of extended value chains, analysing upstream the capabilities and performance of suppliers and their suppliers, and downstream customers and their customers. Being able to make such analyses and reaching appropriate courses of action require very different information, in many cases not readily found within the firm's own accounting records or in one's typical understanding of related parties' activities.

CASE STUDIES: SUCCESSFULLY APPLYING VALUE CHAIN ANALYSIS AND OUTSOURCING

*There are many examples of the economic benefits and cost-savings emanating from value chain analysis and potential outsourcing. In the late 1970s and early 1980s when Lee Iococca assumed the presidency of **Chrysler Corporation**, one of his first actions was to 'unbundle' much of the backward integration that Chrysler and other car manufacturers had historically maintained. By shedding much of the metal-bending, component and sub-assembly manufacturing, Chrysler was able to reduce its fixed-cost structure, lower its break-even point, and increase its flexibility to respond to shifts in* *market demand. By shedding these activities, Chrysler was able to concentrate on auto-mobile assembly, such that it was able to achieve the low-cost manufacturing position amongst the big three automobile manufacturers in the United States, even though it was the smallest of the three. It is interesting to note that both Ford and General Motors have recently 'unbundled' major portions of their component and sub-assembly busi-nesses, in the hope of increasing their flexibility and lowering their cost structure.*

One might argue that Chrysler did not reach the decision to 'unbundle' totally in a vacuum. The Japanese car manufacturers have had a similar kind of structural rela-tionship with their vendors. As a result, they too have had similar flexibility, at least to an extent, to reduce the requirements of their vendors in times of slow activity. The philosophy of lifetime employment, both within the Japanese car manufacturers and upstream with their suppliers, puts some limits on the degree of flexibility that they have to reduce their level of activity, headcount and output.

*Before one thinks that all companies should 'unbundle' any basic manufacturing that they do and push it back on to their suppliers, one should understand the story of **Harley Davidson** and other companies like it. As Harley Davidson effected its own version of just in time – its MAN (materials as needed) programme – their factories were rearranged, unnecessary and wasteful work was eliminated, the business became more proficient and their labour requirements lessened. However, Harley Davidson had made commitments to its workers that none would be laid off as a result of the pro-ductivity improvements emanating from MAN.*

Harley's solution was to reconsider all of the work that was being done by its vendors, then take back the work that it could do itself. In making this analysis, given the com-mitments that it had made to its employees, it considered its labour costs as fixed. There-fore the 'make or buy' comparison that was made compared the purchase price of the vendors with only the material and other miscellaneous variable costs that Harley would have incurred, had they manufactured the item themselves. The effect of this analysis was to prompt Harley Davidson to pull back a considerable amount of work that they had formerly been purchasing from vendors. As Harley's MAN initiative pro-gressed, the company sought other related kinds of work that its workers could perform in a sub-contract relationship to other manufacturers.

*As the relationship between automobile companies and their suppliers has shifted, such that the suppliers are producing more components and sub-assemblies, not only has a stronger relationship developed upstream with the vendors, but much of the en-gineering development has been placed on the vendors as well. Suppliers such as **Johnson Controls** and **Lear Seating** are considered experts in seating and passenger ergonomics: the product that they deliver to all the car companies is a self-contained seating package. It therefore makes sense for them to assume more responsibility for the engineering and product development of such major sub-assemblies. This is a very different relationship to the one that formerly existed, when the major car manufac-turers did virtually all of the design work for every facet of the car.*

There are examples of companies that have done just the opposite of what the car companies have done. Nike would not consider outsourcing its market research and product development activities, yet has virtually no problem using contract manufac-turers around the world to produce its products, and a distribution and warehousing system run by others.

Information requirements for value chain analysis and outsourcing

One approach that has been deployed very often in the past few years is the idea of outsourcing a firm's IT activities to a third party, such as EDS, Andersen Consulting, IBM or others. Many companies have found that the high technology and rapid change around their IT activities has been such that it is difficult for line managers to stay up-to-date. Understanding between IT functions and managers has been strained. Budgets have seemingly become black holes. In an effort to focus on what one does best and 'unbundle' much of the rest, a number of large corporations have outsourced much of their information systems and technology activities.

Where and how a firm spends and makes money, and how that may be measured and improved, requires information cut in new and different ways. It is necessary to think and use cost information in a value chain orientation rather than according to functions and cost centres. Understanding costs and benefits, and considering costs differently depending upon the specific decision to be made, such as Harley David-son's 'make or buy' decision, is not easy. It requires a good information foundation and the ability to utilize that information intelligently.

Kaizen costing

Leading Japanese manufacturers make a sharp distinction between target costing, taking significant costs out of products and processes during the product concept and development phases and, driven by the necessity to make profits in a market-driven pricing environment, *kaizen costing* or continuous improvement costing. Kaizen costing occurs during the actual production operations stage between major new product introductions or major cost reduction initiatives across all aspects of the business. Kaizen, or continuous improvement costing, means just what the name implies: that one is continually attempting to identify the opportunity, even if quite small, to take additional costs out of a business.

Kaizen – a corporate culture of continuous cost reduction

One way that companies accomplish this is to institute a culture of continuous cost reduction. That is certainly what Toyota has done, as represented by its 1993 annual report. One could also argue that it is what Motorola, Allied Signal and GE are also doing, in conjunction with their respective quests for six sigma quality levels. If poor quality results in a whole set of explicit and implicit costs, then one may assume that heightened quality will have the opposite impact.

Japanese companies encourage their employees to make suggestions regarding ways to improve a business. Every employee is encouraged to get involved and make suggestions. The number of suggestions that a company such as Toyota receives numbers in the hundreds of continuous improvement suggestions per employee per year. Although there may be modest monetary incentives involved, it is much more a collective understanding of the degree of competition that the company can sense, which drives this behaviour.

Taking costs out of a business – i.e. reducing costs – is, and becomes, everyone's job in such a cultural environment. The intent is not just to reduce costs arbitrarily, but to do so in the context of the larger business picture, meeting price in the market place, being able to have resources to re-invest, making money, and building a business for the future.

Asset economics

Businesses do three things: raise money through financing, invest in the business, then use the investments to generate a return, represented by the profits and cash flows. There is no virtue in investing in more assets than are absolutely necessary. To do so means that more financing has to be secured, and with it the concomitant costs of that financing, which have to be covered by the returns before there are any residual returns for the investors. Surprisingly, many businesses look upon size, represented by total assets, as a measure of strength, yet this can often simply highlight another area of potential waste.

There are two major investment categories: *working capital*, represented primarily by the receivables and inventories, partially offset by the payables, and what I am going to call *foundational assets*. The term 'foundational assets' includes property, plant, equipment, investments in other businesses and other investments, the premium paid for other businesses, and more intangible assets such as the long-term potential represented by a firm's intellectual capital and brand recognition. This section focuses on removing waste in the more 'classical' assets: accounts receivable, inventories and fixed assets, although brief comments will be made regarding several of the other asset categories.

Classical techniques for removing waste and reducing costs

Improving the efficiency of accounts receivable

Accounts receivable carry an associated cost to finance them, the administrative costs of processing them, and the risks associated with not collecting them. Most companies take this as a given, yet to the extent there are customers who pay on time or even early, shortly after payment is due, or have stretched their payables considerably, these differences may be significant. The processing cost of repeatedly billing delinquent customers adds to their overall costs. As with costs associated with servicing different customers to different degrees, these differences in payment and collection experiences can add an additional element of profit or loss distinction to customer categories and specific customers.

Reducing the costs of inventory

The cost of carrying inventories is often higher than one thinks, and may be the difference between profitable and unprofitable products and customers. In addition to the financial costs associated with carrying inventories, there are also people and facility costs associated with storage and moving, the risk of obsolescence and damage, insurance and taxes, and a host of other associated costs. When one goes through all of the accounts that relate to inventory, it is not unusual for manufacturing companies to find their inventory carrying costs in the order of 25–35% of the value of the product. This high cost, coupled with slow inventory turns, can have a significant, implicit impact on profit margins.

For example, if a firm turns its inventory three times a year, and has a cost of carrying inventory of 30% of the value, then the effect is to reduce the marginal profitability by 10%. As turns go down, costs go up. A company such as Boeing turns its inventories less than twice a year. Given the nature of its products, it may have inventory costs significantly higher than 30%. The impact on margins is great. Faster inventory turns and lower costs of carrying inventory reduce the economic impact of carrying inventory. In the case of JIT manufacturers, whose vendors deliver their inputs to the manufacturer just when they are needed, perhaps even to the place on the factory floor where they are needed, inventory turns as high as 40 or 50 times per year, and reduction of inventory carrying costs, such as material handling, storage, obsolescence and damage, can result in virtually no marginal impact on the cost of the products. It is the economics of these differences that need to be understood, both for product cost and profitability purposes, and to motivate an organization to take the necessary action.

Utilizing capacity

Property and plant are particularly affected by improvements in material management. If a company reduces its inventory by increasing its inventory turns from three to ten times, it has reduced its inventory by two-thirds. To the extent that that inventory consumed considerable space, it effectively frees up such space. There is frequently a great deal of wasted space in many Western manufacturing plants – notably wide aisles and excessive room around machinery. Not having good cost information regarding such space makes it difficult to determine its implications. By comparison, Japanese manufacturing plants are about two-thirds the size of Western plants for the same manufacturing throughput. The implications are lower investment cost, depreciation expense, ongoing maintenance, and other related costs.

Information requirements for asset economics

These kinds of analyses derive their potential value from a good information system. If it does not exist, or is flawed, the possibility exists that the benefits will fall short of those that could result had there been better information.

As with some of the other areas of cost opportunity that we discussed earlier, moving in one direction, tightening up on accounts receivables, reducing inventories to a minimum, and maximizing space utilization may not always be the correct course of action. In the case of fixed assets, and particularly equipment, classical thinking has been that one does not add capacity until the existing capacity has been utilized fully. However, in the context of customer-driven flow processes requiring a high degree of flexibility, some companies are reaching the conclusion that it is better to have excess capacity, represented by extra equipment available all the time, to be able to respond to the uncertain diverse demands of the customer base. This means that the value of fast response and flexibility, in terms of customer orders and profits generated, more than offset the economic consequences of carrying excess tooling and equipment. It takes an extremely well-developed and flexible information base to permit these kinds of analyses.

BENCHMARKING

Using information for strategic cost reduction in your organization

Cost and profitability analysis

1. Has the company reanalysed its manufacturing overhead cost assignments to products in the past five years?
2. Does the company utilize very broad (e.g. labour, machine hours, material costs) overhead cost drivers?
3. Has the company made an attempt to reassign non-manufacturing operating expenses to products as appropriate?
4. Has the company assigned its non-manufacturing operating expenses to its various markets, channels, and customers such that customer profitability may be calculated?
5. Can the company rank order its customers by profitability, including the assignment of all costs to those customers?
6. Has the company made any attempt to assign working capital and fixed assets to products and customers as appropriate?

Waste elimination and lean operating

1. Has the company applied process analysis thinking to its manufacturing operations, or to its non-manufacturing activities?

2. Has the company initiated any sort of waste identification and elimination initiatives?
3. Are the customers' wants and needs central? Do they truly emphasize what is made and when?
4. Does every employee understand the distinction between 'pull' and 'push'? Does the business emphasize 'pull'?
5. Has a 'set-up time' reduction programme been put in place? Is it within or outside manufacturing?
6. Does the company really know what its aggregate and individual set-ups cost? And for inventory-carrying costs? Are there programmes in place to reduce these costs?
7. Does 'lean' thinking prevail in the company? Does it influence management action?

Flat, focused organizations

1. Has the company made an explicit effort to reassign indirect, support personnel to more direct activities?
2. Has the company broadened job classifications and responsibilities to provide for wider responsibilities?
3. Has the company initiated a training initiative?
4. Have spans of control been widened?
5. Have the number of levels in the organization been reduced?
6. Has the percentage of costs that may be assigned directly to products increased? Can the company calculate the change?
7. Have costs been reduced as the result of an explicit effort to flatter the organization? By how much?

Product cost planning (target costing)

1. Has the company initiated a target cost planning process, to replace a more traditional 'cost plus' methodology?
2. Is there a formal process for gathering customers' wants, needs, and their 'willingness to pay' for functionality?
3. Is there a similar process for gathering competitive product and cost information? Is there an attempt to ascertain competitors' future product/cost intents?
4. What proportion of cost management time and cost is devoted to concept/design stages as contrasted to prototype/production stages?
5. Who is involved in the product/cost planning process? Is it truly a cross-functional team?
6. Have the company's underlying cost systems been modified to provide a foundation for product cost planning?

Supplier management, value chain analysis, and outsourcing

1. What proportion of the company's costs are represented by purchased materials and supplies? Does the company focus a comparable level of cost management attention on this category?
2. What kind of programme is in place to really understand the root cause of vendors' prices? What attempt is made to reduce them, and how?
3. Does the company have in place a product standardization and simplification initiative where appropriate?
4. Does the company think in terms of vendor partnering? What does this mean? What are its benefits? Are there any risks?
5. Has the company revisited its 'extended' value chain? Who makes money? Who does not? Why is this the case?
6. Has the company considered its own internal value chain? Where along the chain does the company truly add unique value? Where is value not added, or even dissipated?
7. Has the company undertaken an analysis of those activities that it might outsource, and those it might insource?

Kaizen costing

1. Has the company made continuous cost improvement an integral part of its corporate culture? What are some examples that demonstrate this?
2. Is there a suggestion system in place that emphasizes and rewards cost reduction ideas at all levels of the organization? What role does senior management play in implementation?
3. Does management keep records, utilizing techniques such as *pareto analysis* and *root cause analysis* to monitor cost reduction accomplishments?

Asset economics

1. Relatively speaking, does the company put as much emphasis on asset management and reduction as it does on cost management and reduction? If not, why not?
2. Has the company calculated the full cost of carrying an extra day of accounts receivable?
3. Has the company calculated the aggregate full cost of carrying inventories? What does this represent on a unit cost basis?
4. What would be the profit and cash flow implications of reducing inventories by 50%?

5. What are the real carrying costs of property, plant and equipment? What drives these costs?

6. Does the company have in place a programme to explicitly reduce the amount of property, plant and equipment it utilizes? What results can it show from its efforts?

SUMMARY

Using information for strategic cost reduction

There are innumerable ways by which better information may facilitate better cost reduction. The benefits of accurate, reliable information for cost reduction is that it:

- improves understanding of which products and customers make money and which do not;
- shows where non-value-adding waste exists throughout the business process; and
- gives ways in which it may be reduced markedly, such as through rearrangement, reorganization and set-up reductions.

In an increasingly market-driven competitive environment, there is no other way to operate than to utilize product cost planning and target costing practices. A major component of costs in many businesses is the input from vendors. Standardizing demands placed on them, reducing the number of vendors, and simplifying the procurement and delivery process has major impact. In addition to traditional suppliers, the idea of outsourcing non-core activities may also be economic. Finally, asset management has become more critical in recent years, with the realization that money tied up in idle assets is as equally wasteful as unnecessary expenses.

To truly achieve major cost reductions requires a review of the whole process of planning, budgeting, reporting and analysis. This is so that instead of looking backward, comparing how one has performed relative to a predetermined estimate or standard, the favoured approach is forward thinking as to how better analysis may lead to new insights, reduced costs and assets, and increase economic value as a result.

Section D

Minimizing Risks

11

Information and the Management of Risk

Financial disasters threaten the competitiveness – and survival – of even the strongest businesses, and recent years have been fraught with high-profile examples of the dangers and risks of financial mismanagement. In this chapter, **Stewart Hamilton** emphasizes the importance of effective control systems, explaining that the lessons learned in the financial sector are generally applicable to any business.

CASE STUDY: THE COLLAPSE OF BARINGS BANK

Perhaps it was inevitable that sooner or later there would be a major crisis involving derivatives trading. In fact there was not one but three in quick succession: Barings, Daiwa Bank and then Sumitomo.

In the first, and arguably the most spectacular (although not the biggest) of these, Barings Bank, the oldest merchant bank in London, collapsed on February 27, 1995 after losses in its futures trading business in Singapore of £830 million. The bank, very small by international standards, had lost an amount equal to more than twice its capital base.

Nick Leeson, a 28-year-old trader based in Singapore with dual responsibility for trading and settlement functions, had been able to run up the losses, unsupervized and without the knowledge of his superiors either locally or in London, in unauthorized dealing in Nikkai 250 index options on the Singapore exchange. He had managed to conceal the losses by creating a fictitious account in Barings computer system, which remained undetected for many months. The problems were initially ascribed to the irrational or criminal behaviour of a single individual operating alone, thus conveniently deflecting attention from failures of management control and information systems.

With the Barings collapse, the term 'rogue trader' firmly entered the financial lexicon, as the UK Chancellor of the Exchequer, Kenneth Clarke, sought to reassure the world that there was no problem with the financial system as a whole. Nick Leeson had been fingered as the fall guy and all could relax. In fact at this stage one could almost feel sorry for Peter Baring, the chairman, for presiding over the collapse of the oldest merchant bank in the city of London, which could count the Queen among its clients.

On that fateful February weekend, there was hectic activity in Threadneedle Street, some of it bordering on the farcical as those seeking anonymity tried to enter the Bank of England by a locked back door, as the heads of major banks sat down to see if a rescue package could be put together. This attempt failed because the extent of Barings' total risk exposure as a result of Leeson's activities – and therefore potential losses – could not be quantified, demonstrating the inadequacies of their information management system.

Even more frantic was the activity back at the offices of those bankers summoned to assist, as their staffs tried to ascertain their exposure to Barings Bank and to find out if they too had a Leeson. While no similar cases were reported, some members of the rescue team discovered that their own systems were inadequate in that they could not determine quickly and accurately the extent of their counterparty exposure to the Barings group as a whole.

Subsequently it was generally agreed that the Barings collapse had done more to highlight the need to improve the standards of risk management and control within financial institutions than all the previous exhortations of the various regulators combined. After the publication of the Bank of England's Board of Banking Supervision's (1995) report on the events leading up to the collapse of Barings, most major institutions set in train thorough reviews of their own controls and procedures and made significant strides in introducing some variant of the 'Value at Risk' model to assess their overall risk exposure to derivative trading.

Nevertheless, on February 28, 1997, almost two years to the day after the collapse of Barings Bank, the National Westminster Bank, one of the big three clearers in the UK, announced that it had suspended a senior trader after discovering a loss of £50 million in the trading book at NatWest Markets, its investment banking arm. Pricing errors had been found in its interest rate options book after the departure of a junior trader, Kyriacos Papouis, to join Bear Sterns a few months earlier. NatWest called in external accountants and lawyers to investigate the circumstances and subsequently the reported loss widened to £90 million (see Galbraith, 1990).

How embarrassing then, for National Westminster Bank and their subsidiary, NatWest Markets, to have to admit that some of the losses incurred through overvaluing their option book pre-dated the Leeson fiasco, casting serious doubt on the effectiveness of their internal review of operating procedures and controls, and about the performance of their auditors.

Overview

As J.K. Galbraith noted:

There can be few fields of human endeavour in which history counts for so little as in the world of finance.

The events of the 1990s must underscore that view. Recent years have seen an unprecedented number of high-profile financial scandals, many involving the use of derivatives, in almost every country that boasts a stock market or banking system.

> **"The key lessons for the financial sector of recent years are general management issues relating to the use of business information in managing risk – they are therefore highly relevant to all firms"**

Such events hit the headlines for a few days or weeks and then tend to be forgotten. Sometimes they are followed, often months or even years later, by the publication of some official report or the launch of a prosecution, which re-awakens interest for a short time. More often they are forgotten, and as a result the lessons which are there to be learned go unheeded.

While the details have differed in each case, certain clear commonalities can be identified, and the lessons from these applied to all organizations whether in the financial sector or not. In almost every case there has been present one or more of the following factors:

- Inadequate board oversight and knowledge.
- Poor accounting, information and control systems.
- Inadequate supervision, auditing and regulation.

Financial scandals have been with us for centuries, of which the South Sea Bubble, Tulipomania and John Law's Louisiana scheme are but a few examples (*see* Galbraith,

1990). What has changed, however, is the fact that we now operate in a global marketplace, that modern communications are so quick and comprehensive that such events can no longer be passed off as little local difficulties. What a trader does in one market can have repercussions around the world. A further factor is that the financial marketplace has become much more complicated with a whole range of new products and techniques, particularly in derivatives, the use of which has mushroomed in recent years.

In fact the financial world has been transformed, not just by the new instruments, but by the rapid development of communications technology and computing power,

> "**Modern IT and communications technology have amplified financial risk and the potential for damage – it is perhaps unsurprising, therefore, that better, more efficient information systems hold the keys to controlling risk**"

allowing 24-hour trading around the world. Consequently, the speed at which risk positions can be built up has increased dramatically, as has the need for new knowledge and skills among those managing what has become a truly global activity. Thus the nature and extent of risk has fundamentally altered. As Richard Leftwich of the University of Chicago has said, "Whereas a company cannot shift a factory from Atlanta to Alabama overnight, with derivatives it can fundamentally transform its riskiness at the stroke of a computer key".

What is certain is that the acceptable knowledge levels of the past are no longer sufficient. Similarly, information systems designed for more leisurely times have proved inadequate in this fast-moving environment. The annual budgeting cycle and the monthly and quarterly reporting format have proved insufficient to the task. This makes it all the more important that we learn from the new experiences.

In this chapter we will:

- Examine the factors that trigger dislocation using a number of high profile examples.
- Highlight the importance of effective control systems and the action that management needs to take.

Dislocation of management information systems

Most organizations have their own distinct management information system which, while evolving or changing over time, provides the data for the management of day-to-day operations, and with which those involved feel comfortable. It allows them to make the necessary judgements and decisions in part by exercising a degree of 'gut feel'. The normal lifecycle of collection, organization, processing (involving both analysis and refinement) and maintenance of information, which requires it to be updated and refreshed, continues almost imperceptibly and unnoticed.

While this process remains undisturbed, both the board and senior management have the information as and when they need it, and can have confidence that there are unlikely to be too many surprises. Unfortunately, too few systems are robust enough to cope satisfactorily with what I call *dislocating events*, or the *triggers of dislocation*. These can be defined as events that alter dramatically the status quo and include events such as mergers and acquisitions, reorganizations and rapid growth, all of which impact on the established management information systems. In themselves, these are often high-risk transitions and therefore require high-quality information for their successful management. Changes in IT and information systems, departures of key personnel, and new product introductions can have similar effects.

Figure 11.1 sets out the interactions of these change events:

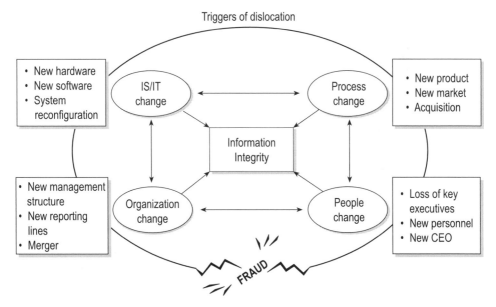

Figure 11.1: *Triggers of dislocation*

Triggers of dislocation and the Barings collapse

In the Barings case, each of these triggers was pulled. Barings had acquired a new business with new products (process); a key member of staff had left taking his expertise with him (people); the organizational structure had been changed, and the IT system had been adapted to cope with the new activities. While these were not contemporaneous events, they all occurred within a short time span, and the cumulative effect was disastrous.

The Barings collapse was followed by two formal enquiries, the first by the Bank of England's own Board of Banking Supervision (BOBS) and then by the inspectors appointed by the Singapore Minister for Finance. When published, the two reports, despite having somewhat differing emphases, were in agreement in identifying fundamental lapses in control and understanding of the trading activities being carried out as key contributory factors in allowing Leeson to incur £830 million of losses in the course of a very short period of time. A closer inspection of each factor in the Barings collapse highlights how lack of robust information systems contributes to triggers of dislocation.

Process: understanding the new products

Barings, a very traditional English merchant bank, in the aftermath of the City of London's 'Big Bang' had acquired a small (about 20 people) brokering operation, Henderson Crosthwaite, run by an ambitious and aggressive trader, Christopher Heath. In doing so, Barings had effectively diversified into a new market, with its very different culture and a new range of products (derivatives), with which both senior management and the board were unfamiliar. The necessary 'gut feel' element of control did not extend to this new business.

This new business, subsequently renamed Barings Securities, expanded very rapidly opening new offices around the world and contributing substantially to the group's profits. Indeed, at one point it was contributing more profit than the traditional banking activities, and Heath effectively ran it as his personal fiefdom. Provided it continued to be successful, the senior management of Barings was content to leave it to Heath. This was despite that fact that misgivings had been expressed from a number of sources about the inherent risks of derivative trading, and banks were encouraged to make sure that these were understood at board level.

In his speech to a G30 seminar on derivative financial instruments, Brian Quinn, then an executive director at the Bank of England, said that "the primary responsibility for understanding these products lies with the management of the individual firm" (Bank of England, 1993). With the benefit of hindsight, this turns out to have been little more than the expression of a pious hope. After the collapse, it emerged in evidence given to the House of Commons Treasury Committee by Peter Norris, ex-Chief Executive of Barings Investment Bank, that *no* members of the Board of Barings plc were knowledgeable about derivatives trading. It follows that they had little understanding of the risks being taken by their subsidiary, or of the improbability of the reported level of profitability.

Christopher Heath, the CEO of Barings Securities deposed before the collapse, has since claimed that the collapse would not have happened had he still been around as he would have realized quickly that something was amiss.

People: the knowledge gap

When the profits of Barings Securities declined dramatically because of market conditions, Barings fired Heath, who had a thorough understanding of the business and replaced him with a traditional banker, Peter Norris, who did not. The departure of Heath and most of his team left Barings management bereft of anyone who really understood the derivatives business, rendering them vulnerable.

After his appointment, Norris tried to bring the trading operations into line with the more formal culture of the traditional business, imposing stricter controls and reporting practices, but he was clearly never comfortable with the gung-ho style that characterized the futures trading activity. In addition, he lacked the instinctive knowledge of the mechanics of the derivative business that might have alerted him earlier to the problems in Singapore. A further impediment was that Leeson was regarded as a 'star' because of the apparent profits he was generating – and no-one wanted to upset him. In these circumstances he escaped the degree of scrutiny that might have exposed his activities earlier. A further factor, because of Barings' unusual capital structure, was the high proportion of profits that were available by way of bonuses to management, and many senior managers in London, as well as Leeson himself, stood to gain handsomely from Leeson's performance. They wanted to believe the reported levels of profit.

The cult of the individual and the high profiles and remuneration packages on offer must, in itself, give cause for concern. The absolute levels of bonuses paid, however offensive in the eyes of ordinary mortals, are not the main issue. Rather the question of what has been described as *asymmetric risk* presents the potential for encouraging aberrant behaviour. If you are approaching the bonus assessment day and you have not quite reached your target, is the temptation not to take an unnecessary risk to make sure that it is achieved? This point was addressed in a paper published by the Bank of England in 1997, where it was argued that "a remuneration scheme, which gives perverse rewards to risk taking behaviour, may put the control system under great stress," (Davies, 1997).

Organization change

In the Barings case there were three different organizational structures in as many years, which resulted in confusion. As a consequence, it was unclear to whom Leeson was supposed to report. The Bank of England enquiry stated that "No-one in management accepts responsibility for Leeson's activities between October 1993 and January 1995 . . .", and goes on to note that ". . . some members of management believed that the responsibility for certain activities (e.g. equity derivatives) rested with other managers, who deny they had such responsibility. This resulted in confusion . . ."

One result of the growth of the global corporation has been the increasing complexity of the management structures necessary to monitor and control widespread operations. Many different approaches have been taken, and most involve some sort of matrix structure whereby individuals report to more than one superior. This may arise, for example, where a group allocates profit responsibility by product line across national boundaries, but where there is still need for country management. Frequently such structures create conflicts of interest, particularly where issues of transfer pricing and profit allocation are involved. Often these problems are compounded by inadequate information systems that were not designed to cope with such complexity.

In another example of reorganization triggering dislocation, a major European company, when it moved from a country-by-country organization to a pan-European product line structure necessitating a complex reporting matrix, discovered that it had completely incompatible reporting systems, including three different inventory management systems. For some 18 months afterwards, management was 'flying blind' with unreliable performance data and much duplication of work. The CFO subsequently admitted that insufficient thought and resource had been put into the change process.

A further complexity seems to arise with remote operations. It is perhaps not a coincidence that many of the problems have arisen far from the head office. The old adage of 'out of sight, out of mind' would appear to apply. What is certainly true is that remote operations pose their own difficulties. Management by walking around is impractical, getting a feel for local conditions and risks is less easy and requires determined effort, and even mundane issues such as time differences create problems for effective control.

Information systems and information technology change

Barings Securities had expanded rapidly and its management information systems had not kept pace with the increased demands made on it. The company was driven and motivated by the traders, and back office staff had low status. There had been a history of problems with the settlement systems, and on an earlier occasion Leeson had helped to sort a mess in Jakarta, gaining a reputation for being a useful pair of hands in the process. There is also evidence of underinvestment in the necessary infrastructure. Ian Hopkins, formerly head of Group treasury and risk at Barings Investment Bank, has claimed that insufficient resources were devoted to control matters in an attempt to keep costs down.

After Leeson was sent to Singapore, he had responsibility for both back and front office operations. Initially when an error arose, he was able to create a fictitious account, the now infamous 'five eights', to hide it. Later he used it to cover his unauthorized trading activities and mounting losses. Data concerning account 88888 was included in the margin report sent daily to London. However, because the account number was not on the computer master file, it was dumped into a suspense account.

There was a further problem in that the software used in Singapore was incompatible with that in London. As a result, the system was reliant totally on information generated by Singapore and then transmitted to London where it could not be duplicated and checked. If the suspense account had been investigated (which it was not), or if the reporting format had been structured to highlight significant amounts and totals for accounts, account 88888 may have been discovered much earlier and the collapse prevented. The irony is that the information was available but not in a form that allowed a clear picture to emerge.

BENCHMARKING

Assessing your organization's exposure to risk factors

Clearly any risk assessment is a vitally important – and frequently highly complex and sensitive – process. This section is intended to start focusing thinking on the four areas that may trigger dislocation.

Process issues

Consider whether the risks inherent in acquiring a new business, developing a new product, or entering a new market are fully understood. For example:

⫸ What action has been taken to analyse and understand these risks?
⫸ At what level in the organization are the risks understood?
⫸ What plans are there to control these factors?
⫸ What review procedures are in place to monitor these risks?

People issues

Assess whether there is a *knowledge gap* within the organization, and whether people's work is understood and managed as effectively as necessary. In particular, consider:

⫸ To what extent would the company be exposed if key staff left?
⫸ Are there individuals that are exerting undue influence on sections of the business – perhaps unwittingly and through informal methods? (Beware the cult of the individual!)
⫸ Are new personnel at all levels of the organization *integrated* satisfactorily into the business, for instance understanding the necessary control procedures, systems and organizational culture?

Organization change issues

Change is constant, even without major high profile events such as mergers or restructuring programmes, and its effects need to be reviewed regularly. For instance:

⫸ They may be complex, but are reporting arrangements *adequate*? For example, can managers direct the activities of their team, providing the necessary support and setting the required standards? (This may also include ensuring that the necessary appraisal, training and remuneration processes are not flawed.)
⫸ Are there areas of the business (perhaps including highly successful ones) that are largely ignored or disconnected from the rest of the company? What can be done to integrate their activities into the business?
⫸ If there have been new developments (e.g. a new management structure or reporting arrangements) are the new responsibilities understood and accepted?

Information systems and information technology change issues

Investment in the management information infrastructure is vital and the responsibility of senior management. Some key issues to consider include:

⮕ Are management information systems keeping pace with the demands that they are facing?
⮕ When will new hardware and software need to be introduced? When should planning start and what action will be required?
⮕ Are there sufficient resources?
⮕ Are there persistent 'black spots' – priority areas where the system needs to be improved, overhauled or replaced?

The importance of effective control systems

While dislocating events may cause difficulties, the potentially damaging effects can be mitigated by the existence of good control systems, which can either alert management to problems or prevent them happening. Unfortunately, with Barings this was not the case.

> **"In the case of Barings Bank, almost everything that could go wrong did. Most organizations do not experience such dramatic outcomes, but great damage can be done if insufficient attention is paid to the likely effects of dislocating events"**

Although Barings' management in London had tried to impose controls and restrictions on trading, these were geared more to the traditional business and, as events unfolded, proved quite inadequate. When Norris took over, he did improve Barings Securities' control systems, introducing some of the traditional disciplines. However, the risk control function was still designed to cope mainly with agency, rather than the growing proprietary, business. The controls that Norris was implementing continued to lag behind the requirements of a changing business. Since proprietary trading, especially in derivatives, was at the forefront of development, it was here that controls were most underdeveloped. This allowed Leeson to have responsibility for both front and back office functions in Singapore, in itself a startling breach of one of the first principles of internal control – segregation of duties. There were glaring failures at a much more senior level in London. Little control was exercised over cash transmitted to Singapore to finance margin calls. There was no effective investigation of why the outstanding balance had grown so large or why Barings was funding client margin calls.

The BOBS investigation found that ". . . funds were paid away without any independent check on their validity . . . with no attempt to reconcile the request to any known trading positions," and that "there was no specific requirement for higher authorisation by a more senior employee for high value transfers." Indeed, the chief operating officer of Barings was "not familiar with the funds movement authorisation procedures within the group" and he did not get involved with "the day to day operational issues". However, Barings was not alone in suffering from failures in control systems. In a number of other cases, similar problems arose. Given the number and scale of these disasters, it is worth asking the question, why do these problems persist? In my view, the reasons are clear and worth examining in detail.

The task facing management

It may be unrealistic to expect every board member to be knowledgeable about every aspect of a company's business. However, it is incumbent on them to be informed sufficiently about what is being done so that they can make rational decisions as to the degree of risk that they wish to accept. It is particularly important that they are sensitive to the possible *dislocating effect* of management decisions. Good companies plan well ahead for such events and devote sufficient time and resources to minimize the adverse side effects of major change, and by doing so significantly reduce the risks.

While the Barings outcome was extreme, the effects of ill-managed change can be sub-optimal performance if the quality of information is affected. Getting the right amount of information, which is also reliable and provided at the right time, is the key to optimizing performance and minimizing risk.

 **SUMMARY**

Information and the management of risk

Risk is clearly part of business life, and management has a duty to shareholders and others to manage and control it in such a way that the profitability and continued existence of the company are not jeopardized. It is important that management creates a climate in which robust controls are the norm, and unprofessional and uncontrolled behaviour are not tolerated. Furthermore, in the aftermath of the events we have been discussing, boards are under pressure to publicly disclose and discuss their risk strategy and the adequacy of their internal control systems. In order to do so, there is a clear need for a systematic approach to the assessment and measurement of risk, and the establishment of a framework in which to manage it.

Information follows a normal lifecycle of collecting, organizing, processing and refining; as long as this process continues the management of the business has the information needed to develop success or, put another way, to avoid disaster. However, factors emanating from four types of change can trigger dislocation in this cycle – sometimes imperceptibly at first – but the results can be catastrophic. The four potential triggers are process, people, organization and IS/IT changes.

BEST PRACTICE

Using information to manage risk

The following checklist provides a short guide to using information to manage risk:

1. *Assess the level of exposure in your business to dislocating events* – this can be approached by considering some of the issues mentioned earlier in the benchmarking section. In particular, focus on the four areas that can trigger dislocation:

    - process changes
    - people changes
    - organizational changes
    - IS/IT changes.

2. *Maintain awareness* – in particular, ensure that the senior management of the firm *maintains* an awareness of the key issues and principles of the business, rather than becoming distracted or out of touch with evolving circumstances. This is the starting point: it is vital that the management of the firm move on from this point to establish a robust, flexible system that can detect (if not absorb) the potential for dislocating events.

3. *Adhere to the three basic principles of risk management*:

    i.   Ensure that risk management is seen as an essential part of the company culture and accorded the highest priority at all levels right up to the board.
    ii. Provide sufficient resources to ensure that the necessary policies and procedures are put in place, and communicated throughout the organization. These need to be reviewed regularly and documented clearly, as risk management is a dynamic process.
    iii. Design and maintain management information systems to produce the right information in the right form and at the right time, to ensure that the risks can be controlled, particularly at times of change.

In the next chapter we shall see how successful companies achieve this.

References

Bank of England (1993) *Quarterly Bulletin*, November. Bank of England, London.

Board of Banking Supervision Report to the House of Commons, July 18, 1995, 1.41, page 7. HMSO, UK.

Davies, D. (1997) *Financial Stability Review*, Spring. Bank of England, London.

Galbraith, J.K. (1990) *A Short History of Financial Euphoria*. Penguin, Middlesex, UK.

12

Controlling Risks

The previous chapter emphasized the importance of effective control systems and outlined the threats to management information systems from dislocating events. In this chapter, **Stewart Hamilton** continues this theme and provides practical techniques for assessing, managing and controlling risks.

CASE STUDIES: WHEN MANAGEMENT INFORMATION CONTROLS BREAKDOWN

At Morgan Grenfell Asset Management, a fund manager, Peter Young, was apparently able to bypass the in-house rules and invest more than the authorized amounts in unquoted equities. Furthermore, he was able to set up a number of Luxembourg 'front' companies to disguise his activities and continue to report excellent performance figures. A Deutsche Bank director said "there is a clear structure, and there was a break-down of controls and supervision."

It has been argued that whatever Young's motives were, a contributory factor was his need to maintain his position as a 'star' trader and this may have tempted him to try to artificially improve his performance. At the time of writing this case is still the subject of various enquiries, some criminal, and doubtless more details will emerge. In the meantime the affair embarrassed Deutsche Morgan Grenfell and cost them a great deal of money, now estimated at $700 million, directly by way of compensation to investors and potential fines, and indirectly through loss of clients. It also served to highlight the need for controls to be reviewed regularly and enforced rigidly.

With Daiwa Bank, the story was similar, although in this case the deception covered a period of some 11 years. Commenting on Toshihide Igichi's activities, Masahiro Tsuda, the general manager of their New York branch, said "We are deeply embarrassed that our internal controls and procedures were not sufficient to prevent this fraudulent action." At NatWest Markets, where there was no attempt at concealment, Martin Owen, the chief executive, admitted "We have found a major deficiency in controls."

Overview

An analysis of recent financial scandals would suggest that the main problem has been incompetent management, poor internal control and information deficiencies. That was certainly the case at Barings Bank. Until the collapse, Barings management in London believed the trading conducted by Barings Futures Singapore to be essentially *risk-free* and *very profitable*.

There is little doubt that these disasters have focused the minds of many managers, particularly in the financial services industry, on the need to better manage risk.

The acceptance of risk

The acceptance of risk has always been an integral part of business activity. Indeed

> "All companies must of necessity undertake a degree of risk in order to deliver a satisfactory return to their shareholders and to achieve long-term growth"

the willingness to take risks of a personal and financial nature is one of the hallmarks of the entrepreneur. Equally, it is recognized widely that there is, or should be, a relationship between the level of risk taken and the likely reward, with the greater risk requiring the higher return, a fundamental truth that seemed to escape the senior management and board of Barings Bank.

Good managers understand this, and take steps to ensure that the risks taken in the course of their business are measured ones, with the consequences of the likely outcomes being well understood. Risks that are avoidable are clearly identified and eliminated; those that are not are minimized – 'laid off' to the greatest extent possible. Such companies also take a broad or holistic view of risk and not just the financial perspective, and actively manage the risk process. A study reported in January 1999, and commissioned by Pricewaterhouse Coopers, concluded that while in continental Europe risk has somewhat negative connotations, with strategies oriented mainly towards avoiding and hedging risk, Anglo-American companies view risk as an *opportunity* and consciously accept effective risk management as a means of achieving corporate goals.

An organization needs to determine its *risk appetite* and *risk bearing capacity*. In other words, it must articulate the nature and extent of the risks that it is willing to accept in its particular business. This must be done in the context of a thorough understanding of the business process and environments in which it operates, permitting the assessment of the likelihood of risks becoming reality and the effect that these would have. Only then can appropriate measures be taken to minimize the incidence and impact of such risks.

While certain risks have to be taken if a company is to achieve the necessary return for its shareholders, one important aim of a risk management system is to identify accurately *essential* risks within and outside the corporate environment, and allow for the taking of informed decisions. In that way, unnecessary surprises are avoided. Examples of essential risks might be the loss of a major customer, the failure of a key supplier, or the appearance of a significantly better product from a competitor.

Like any other component of business practice, risk has to be managed. Experience shows that there are four key elements to a top-class risk management process:

1. Risk has to be accorded a high priority within the organization, with the lead being given by the board of directors.
2. There must be well-documented risk management policies and procedures that are reviewed and monitored regularly.
3. An integrated risk management framework needs to be in place.
4. There must be effective communication of these policies and procedures throughout the organization.

Clearly risk is an inevitable part of conducting business and this chapter outlines practical techniques for risk assessment, monitoring and control.

Understanding the need for risk management

A necessary condition for any effective risk management system is *recognition* of the need for one at the highest level in the organization. While this may seem self-evident, the facts would indicate otherwise. Research by Ernst & Young in December 1998 suggested that in Europe at least, risk management has not been accorded the priority that many would believe it deserves. After interviews with 'hundreds of senior executives' they concluded that fewer than 50% of the companies surveyed had appointed a designated risk manager, over 25% had not effectively assessed their major business risks, and over 30% did not have a formalized approach for identifying and registering risks that they faced.

This despite the fact that the focus on risk assessment and management has never been so intense as it is in the wake of many recent high profile disasters, of which Barings was only the most dramatic and by no means the largest, in terms of cash loss. There has been a growing clamour for more regulation or supervision in almost all parts of the world, and pressures on managers to report the extent of their company's risk exposure have been increasing. Indeed, from the end of the year 2000, under proposals being drawn up by the Institute of Chartered Accountants in England and Wales (ICAEW), companies listed on the London Stock Exchange will be required to include in their annual report a statement on the extent and effectiveness of their internal control systems designed 'to safeguard shareholders' investment and the company's assets'. This reflects similar initiatives in Australia and Canada, and the obligatory risk section of the SEC form 10K in the USA.

Whilst external pressure from investors and regulators is understandably a catalyst for putting in place appropriate systems to assess and manage risk, basic principles of good stewardship demand that boards and senior managers place the issue high on their list of priorities. Proposed regulation apart, it must be a matter of prudent common sense to have a coherent risk policy, and an appropriate system to ensure that it is adhered to, if only to avoid the sort of negligence cases emerging in the USA.

Creating the climate for risk management

It is, of itself, not sufficient to recognize the need for a risk management policy and associated control systems. The ethos of the entire organization must embrace a culture that places due emphasis on appropriate behaviour with regard to ethical standards and the stewardship of the company's assets. Essential to the success of any system of risk management is that it becomes a fundamental part of the culture of the company and as such is accorded the priority and resources it deserves. This requires a commitment by directors, managers and employees to the principles of ethical behaviour, and the development of an environment in which good controls are the norm. Too often control systems and their implementation are seen only as an additional layer of overhead, and not as something that can and should add value by ensuring the effective utilization of assets and the avoidance of waste.

Worryingly, a 1996 survey of 100 American companies with turnovers between $250 million and $30 billion, carried out by Coopers & Lybrand, revealed that more than half of the middle managers believed that controls got in the way of getting work done. The conclusion was that rather than seeing it as an integral part of business activity that could help companies achieve their corporate objectives, control systems were viewed as a bureaucratic burden and policing process. Such attitudes are dangerous and should be discouraged through a process of educating people about the needs for controls as a fundamental plank of a business's success.

For any risk management system to be effective, it requires the communication throughout the organization of what is regarded as *appropriate business behaviour*, and what controls are necessary to ensure that the standards are adhered to. This may be achieved through formal codes of conduct with appropriate disciplinary procedures, and reinforced by the example set by the leadership of the organization. This becomes all the more necessary when organizations are growing rapidly and there is a constant influx of new employees who need clear guidance as to what behaviour is acceptable and expected.

CASE STUDIES: APPROACHES TO RISK ASSESSMENT

The much publicized and bitter experience of the major Swiss bank UBS in its dealings with Long Term Capital Management, and the substantial losses incurred, led it to conduct a thorough review of its risk assessment and management processes. The results of this review are set out in the 1998 annual report in considerable detail. In the report UBS states that:

Effectively managing and controlling risk depends on a sound process for identifying the risks which UBS faces, as well as establishing a comprehensive set of limits and procedures to control these risks. UBS puts these limits and procedures in place to ensure that its exposure to risk is consistent with its risk appetite and risk bearing capacity and with its assessment of management's capabilities to manage and control the risks in an effective manner. In this context, internal capabilities, such as the availability of suitable IT processing systems and staff knowledge and experience, and the external environment are taken into consideration.

UBS then continues by detailing the assessment processes put in place. Such candour from a leading institution must be welcomed, providing a benchmark for others.

It is not only financial institutions that are placing risk management higher up the agenda than previously: a leading European pharmaceutical company has recently launched a major initiative to systematically survey and assess the risks facing it in all aspects of its activities. The result of this initiative was the promulgation of a detailed policy statement, from which the following extracts have been taken:

Risk Management Policy for the Group

The management has adopted a Risk Management Policy. Stated below are the risk management objectives and practical implications, with respect to managing risks, which are to be applied by all Companies and units within the Group. These practical implications should also be applied by joint ventures, contractors, licensees and suppliers as far as the company risk management is concerned.

The risk management policy shall underpin the company's overall vision and mission and assist in ensuring that plans can be met, by creating a stable risk environment as reasonably possible.

Mission Statement

The company's mission is to develop, manufacture and market pharmaceuticals and related products of high quality which fulfil important medical needs and ensure customer satisfaction.

Risk Management Policy Statement

In our existing business we will always encounter risks of varying magnitude. Risks are a part of human as well as business life. The company's vision is to devote its resources to provide efficient pharmaceutical products that reduce health and medical risks.

In our striving to develop, manufacture and distribute high quality products to society we must continuously identify all substantial risks inherent in our business as well as risks that can impact on the company from the outside. Only risks which we know can be assessed, controlled and monitored.

This requires that every manager must make sure that all risks that substantially can affect his/her area of responsibility are known and appropriately treated.

The company will protect all its assets (employees, customers, trust/confidence/image, brands, know-how, property and liquid assets) and its operations from injury, damage or loss to the best of our ability by applying leadership skills, scientific knowledge and best industry practices.

Managing risks

All organizations necessarily face myriad risks as they go about their business. Many of these risks are small and are likely to have little impact on the overall financial health of the organization, but there are others that could occasion significant loss and, in extreme cases, bring the company down. It is therefore essential that a systematic approach be taken to the assessment of risk.

The basic stages of establishing a sound system of risk management are straightforward, as outlined in Figure 12.1. Once the board has established and promulgated the overall risk policy of the organization, management must then analyse the risks facing the company through a systematic process of risk identification and, whenever possible, quantification. Thereafter, consideration should be given to the possibilities of risk avoidance and mitigation, and the establishment of effective systems for ongoing risk monitoring and control.

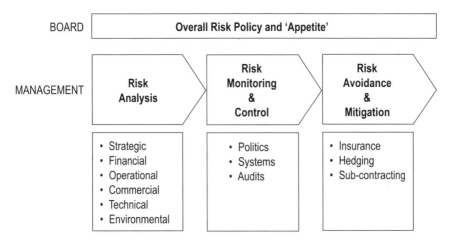

BOARD — Overall Risk Policy and 'Appetite'

MANAGEMENT —

Risk Analysis

Risk Monitoring & Control

Risk Avoidance & Mitigation

- Strategic
- Financial
- Operational
- Commercial
- Technical
- Environmental

- Politics
- Systems
- Audits

- Insurance
- Hedging
- Sub-contracting

Figure 12.1: *Overview of the risk management process*

Risk analysis

Risk identification (defining the scope)

It is necessary, when attempting to identify risks, to define the categories into which they fall. This allows for a more structured analysis and reduces the chances of risks being overlooked, which a 'laundry list' approach does not. While there is no consensus as to what these categories should be, and there will be degrees of overlap, the following groupings are helpful: strategic, financial, operational, commercial, technical and environmental. Table 12.1 expands these categories and provides some examples of the risks that should be considered.

For example, under the strategic risk heading might come a change in consumer preference, say from red meat to lighter meats or fish. Similarly, customer aversion to cosmetics tested on animals has had a major impact on sales of certain products. The current reaction to genetically modified foodstuffs in Europe has affected not just Monsanto and other producers, but also the retail chains stocking such produce. With regard to environmental risks, it must have come as a shock to Shell the extent to which their confrontation with Greenpeace over the disposal of the Brent Spar platform affected forecourt petrol sales in Germany, despite the fact that they believed that they had come up with the most environmentally friendly way of disposing of their redundant oil platform. Perceptions often take the place of facts. Similarly, I know of a number of industrial manufacturing companies that have had to shut down certain operations because they could not meet the new EU requirements on air pollution emissions at a cost that justified the investment.

These lists are illustrative and not exhaustive, and all companies should draw up their own list of issues reflecting the nature of their business and the environments in which they are operating.

Table 12.1: *Potential factors contributing to risk, on which management needs to maintain and review information*

Strategic	Financial	Operational	Commercial	Technical	Environmental
Poor marketing strategy	Treasury risks	Product failure	Supplier failure	Equipment breakdown	'Green' pressure group activity
Poor acquisitions strategy	Inadequate assessment of counter-party	Design failure	Loss of key executive	Infrastructure failure	Regulatory change
Changes in consumer behaviour	Weak credit assessment	Project failure	Failure of joint venture partner	Fire	Accidental pollution
Political or regulatory change	Sophisticated fraud	Client failure	Sub-contractor failure	Explosion	Public perception
	Systems failure	Breakdown in labour relations	Failure of legal compliance	Pollution	
	Poor working capital management	Expropriation of assets	Onerous contract conditions	Drought or flood	
	Inappropriate accounting policies	Political upheaval		Other natural disasters	

Risk assessment and mapping

Risk assessment is more difficult than risk identification. Risks that give rise to frequent losses (for example, increasing the incidence of bad debts or the level of warranty claims) are easiest to calculate based on past experience, whilst very infrequent losses are hard to quantify in probability terms. Risks with a likelihood of arising once in a hundred thousand over the next three years or more (e.g. an earthquake or a political uprising) do not have much meaning for a company trying to meet shareholders' expectations next quarter. It is more important to quantify the potential consequences of identified risks and define alternative courses of action to manage, or mitigate, such risks.

Not all risks have the same impact and therefore quantifying their effects, even in the most general of terms, is essential. At its simplest, this might be a ranking on a scale from 'inconvenient' to 'catastrophic'. Once this has been done, the risks in each category can be mapped to both likely frequency and potential impact, with the emphasis on materiality (*see* Figure 12.2).

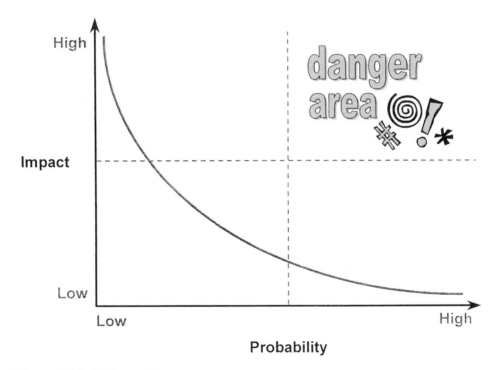

Figure 12.2: *Risk mapping*

In our pharmaceutical example, each business unit and functional head was asked to do an individual assessment for their part of the business and then plot the results. Managers were required to assess the likelihood of the risks in each defined category by assigning probabilities in percentage terms, or more qualitatively on a high, medium or low basis. They were then required to estimate in financial terms the impact of such an occurrence on a worst, average and best outcome basis, and to consider a time horizon. Once the risks had been plotted, those that could be insured or offset were clearly identified and the costs of laying-off quantified. The management could then decide the extent to which they should be self-insured, in the context of the company's overall resources.

Clearly, companies would wish to operate in such a way that activities in the top right corner were avoided, or alternatively ensure that the probable rewards justified the risks.

Another way of looking at the risks faced by an organization is to segregate them by potential impact and controllability. The grid in Figure 12.3 is used by a major bank to assess risks in certain parts of its business. In this example they were looking at the introduction of a new financial product, a form of warrants, that they hoped to cross-sell to existing corporate clients.

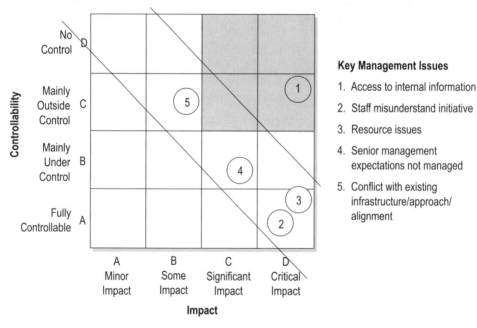

Figure 12.3: *Controllability/impact*

Once that had been done, they used a checklist to record the risk, its probability and impact and the mitigating steps to be taken, as Table 12.2 shows.

Whichever method or model is adopted, the main concern is to ensure that there has been a systematic and thorough review of the risks in all categories, and that appropriate decisions are taken to accept that risk or not, to offset it or to see that it is rewarded appropriately. Companies undertaking such analysis have found it useful to push the assessment process right down the organization as those closest to the process or customer often have a greater understanding of the risks being faced on a day-to-day basis, than those in more senior positions.

I recently acted as a facilitator in a discussion of risk management for the

Table 12.2: *Risk mitigation*

Risks	Criticality	Controllability	Action Required
Access to information internally	D	C	Communicate project to seniors request support if required
Staff misunderstand initiative	D	A	Effective communication plan
Resource issues	D	A	Raise issue with sponsor to ensure resources are allocated
Senior management expectations not managed	C	B	Regularly inform through business reviews
Conflict with existing infrastructure/ approach/alignment	B	C	Senior support where required

managing directors and financial controllers of a group of subsidiaries of an international construction company, about 30 in all. For the purposes of the discussion they were split into teams of five, making sure that no group had two from the same company. They were then asked to come up with the three most significant risks facing their part of the organization. The results were instructive. Not only did they, in aggregate, identify 12 or so different risks, but these included several that had not previously crossed the minds of the senior executives present. Examples were the poaching of key personnel by competitors, proposed changes in safety requirements, and an alteration to the taxation provisions affecting sub-contractors.

Risk avoidance and mitigation

Companies can mitigate the risks they are facing in a number of different ways. These

> **"Good quality procedures are fundamental to proactive risk management. Doing right things right in day-to-day business processes reduces risks and costs"**

can include risk sharing by taking on joint-venture partners, by sub-contracting potentially difficult tasks, or by ensuring, through appropriate contractual agreements, that part of the risk remains with the customer. This last measure can be important when entering uncharted waters (such as the introduction of new technology), particularly when involved in government programmes.

In risk mitigation, the first priority should be the elimination, as far as possible, of non-commercial risks, in other words those risks that, if they are triggered, can lead only to costs. These can be divided into four main categories:

- personal injury risks
- property damage risks
- legal and contractual liability risks
- business interruption risks.

Eliminating these risks can be achieved through quality assurance programmes, environmental control processes, the enforcement of employee health and safety regulations, the installation of adequate fire safety and protection, and the maintenance of appropriate levels of security to prevent crime, sabotage, espionage, threats to IT systems and threats to personnel.

Personal injury risks

Personal injury risks include all risks of bodily injury, mental anguish, pain and suffering to personnel, customers or third parties. Examples are work-related injuries, discrimination on a race or gender basis, exposure to hazardous materials or emissions, fire, explosion, travel accidents, product-related risks, assault, extortion and kidnapping. (Personal injury cases can lead to legal action, which is a risk category of its own.)

Property damage risks

Property damage risks are fairly easy to identify. They involve any potential loss of or damage to property owned by, or in the care, custody or control of, the company. Typical risks are fire, explosion, machinery breakdown, flood, storm, theft, vandalism, sabotage, and accidental contamination or pollution. In recent years, both Perrier and Coca-Cola have discovered the impact of the latter two. As a category, they are reasonably easy to insure against – but at a cost.

Legal and contractual liability risks

Legal and contractual liability is a growing area of corporate concern. These risks are 'moving targets' given the rapid changes in public attitudes, international legislation and the volatility and unpredictability of court rulings. Significant risks for a company would include product liability, environmental liability, and patent infringement, as well as the more normal employers' liability.

An essential part, therefore, of any risk management system is that of legal control, which involves the monitoring of changes in laws and regulation and the monitoring of contractual obligations. Equally important is the consideration of legal liability in purchase and sales agreements and due diligence in connection with acquisitions and divestitures.

Business interruption risks

Companies need to consider how R&D, manufacturing or supply of materials or finished products could be interrupted, and what effects that would have. For example, how long could an important brand be allowed to disappear from the market without irrevocable damage being done? All companies should have contingency plans in place for eventualities such as a major fire at a production or distribution facility. It was instructive to see how some businesses were able to continue to operate quickly after an IRA bomb blast in the city of London, whereas others were out of commission for months.

There are a number of other risks that lead to financial loss without being triggered by personal injury or property damage. There is a grey area between non-commercial and commercial risks, in addition to the risks normally controlled by the corporate policy on financial management (e.g. credit risks, interest rate and exchange rate exposure, and use of financial instruments such as options and derivatives), which includes embezzlement, computer crime and industrial espionage.

Insurance

For many companies, the primary method of risk management has traditionally meant buying insurance above a substantial corporate deductible (excess). This is not always the best or most cost-effective solution. Whilst the insurance markets are still, after more than 200 years, the most efficient way to cover the risk of catastrophic events, not all risks are insurable and those that are might command a level of premium that cannot be justified. It follows that companies must look beyond what the traditional market can provide and seek alternative risk mitigating solutions.

Companies need to have regard to maintaining sufficient liquidity to meet reasonable levels of loss, and therefore it is important to maintain tight financial controls and have resources in place to meet sudden capital needs. The use of the captive insurance vehicle is a possible alternative – even for the long-term financing of substantial 'uninsurable' risks.

Risk awareness – monitoring and control

The key requirement is to increase risk awareness throughout the organization, at all levels, through the dissemination of information, the publication of guidelines and a programme of education as to the need to reduce and control risks. This process has to be accompanied by the institution of appropriate control procedures and risk measurement systems.

Whilst it may be obvious to most managers that there is a need to manage risk, this is not always the case further down the organization. A complete system of risk management requires *every employee* to be conscious of the fact that unnecessary risk taking must be avoided. In some industries, e.g. aircraft maintenance, this is so obvious that it hardly needs mentioning, but in others it requires a major educational effort. Everyone must be aware that issues of risk affect not only the organization's overall performance, but could, in a more direct way, cost them their jobs.

Internal controls

A sound system of internal control is a fundamental prerequisite for any risk

> **"The purpose of internal controls is not to eliminate risk but to manage it in the pursuit of profits, in accordance with the risk policy guidelines laid down by the board"**

management system. Because business is a dynamic activity, a company's operations are constantly evolving and the nature of its risks changing as a result. It follows that the internal control system must be capable of being adapted quickly to meet new circumstances as they arise. This can be done only through a regular reassessment of the nature and extent of the risks being faced, and the implications any changes may have for information gathering and dissemination. It is also essential that the system includes procedures for identifying and reporting any material weaknesses in the control process at an appropriate level.

The Institute of Chartered Accountants in England and Wales (ICAEW) draft guidelines, issued in connection with the proposed new UK reporting requirements, suggest that in determining what constitutes a sound system of internal control, the following factors should be considered:

- The nature and extent of the risks that it regards as acceptable for the company to bear within its particular business.
- The threat of such risks becoming a reality.
- If that happened, the company's ability to reduce the incidence and impact on the business.
- The costs and benefits related to operating relevant controls.

As discussed in the previous chapter, the internal audit function should have a major part to play.

Maintaining information integrity

In the previous chapter, we saw how maintaining the integrity of the management information system was essential to the proper functioning of any organization, and it follows that it is a precondition for a successful risk management process. Without accurate and timely information, no risk management system can hope to work. In addition, the threat of dislocating events also adds to the burden of risk; consequently, any system must plan for the possible impact of such events. For example, a period of rapid expansion in activity with the hiring of new personnel brings its own problems. It can take a great deal of time to train new staff members to carry out their functions efficiently, never mind inculcating them with the company's values. It is also the case that the recent trend of 'downsizing' has, in many cases, eliminated the layer of experienced middle managers who acted both as mentors and as key components in any control system.

All good risk management systems rely on the integrity of the information provided, and it follows that management information systems must be aligned to the risk characteristics of the business. Any control system must therefore be designed to minimize the probability and impact of the identified risk events. These systems have to be organized to ensure that the relevant information reaches the right people at the right time in such a way that deviations from expectations are highlighted, so that they can be investigated and corrective action taken. In order to do so, managers must have a clear picture of the risks faced, and identify the information that they need to ensure that monitoring and control is possible.

In today's complex world it is necessary to have a broad and complete system of information-gathering that includes non-financial data such as quality and customer satisfaction. Few companies have yet organized their information systems to provide the required data, but information such as manufacturing defect levels, customer returns or rejections, and employee turnover, can highlight possible critical points.

It also has to be borne in mind that while information has value, there are costs associated with data-collection, -processing and -analysis, and therefore any system should focus on those that are *necessary* to achieve the desired objectives. It also has to be recognized that although the accuracy of information may increase over time and collection costs will rise, the value of that information as a management tool diminishes the further away it is from the actual events to which it relates. Skill and judgement are required to use information as early as possible to maximize effect and minimize cost, as Figure 12.4 illustrates.

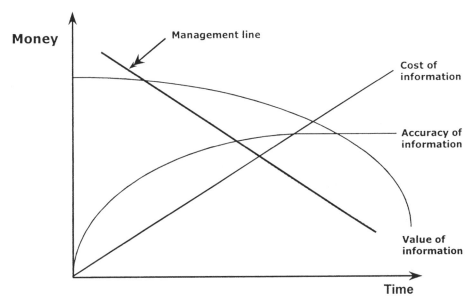

Figure 12.4: *The relationship between the time, value and cost of information*

Any information system must include appropriate performance indicators that allow management to monitor the key business activities, thus enabling them to identify developing problems and take the necessary corrective actions. Such indicators

> **"Data has a cost; information has *value*"**

could include defect rates, customer complaints, order intake levels, sales enquiry conversions and so on. Proper documentation of policies and procedures must be prepared and communicated throughout, with regular audit and re-assessment. It is no use, as often happens, for resources to be devoted to the preparation of a glossy manual only for it to subsequently gather dust, unread and unused, in managers' offices.

Risk management structures

Some companies are already putting in place a systematic approach to the assessment and management of business risk on a widely defined basis. Potential major events that threaten the assets (i.e. personnel, property, funds, products, trademarks and reputation) of a company are not always obvious to the average employee or the line manager, and even when some are appreciated it is more likely to be in relation to their direct sphere of operations. In order to get a clear overall picture, someone in the organization must be given the responsibility of taking a holistic view of all corporate risks and putting these into a management perspective. This is the primary role of the risk management function. Some companies have appointed a designated risk manager reporting directly to the board or audit committee; others have set up risk management committees, task forces or working parties to conduct an overall risk review and to make recommendations for the implementation of appropriate new systems.

Counting the costs

An important element in the risk management process is assessing the costs of risk financing. This involves accounting for all costs related to risk, such as avoidance costs, necessary investments in physical protection, insurance premiums, 'self-insured' losses, and additional information systems and personnel. This should, in part at least, allow a company to measure the effectiveness and efficiency of its risk management function. It is, however, hard to identify and estimate which losses did not occur because of the activities of the risk management function. Instead, it has perhaps to be taken on faith that the introduction of a risk management function and the associated investments in increased safety and well-being of the corporation ensures an atmosphere in which the sustainable development of shareholder value can be achieved without sudden surprises.

Risk management audit and review

All systems, risk management included, require regular audit and review. Organizations change, often quite rapidly, and the triggers of dislocation discussed in the last chapter are as relevant in this context. It follows that a regular risk management audit is an essential part of the overall control system to ensure that all parts of the organization follow the laid down policies and procedures.

Living with the aftermath

Things will go wrong! Despite the best practices and procedures, from time to time events will occur which put the company at risk, either financially or in terms of reputation. Examples include the Exxon Valdez oil spill, the Brent Spar pollution row and, most recently, the outcry in the UK over genetically modified foods. Such events give rise to crises within the affected organization. Perhaps the key role in crisis management is that of public relations. At such times, the media will be demanding information about the incident and in particular will want to know about the company's proposed course of action. The inept way that Shell handled PR over the Brent Spar incident was in marked contrast to Swiss Air's actions after the crash off the Canadian coast. Companies need to make contingency plans for such eventualities, and in particular must have designated spokesmen who are thoroughly briefed and who have an overall awareness of the issues involved and can answer internal and external questions regarding the actual occurrence, and the remedial or other actions intended.

This helps to limit the consequences of such an occurrence and minimize the damage – both financial and otherwise. Companies will have to learn to live in the glare of publicity and develop the appropriate skills to cope, which may involve media training for senior executives, clear understanding of legal protection management, and the ability to articulate clearly and convincingly the risk management policies and procedures of the organization. Post-crisis or post-accident investigations and appropriate feedback are an essential part of the risk management process to ensure that we can learn from history.

 ## SUMMARY

The ethos of control

Control systems do not function in isolation. They have to operate within an organizational culture that nurtures and encourages appropriate behaviour. In Robert Simon's *Levers of Control* (1995), this is described as beliefs systems. Controls are much more likely to be effective in an environment where the need for them is regarded as a normal and necessary part of the proper conduct of business, and for the minimization of risk. Even when control systems are in place they do not necessarily function properly.

No matter how well defined, they have to be reviewed and policed regularly, especially in the light of one or more of the triggers of dislocating events outlined in Chapter 12, when they can be at their most vulnerable and where the comfort factor has been disturbed. The Morgan Grenfell case showed that even where controls exist, they can be overridden, and highlighted the need for proper levels of supervision. Those involved most directly are not always the most appropriate to ensure that the controls are in force. This is because:

- Too often they are too busy with their own work to be willing to spend time in that way.
- They may be too familiar with existing practices to give it much thought.
- There is an unwillingness to devote the resources required.

However, if controls are to be effective there is a need for regular and independent review. Unfortunately, it remains the fact that in many organizations internal auditors are perceived as overheads and not as essential parts of on overall control structure. In a survey of 186 of the top 500 UK companies carried out by the accounting firm, Ernst & Young in 1995, they found that 40% of the companies had no internal audit service, and concluded that company directors are "dangerously complacent" over internal control. And this was *after* the Barings collapse!

Even where internal auditors are employed, they may not enjoy sufficient status to carry out their work effectively, or have ready access to a top management that is willing to listen to them. Finally, there is the problem of complacency. Management pays little attention to the accounting and reporting process until something goes wrong. It is perhaps analogous to the supply of electricity: it is taken for granted until a fuse blows – and only then do people realize that the wiring might be quite complicated.

 **BEST PRACTICE**

Measures for controlling risks

There are a number of measures that can be taken to control (meaning identify, assess, minimize, manage and mitigate) risks, and the triggers of dislocation that can cause them. These include:

Accepting that risks exist

This means understanding that risk is a fundamental part of business activity and ensuring that risks are taken that are *measured*, with likely (and possible) consequences fully understood.

Creating the right climate for risk management

Accepting that risks exist is important because it provides a starting point for the other actions that are needed – and foremost among these is the need to create the right climate for risk management. The organization needs to understand *why* control systems are needed. This requires communication and leadership so that standards and expectations are set and clearly understood.

Understanding the key elements of the risk management process

It is important that risk is given a high priority within the organization with the lead taken by senior management. Furthermore, risk management policies and procedures must be established (and reviewed and monitored regularly), and the integrated risk management framework needs to be implemented and communicated throughout the business. The overall risk management process needs to comprise the following stages:

- *Risk analysis* – this includes defining the scope of the risk, and in particular assessing the following potential sources of risk: strategy, finance, operations, commercial activities, technical developments, and environmental issues. The next stage is to assess and map the risk; this includes understanding where it lies, how critical it is, how feasible it is to control, and what action is required.
- *Risk avoidance and mitigation* – when mitigating risks, the first priority is to eliminate those risks that will lead only to costs. These include personal injury risks, property damage risks, legal and contractual liabilities, and business interruption risks. As well as establishing the necessary processes, these can also be mitigated by sharing the risk with a partner (e.g. through a joint venture or other type of commercial agreement).
- *Risk monitoring and control* – this is also an essential part of the risk management process, and it builds on the need to ensure that *every employee* is aware of the fact that unnecessary risk-taking is to be avoided. This can involve disseminating information, preparing and communicating guidelines and instituting control procedures and risk measurement systems.

Maintaining information integrity

Risk management systems rely on accurate, timely information in order to work effectively. Yet information systems themselves can be subject to dislocating events, heightening the risk and potential for damage. It is therefore vital to ensure that the management information system is aligned to the risk characteristics of the business, and that the control system takes into account and minimises the likely impact of identified risks. This requires:

- Managers to have a clear idea of the likely areas of risk, and an understanding of the information that they need to receive to control this risk.
- Information to reach the right people at the right time (this requires an awareness of the cost and time issues of providing information).
- Deviations from expectations to be highlighted clearly, enabling investigation and corrective action to be taken.

- A broad and complete system of information-gathering that provides financial and *non-financial* data.

Reference

Simons, R. (1995) *Levers of Control*. HBS Press. Boston, USA.

Part Three

**How your Company can Compete
with Information**

13

Competing with Information – a Diagnostic for Managers

The Information Management Diagnostic developed by **Donald Marchand** is a tool for discovering the business value of information. This chapter explains how general managers can use this diagnostic tool to better understand the role of information in their business and improve their management of this valuable asset – notably by using the tool to implement the strategic information alignment (SIA) framework.

Overview

In the first part of this book we suggested that in the years ahead, as companies learn to compete with information and new technologies, managers will have to rethink their business strategies, practices and implementation approaches. For general managers, the focus of attention must shift in three ways.

First, the mindsets of general managers need to include information and knowledge as key assets in the business along with the enabling tools of information systems (IS) and information technology (IT). Managers will have to ask how do new ways of using information and technologies transform the more traditional view of business change as primarily oriented towards strategy, structure, processes and people?

Second, general managers must appreciate the differences between managing *with* information and the management *of* information in their company. Everyday, managers are inundated with information and communications in the form of e-mails, faxes, voice mails and express delivery mail, since they manage their company at a distance *with* information about customers, operations, finances and people. However, general managers are far less comfortable with the management *of* information, which focuses on how well a company competes by using and deploying information, systems and technologies better and faster than its competitors.

Third, general managers must not confuse the *tools* for the management of information with the *content*, *use* and *value* of the information employed by people in the company.

Earlier in the book a differentiation was made between:

- *IS applications software* to operate business functions and processes.
- *IT systems*, technical staff and the infrastructure supporting a business; and
- *information management (IM)* dealing with the ways in which the business is represented through information, the quality and integrity of the information, and the uses of information to create business value for the company.

Now we will move beyond the questions of *why* we should manage information and *what* information to manage, to *how*. In particular, this chapter will address the question *how can information management practices be benchmarked, evaluated and transformed?* We will focus on the ways that information is used in a company, rather than on the deployment of new technology. The distinction is important: to succeed, general managers have to focus on *how people use information to achieve business results*, not simply on applications of new tools and techniques.

Creating business value with information: applying the SIA framework

In Chapter 2, the four ways of using information to create business value and the 'cross' diagram (*see* Figure 13.1) were introduced. This diagram is used to map

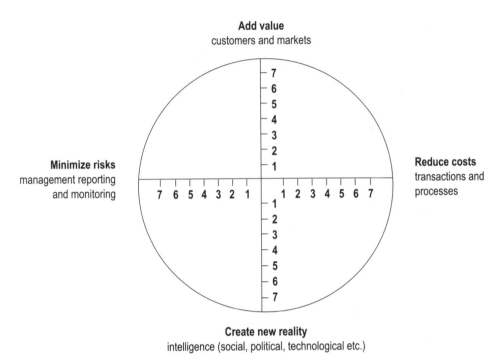

Figure 13.1: *Four ways of using information to create business value*

information practices along each of the four axes as well as to develop a composite picture for a business unit (BU) or a set of BUs.

This evaluation along each dimension, as well as the connections between each dimension, reveals an *information management profile* for individual BUs. This profile can be compared to the profiles of other BUs within a large company, with other units of direct competitors or with those outside a company's industry. The profile provides a clear picture, which managers can use to evaluate the perceived effectiveness of the information management practices of their BUs. In addition, they can also assess the strengths or weaknesses of their BU's information management capabilities, in the context of their expectations about business changes that will require different information management practices in the future.

To start the exercise, managers are presented with representative IM practices along each of the four axes, as shown in Figure 13.2.

Along the *Minimizing risks* axis, there are three types of risks that companies generally collect information to evaluate and control: financial, operational and commercial. The ranking ranges from companies where IM practices are weak to non-existent, to companies that focus on one type of risk – e.g. financial risk – to the exclusion of others, to companies that develop IM practices to manage all three types of risks.

Along the *Reduce costs* axis, the range of practices extends from companies that do not focus on process management to companies where process improvements are

Adding value

7 Information about customers and markets aggressively collected and used in real-time and company-wide
6 Customer satisfaction constantly evaluated and used company-wide
5 Real-time collection of customer information combined with market forecasts are in place and used regularly
4 Use market surveys, focus groups and customer surveys regularly
3 Provides surveys of customers; follow-up is uneven
2 Information about customers and markets collected but not used
1 Information about customers and markets not collected

Reducing costs

7 Global, regional process focus is implemented and continuously improved
6 Process focus dominates demand/supply chain management inside/outside company
5 Process/quality focus is company-wide and beginning to focus on customers and partners
4 Process improvements are beginning to be company-wide
3 Process/quality programme in place in specific functions
2 Process management mindset just beginning
1 Functions dominate processes; little evidence of process focus

Creating new reality

7 Sensing for innovation is continuous and company-wide
6 Product generation is key process for business survival
5 External scanning of best practices and innovation is strategic to company managers
4 Balance of product and process innovation is achieved internally
3 Senior management committed to product/process innovation; implementation is uneven
2 Innovation and discovery are focused in R&D, not other functions
1 New product/process ideas not sensed or processed; little focus on innovation

Minimizing risks

7 Key focus on management of operational, financial and external risks
6 Heavy focus on financial and operational performance and risks
5 Predominant emphasis on financial performance and risks
4 Balance of financial, operational and external reporting and controls
3 Financial, operational and external risk controls in place; reliability not known
2 Financial controls are in place; operational and external risks not controlled
1 Financial, operational and external risk controls are weak to non-existent

Figure 13.2: *Ways of using information: representative practices*

taking hold in selected functions, and on to companies where process management is global and continuously improved.

Along the *Add value* axis, the range focuses on companies where customer information is not collected or used, to companies that perform regular surveys and other forms of market research, up to companies that aggressively collect customer information company-wide and in real time.

Finally, along the *Create new reality* axis, the range varies from companies that confine innovation to specific departments such as R&D or marketing, to companies that try to balance product and process innovation, to companies where new product generation or continuous innovation is critical to survival in their industries.

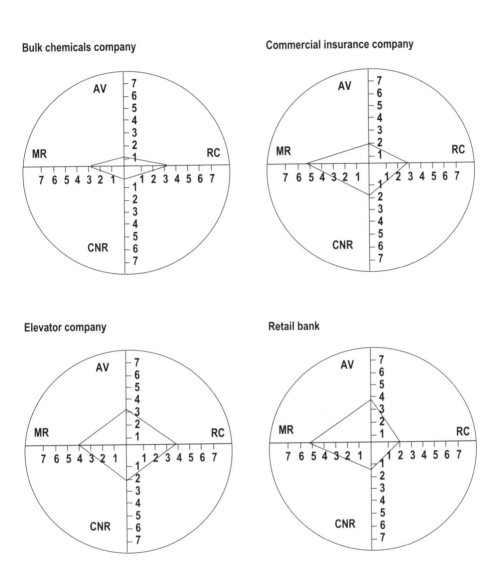

Figure 13.3: *Current information management profile*

Examples of companies and their positions on the four axes are given in Figure 13.3. Each of these rankings along the four axes provides a point of departure for the evaluation of a BU's information management practices and capabilities, as well as providing a basis for benchmarking IM practices among competitors or outside the industry.

BENCHMARKING

Five key questions to focus information management on building competitiveness

Once managers begin focusing on the range of IM practices along each axis, and the wide variations among BUs in the same industry (or even the same company), it is then possible to uncover strengths and weaknesses in existing capabilities, as well as defining what IM practice levels and capabilities will be needed in the future.

1. How does our BU compete with information today and how should it compete in the future?

Figure 13.3 includes four examples of how groups of managers in four companies participating in company-sponsored executive programmes at IMD evaluated their existing IM effectiveness and capabilities. IM practices are rated on a seven-point scale along each axis, with 1 indicating that managers rank their BU IM practices as weak and 7 indicating that they rank them as excellent. Following this exercise, each group of managers is asked to evaluate the strengths and weaknesses of their current IM practices as reflected in their IM Profile.

Figure 13.4 provides the profiles of the same BUs when the four groups of managers were asked *how should our BU compete with information in our industry in the future (three years forward)?* Again, the managers were asked to analyse gaps or new capabilities that would be needed to compete with information more effectively in the future.

While differing in degree, the current IM practices of the four companies are remarkably similar. In each company, the focus of IM is on the management of risks. While this emphasis is understandable for the insurance company and retail bank, it was rather surprising to find that bulk chemicals and elevator companies also emphasize financial and operational risk management. However, in these cases operational risks are critical, since no one likes to be trapped in a malfunctioning elevator or involved in a chemical spill or production accident.

On the axis of reducing costs, the IM focus is quite different in each case. Again, because the bulk chemical company is involved in an industrial commodity business, a great deal of focus is placed on lowering the cost of operations, with process and information flows kept as lean as possible. In the cases of the insurance company and retail bank, these organizations are relatively new to process and quality improvement initiatives. In the case of the elevator company, the emphasis on costs and process improvements has been in place for several years.

When we look at the future IM profiles in Figure 13.4, a very different picture emerges. Except for the bulk chemical company, which emphasizes cost reduction and minimizing risks, the other three companies all plan to increase their focus on IM for adding value with customers and innovation in products and/or processes. In these cases companies must either invest new resources for customer information management or for managing product and process intelligence, or re-allocate resources from their current IS/IT investments.

In developing these profiles and examining their strengths and weaknesses, general managers examine existing IM practices and investments in the context of their changing business conditions in the near future and the appropriate profiles of IM practices and investments that will be needed.

The shifting profile of IM practices from the horizontal to the vertical axis raises serious questions about prevailing IS/IT investments, which in many companies are directed at reducing costs and minimizing risks, especially financial risks. This step in the diagnostic immediately makes general managers focus on what capabilities and investments will have to be developed to substantially improve IM practices for customers or for product and process innovation.

2. How does our BU compete with information compared to other BUs in our company or our direct competitors?

The next step in the diagnostic asks managers to examine the IM profiles of different BUs inside their company or the IM profiles of their direct competitors (*see* Figure 13.4).

As managers develop current and future IM profiles of other BUs, the diagnostic uncovers significant differences among BUs in large companies related to IM needs and directions as well as the similarities and differences between BUs inside a company and their direct competitors.

➤ In a large Swiss bank with four major lines of business, the retail and private banking BUs needed to refocus IM practices from predominantly risk management and control to adding value for customers and product innovation.
➤ In the case of the asset management BU, the emphasis needed to shift towards innovative product development and improved commercial risk management.
➤ For the capital investment BU, the IM profile required much better partnering relationships with large commercial customers and substantially improved customer services.

Each of these shifts in IM profiles among the bank's BUs was also benchmarked against competitors. In each case, the bank's senior managers discovered that

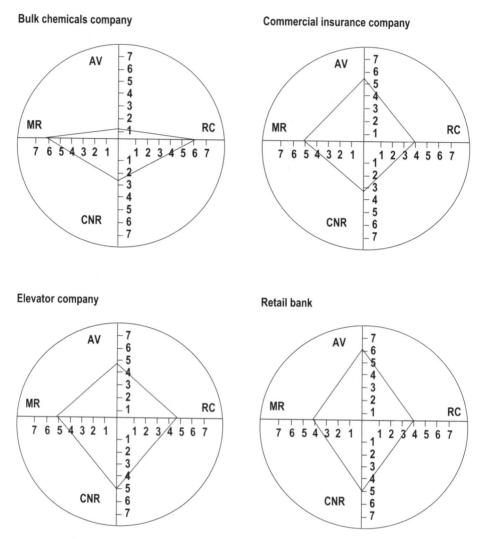

Figure 13.4: *Future information management profile*

competitors were much further along in making new investments to shift their IM profiles towards future sources of potential competitive advantage.

3. How does our BU compete with information compared to companies outside our industry?

IM practices today do not respect traditional industry boundaries for two reasons. First, IM practices are associated with major shifts in business practices over long periods of time. As suggested earlier, IM practices in, for example, risk management or process improvement to reduce costs have evolved over many decades and have been employed in many industries. Best IM practices cut across industries and markets.

Second, the tools of IS and IT supporting new IM practices today are available across all industries. Again, best practices relating to the use of IS/IT for customer or service information management or the innovative use of product intelligence in a company can be found in diverse industries. Therefore it is critical that general managers look outside their industries for innovative IM practices in support of shifts from current to future business directions. Using Figure 13.2 as a starting point, managers can now explore and share their knowledge of IM practices external to their industry.

4. What capabilities do we need to improve or develop for IM to be the best in our industry?

This step in the diagnostic challenges managers to consider what combination of people, processes and IS/IT capabilities will be required over a specific period of time to develop the IM practices to create business value across each of the four axes of their future BU IM profile. In addition, managers also ask what people, processes and IS/IT capabilities they will outsource or reduce in emphasis so as to focus resources on capabilities that help a BU grow and compete.

For example, some manufacturing companies are investing significant amounts in IS/IT to improve information management along the horizontal axis – to control risks and reduce costs – while the future business directions require much better customer information management and product innovation internally. These companies are allocating millions of dollars of investments in new IS software for automating manufacturing, inventory management and distribution processes. At the same time, their senior management believes that business success in their markets will require major improvements in IM practices for creating new products and lines of business, or adding substantial value to customers with closer partnerships and better services before, during and, especially, after sales.

To resolve how much to invest in IS/IT capabilities supporting current versus future IM directions, these firms must re-examine critical trade-offs between current versus future IM demands and business directions.

5. What changes should we make in our business to implement the required levels of IM best practices in our BU and in our company?

This is the step that moves from strategy to action. Here, general managers must decide how they will synchronize the initiatives required to change not only the IM practices of the firm but also the necessary process, people, organizational and strategic changes if IM practices are to enable the creation of business value in the BU and company.

Shifts in IM practices are intimately connected to the fabric of the business. Improving customer information, for example, is not effective in isolation from the IS/IT process or the structural, people and strategic choices that a firm must make. Successfully implementing these change initiatives becomes critical to capturing the business benefits of new IM practices in support of new business opportunities.

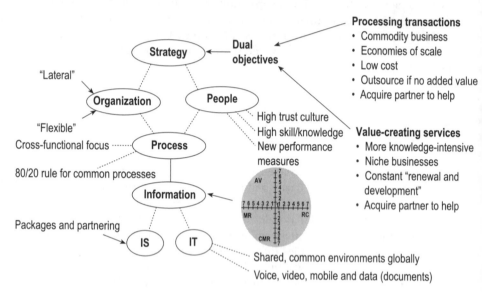

Figure 13.5: *Synchronizing key initiatives in the change process (e.g. a financial services company)*

As Figure 13.5 suggests, a financial services company today must develop two business strategies at the same time: become the low-cost operator for transaction services *and* focus on developing new products in key markets where knowledge- and information-use are critical to success. To pursue these initiatives, a company must develop a high-trust culture where highly skilled knowledge workers can apply their creativity. It must have a flat, flexible organization capable of operating low-cost transaction processes, and must share information for risk management, customer relations and product development wherever it is needed in the firm. It also needs to acquire the appropriate software packages and IT infrastructure to operate in a global environment.

The senior managers of this firm realize that it is not sufficient to work on one or two change initiatives sequentially, but rather to focus on *synchronizing changes* across each dimension of the change process.

The general manager's information challenge

There is a certain irony that at the beginning of the twenty-first century, and well into the 'information age', general managers must discover for themselves through the use of a diagnostic method as outlined in this article, where the business value of information really lies in their organization. A lay person could ask with some justification *shouldn't general managers have known the business value of information all along?*

The answer to this question is not necessarily. To understand the business value of information, a manager must look backwards and forwards at the same time. Looking backwards is necessary to understand how information management has evolved over many decades in the twentieth century. The evolution of IM practices for risk management has occurred over many years. Managers take many of these practices for granted since they are such a 'natural' part of the way we do business. Similarly, IM practices in process improvement initiatives such as total quality, re-engineering and workflow management have evolved over decades. Many managers assume that they are an integral element of the modern business even though many firms have still not used these practices.

So, general managers must re-examine IM practices and assumptions that are embedded in current ways of doing business to determine whether and how they create genuine business value. On the other hand, looking forward is also required for three reasons:

1. The tools of IS and IT are rapidly changing IM practices.
2. Business imperatives, such as continuous innovation, require fundamentally new ways of seeking, sharing and using information in the company.
3. Information, as opposed to data, is sensitive to the context of its use. (For example, customer orders today are more than data transactions; they can also be critical indicators of customer satisfaction for account managers. The focus on customer partnerships provides an important context for the use of order fulfilment information.)

This last case highlights the fact that constant business change brought on by global markets, new technologies and new competitors redefines the contexts in which information can add value to the business. This situation, combined with the fact that information management is one of the least understood issues affecting business performance, means that the process of evaluating and using information often needs to be more systematic and explicit to achieve competitive advantage.

In summary, the Information Management Diagnostic is a valuable tool for discovering the business value of information, based on the proposition that if general managers can better understand information's role in their business they can improve how they manage this critical and costly asset.

14

Open Company Values: Transforming Information into Knowledge-Based Advantages

In this chapter, **Piero Morosini** explains how open company values are central to building sustainable market advantages based on information and knowledge. A company's 'knowledge strategy' therefore needs to create unique ways for managers, employees, suppliers and partners to learn from each other and continuously add value to the business.

CASE STUDY: THE SIGNIFICANCE AND IMPORTANCE OF OPEN COMPANY VALUES –
THE ASEA BROWN BOVERI MERGER

ABB, the Swiss/Swedish electrical engineering giant formed after the 1987 merger between ASEA and Brown Boveri, had to completely re-create its social structure following this event. During the 1987–1996 period, the company more than doubled revenues to US$ 34 billion, with significant productivity and quality improvements driving annual stock price increases in excess of 20%. The initial step taken by the first ABB CEO, Percy Barnevik, was to identify the new company's key social actors. These were the so-called 'global managers': 500 individuals of different nationalities from both ASEA and Brown Boveri, fitting a specific profile. According to Barnevik they were:

. . . people who had demonstrated the ability to lead others, with humility and respect for other cultures. Extremely patient and open minded to understand, appreciate and work within the diversity of traditions and ways of doing things in different countries. Individuals that are 'givers' more than 'receivers', in the sense that they continuously develop people from other parts of the organization. At the same time, tough-skinned individuals with outstanding technical and commercial knowledge, working experience in several countries, good language ability, and the stamina to become 'superstars' in their field.

Notice that character and personality traits – leadership, openness, humility and stamina – come first and clearly dominate this profile. 'Outstanding technical and commercial knowledge' are five words that come far later in the paragraph. Does your company have, or can it attract and retain, significant numbers of social players fitting this profile? If not, chances are that your knowledge management strategy will be implemented in very different ways across geographic locations, functional divisions or even hierarchical divides, which will grow into insurmountable boundaries over time.

Overview

Open company values are the central element in building sustainable market advantages based on information and knowledge. In particular, the way in which an organization aligns key individuals around common global values that promote open learning can make or break any competitive strategy based on knowledge capabilities – no matter how adequate or sophisticated its information systems and technology are.

Most companies trying to capitalize on their knowledge capabilities have, in the past, focused one-sidedly on technology that gathers, processes, analyses and distributes information with ever increasing power. The numbers are staggering – in the USA, the cost of one megabyte of storage capacity in 1996 was around 2% of the 1985 cost. However, total spending on computers and related equipment more than doubled during the 1987–1991 period to US $112 billion. Indeed in the USA, 1991 was the first year when total spending in machines that handle information actually surpassed spending in machines that manipulate physical entities – and the gap has continued to increase ever since (Stewart, 1997).

However, better IT capabilities and IS alone have hardly given companies the knowledge-based advantages they seemed to have expected from their spending patterns. In fact during the 1980s and 1990s, executives, consultants and practitioners have increasingly tried to improve an organization's performance by codifying the knowledge underlying key company processes and routines, and subsequently reorganizing and rethinking them using the innumerable possibilities given by today's IT.

The results? According to substantial empirical and anecdotal evidence during the past two decades, *more than half* of the global re-engineering, outsourcing and similar large-scale initiatives undertaken by large multinational companies fail. Occasionally they fail after initial performance improvements are obtained, or sometimes companies simply find these initiatives too costly to maintain or too unwieldy to manage. What lies behind these stubbornly high failure rates? Why are companies finding it so hard to unleash their market and organizational knowledge to obtain sustainable advantages out in the marketplace? This chapter addresses these issues and outlines:

- What should the main components of a knowledge management strategy be?
- How can we foster open company values that will transform information into knowledge-based advantages?

Understanding knowledge management strategy

One key reason why knowledge management initiatives fail so often is that companies misunderstand what drives knowledge advantages in the first place. Knowledge exists in the minds of *knowers*, i.e. people – individuals, groups and teams – communicating meanings and interpretations of reality. Outside people's minds, knowledge does not exist – only information.

The ancient Greek word for knowledge is *gnosis*. Greek philosophers, such as Plato, distinguished between *theoretical knowledge* and *knowledge through direct observation* and experience. In either case, the word *gnosis* initially denoted a deep understanding of phenomena based on individual intuition and insight. In its original form, 'knowledge' thus referred to a psychological process of learning, a reflective flow of thoughts inside an individual's mind. By contrast, *informationem*, the root of our modern word for information, is a Latin term, in turn derived from the Greek word *morphe*, meaning the concrete representation of the empirical elements of a phenomenon. If an ancient Greek philosopher was to manage a modern corporation, he would refer to all of a company's formalized routines and codified processes simply as 'information' (no matter how sophisticated the means to codify and store it), and would refer to the learning flows inside its employees' *minds* as knowledge.

The centre-piece of any knowledge management strategy, system or structure should refer to the particular ways in which individuals and groups of people learn and communicate, ably supported by the right information resources and technology. Instead, however, companies often start in exactly the opposite direction. They first choose to buy or design a 'knowledge management system', often relying on outside IT specialists, and subsequently move on to train the employees who will use the system by gathering existing company 'knowledge', or by creating, codifying and distributing new information. Companies that think about knowledge management primarily in terms of IT or automation implicitly believe that *real* knowledge is akin to the possession of critical information, which can be stored, codified or somehow *freezed* internally. Indeed, it is common to hear management executives, academics or practitioners talk about *explicit* or *tacit* knowledge, unaware that this might represent a fundamental contradiction in terms. By its very definition, all knowledge is tacit: an individual or group-based psychological experience of learning.

From my perspective, the key issues that any global company's knowledge management strategy must resolve have little to do with IT or automated systems for codifying information (an increasingly necessary but hardly sufficient step). Rather, the main challenge of a global knowledge management strategy is one of promoting effective learning and communication between individuals, groups and teams of widely diverse backgrounds, operating in different and continuously changing environments.

Developing the main elements of a knowledge management strategy

Properly understood, the goal of your company's knowledge management strategy should be *how to create unique ways for your employees, customers, suppliers and allies, to learn from each other effectively in order to continuously create market value.* This challenge can be divided into two fundamental and inter-related elements:

- creating a unique social structure for the company; and
- developing a suitable information infrastructure to support it.

By the latter, we mean not only IT but also the quality of information and the people responsible for gathering, processing and distributing key information inside an organization.

Creating a unique social structure

One central assumption of the modern corporation is that learning essentially is a holistic social activity. In other words, when people get together to learn, the speed and depth of knowledge attained should be considerably greater than what each individual person could achieve on their own. However, although pivotal to understanding why our modern corporations exist and how they create value, this assumption should not be taken for granted. In today's so-called 'knowledge economy', the extent to which any company makes the social learning assumption happen can signal how successful that organization is at creating and managing value in the first place. Here we can see staggering performance differences between companies.

One broad way to estimate the market value of a company's social structure is to compare its total market capitalization (number of shares multiplied by the share price) to the value of its physical and semi-physical assets (such as buildings, hardware, goodwill, securities investments and machinery). In July 1998, companies such as Microsoft (software), Pfizer (pharmaceuticals) and Wal-Mart (retailing) were among the top ten most valuable companies in the world, with a market capitalization to assets ratio of 15, 9 and 3 respectively. In other words, the market value of these companies was between 3 and 15 times the value of its physical and semi-physical assets. However, other companies in those same industries, such as Sun Microsystems, Pharmacia & Upjohn, and Sears Roebuck had ratios of 3, 2 and 0.6 respectively (in the case of Sears, its market value was actually lower than the value of its physical assets).

What constitutes the difference between a company's market value and the value of its physical assets? Why does this difference vary so much across companies broadly competing in the same industries, such as Pfizer and Pharmacia & Upjohn in 1998? The main reason behind these differences lies in the highly diverse quality of these companies' *social structures*. In other words, the ways in which these companies continuously learn and apply this learning to new or existing products, services, brands and market networks, are sometimes seen by the market as either adding clear value to the company's physical assets (as in the case of Wal-Mart in 1998), or occasionally even diminishing their value (e.g. Sears Roebuck in the same year).

Setting up a suitable information infrastructure

Once a company's leaders understand the deep drivers of their social structure, they should move to support it with a suitable set of information practices, resources and capabilities. All these elements are central components of a company's information infrastructure, by which we mean not only IT, but also the ways in which key management information is gathered, analysed, shared and utilized by people inside the organization. The challenge here is one of developing suitable routines and resources to continuously collect and codify key information, and facilitate communications between individuals across the organization's internal and external communities. The main goal of such an information infrastructure is to strengthen and expand a company's social structure of learning (and not vice versa).

Building a unique and successful social structure

A company's social structure is concerned with how it learns, acts, communicates and obtains results in the marketplace as part of a living community. Its purpose is more than economical, it is social including key elements such as:

- social players
- social networks
- open business values
- gnostic rituals
- guiding myths.

The social players are the company's employees, customers, suppliers, allies, competitors and other key stakeholders. They interact and learn from each other through networks, enacted in such forms as meetings, taskforces and project teams. However, what makes an organization's social structure effective and potentially unique is the degree to which its key players – their employees – share open business values throughout their network activities. By open business values, we mean a particular behaviour and way of communicating that is common but highly specific to individuals in a group, which promotes effective sharing of information and transparent learning, and continuously encourages others to do so. In an effective social structure, these open values are not abstract concepts or aspirations, but are clearly recognizable and continuously enacted by its employees in myriad concrete gnostic rituals. Examples of these rituals are the specific ways in which a company's employees handle cross-functional rotations and international assignments of its key personnel; internal performance measurements; quality and amount of time devoted to developing others (and the rewards that go with it); and how they work with the company's key customers, suppliers and allies. Equally important is the fact that inside effective social structures, the employees have transformed top management visions, missions and other overarching principles into myths, such as heroes, metaphors, symbols or memorable events, that can then be transported into their everyday activities.

Figure 14.1 represents the interaction of external, internal and social factors that underpin the vision of a firm as a holistic, living entity. Unlike external or internal factors, a firm's social aspects have been so far comparably overlooked. However, they constitute a central perspective in the understanding of knowledge and learning which will be developed in the following paragraphs.

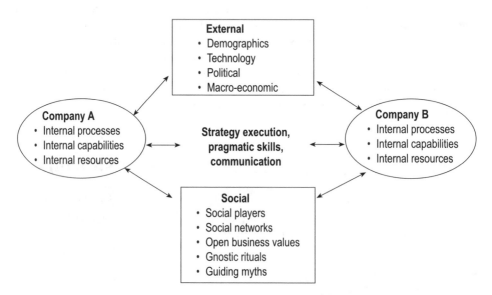

Figure 14.1: *The firm as a holistic, living social entity*
From Morosini (1998).

Social players

The starting point for developing an effective social structure in a company is its social players. Some of the key players in a company are to be found in its leadership team: the CEO, board executives, senior managers and other key executives. Since it is difficult for any global knowledge management strategy to involve all employees from the very beginning, some of the most effective companies in this area have clearly identified a global cohort of leaders underpinning their social structure. However, in order for the company's leaders to embrace and promote openness, their characters and personalities must be of a certain nature that values and understands the benefits of this approach. This was clearly the case in the ABB merger, as Percy Barnevik's quote at the beginning of this chapter highlights.

Social networks

A global cohort of leaders can initiate consistent learning initiatives with unstoppable momentum across boundaries. However, leadership and openness alone are not enough – social networks are also necessary.

CASE STUDY: THE VALUE AND POWER OF SOCIAL NETWORKS

*Typically a company generates about 50 000 defects per million products. The Six Sigma method, which in statistical terms refers to a very high level of quality, aims at reducing defects to less than four per million – an approach essentially akin to the zero-defect or TQM methods. **General Electric** didn't invent it, but were capable of applying it in a uniquely fast and successful manner. In June 1995, GE learned Six Sigma from Motorola during one of the company's regular gatherings of its global managers (coincidentally numbering 500 individuals, as in the case of ABB) and started the first pilot immediately. In November of the same year, following positive pilot results, GE launched 200 Six Sigma initiatives and 3000 the year after, covering every business area from plastics to aircraft engines and financial leasing operations. The role of Six Sigma implementation and expertise was quickly institutionalized, with over 60 000 managers trained in the application of the method in 1997 alone, and global managers' bonuses made dependent on Six Sigma results. GE, with $100.5 billion revenues in 1998, enjoyed operating margins of 16.7% and working capital turnover of over nine turns during the same year, compared to 13.6% and 5.8 respectively in 1994, before the introduction of Six Sigma.*

Why can GE so quickly and successfully learn and apply a common working method such as Six Sigma? During the same time period of three years it took GE to do it, a well-known Japanese automotive giant I have followed could not agree on a common corporate logo for its European subsidiaries! GE's success is due not only to the exceptional quality of its 500 global managers; it also highlights the power of the social network inside a company and between a company and its suppliers, customers and allies. For example, key elements in the GE social network are their regular Corporate Executive Councils (or CEC, involving the company's top 30 executives), global management meetings (including the CEO and 500 global managers), and the Town Meetings (each global manager with their business unit). By systematically enacting these meetings, a new company initiative can cascade face-to-face *from the CEO and CEC to 150 000 employees in slightly longer than one month.*

Open business values

However, key social actors and networks are still not enough to explain the success of companies such as GE or ABB. Another crucial element of an effective social structure is *open business values*. By this, we do not mean the generic 'corporate culture',

> **"A leadership visibly committed to communicating and behaving according to values that promote learning and transparent communication is what I call open business values"**

'organizational beliefs', or 'organizational identity' concepts that have been common-place in recent management literature. Open business values are the degree to which a company's key social actors share, enact and communicate to others basic principles of behaviour which encourage learning, sharing of information and transparent communication. How a company's leaders embrace, act and communicate those basic values are as important as the values themselves. These values are explored below.

Values that open minds to learning

At the outset of the 1987 ABB merger, Barnevik and a group of executives from both companies articulated the company's 'book of values', a 40-page document. The first consideration should be given to the content of the values themselves. In the context of a large merger, this book of values was not so much developed around generic organizational principles, visions or aspirations. What is striking about this document is the *pragmatic, down-to-earth and specific advice it contains to guide the behaviour of the global managers*. For example, regarding the merger process between ASEA and Brown Boveri, it stated:

The true merger process does not come automatically or naturally - it is culturally unnatural and takes management determination.

- *Combat 'us' and 'them' syndrome vigorously.*
- *Strive to mix talents and experiences from the partners.*
- *Listen and take time to understand other viewpoints.*
- *English is the group language, but is foreign to 80-90 percent of our employees - watch out for miscommunication.*
- *Show respect and recognition - do not 'rub in' past failures or poor performance. Look forward.*
- *Inform repeatedly - over-inform.*

Learning from, and communicating effectively amongst, each other was clearly the kind of behaviour expected from the key social players in ABB. They had to start simply by learning to learn from each other before they set out to conceive grandiose knowledge management strategies. Here, the book of values warns them of some of the impediments to learning and communication and provides practical advice on how to handle them. Similarly, when it comes to recruiting and developing other key social players, the document stresses the same values, with the same straight-forwardness:

We must strive to have managers who are 'givers': They attract and develop talented people and thus provide internal candidates not only for themselves but also for other parts of ABB. We cannot afford 'receivers' who always need to recruit from someone else or externally. We must promote a 'giver' mentality among our managers so that we can maintain our policy of normally recruiting and promoting from within the group.

In the case of General Electric during the early 1980s, CEO Jack Welch articulated his company's values in a few statements: speed, simplicity, self-confidence; informality and quality; candour. These values clearly build on each other and could read like an ABB global manager profile. Only when you are self-confident enough can you be candid and open to learn from others; only when you can express yourself with simplicity can you be understood; only when you keep things informal as a group can you move with speed. With these kinds of simple but shared values and mentality, General Electric global managers can move fast and successfully to implement massive initiatives, such as the Six Sigma quality programme, which would be daunting for almost any other company.

Living by your values

The second key consideration relating to open business values refers to how a company's leaders embrace and move to communicate these simple, basic values to others. Here one can see considerable differences in the companies' approaches around very similar principles. After the first ABB global managers had been selected in late 1987, Barnevik organised a plenary 'global manager meeting' in Oslo, the first in January 1988. The central theme of the meeting was ABB's book of values, spelling out the reasons behind the merger, the core business values of the new organization, and how to behave around those values. This was the beginning of Barnevik's continuous series of face-to-face meetings with ABB's global managers. In order to help turn ABB's book of values into actual behaviour, Barnevik made this document the centrepiece of his own communication activities, constantly discussing, following up and enriching its contents with the global managers' group, and urging them to follow suit with their own company constituencies. There is no doubt that the personal involvement of ABB's top leaders, their action-oriented and straightforward communications, were at least as effective as the book of values itself in promoting the same kind of behaviour in the company's global managers.

CASE STUDY: TRANSMITTING VALUES AT GENERAL ELECTRIC

GE's employees started to listen more attentively to Jack Welch's simple speeches on the company's values, following the company's unprecedented restructuring during the early 1980s, which included divestments in over 200 GE companies and massive layoffs of around 135 000 people. The resulting company was considerably less bureaucratic, underlying the CEO's message of simplicity, candour and transparent learning across boundaries. Moreover, Jack Welch personally started a series of communication rituals, variously called 'work-outs' or 'town meetings', in essence nothing more than gatherings of key managers across functional and geographic boundaries, where difficult issues were discussed openly and candid learning was fostered around the CEO's leadership. As a result, there were fewer and fewer places to hide in GE's global managerial ranks throughout the 1980s. However, those individuals who survived their CEO's grinding communications rituals were those capable to imbue in others that simple message of candid, simple and open learning across boundaries. Unlike Barnevik's itinerant global manager meetings, most of Welch's social networking took place at GE's corporate university at Crotonville, where he reputedly spent over 50% of his time, constantly 'working out', coaching and learning from others.

However different in shape, context and frequency, both ABB's and GE's top leadership followed similar principles in order to communicate their simple business values. They both had a very simple and consistent message, articulated around specific actions and rituals that could be replicated by their audience. They also repeatedly hammered it in a direct, face-to-face, relentless and obsessive manner, to a series of well-defined target groups inside the company's social structure, including global managers, key customers and suppliers.

Communications that promote open learning

ABB's and GE's leaders also made sure to *walk-the-talk* during their communications rituals, turning them into opportunities to practice open learning as opposed to inadvertently blocking learning from happening. The latter is a too-often overlooked problem that many companies' top management fail to perceive. Following the fall of the Berlin Wall in 1989, ABB leaders aimed at promoting massive internal technology transfers across transitional economies such as Eastern Europe and Russia, where the company was determined to rapidly acquire large manufacturing concerns but where cultural and organizational boundaries were perceived to be particularly challenging. ABB leaders wanted to do this by empowering their global managers to take on the opportunity to learn from each other, otherwise it was believed that these initiatives would not be sustainable over time. Therefore they ensured that commitment to these initiatives did not come as a result of top management support or any other source 'external' to the global managers.

After ABB's CEO and top leaders initially presented their global managers with these major challenges, some of them were more proactive and effective than others in actually engaging in best-practice and internal benchmarking across transitional economies. Rather than intervening directly to improve the less effective units, or publicly 'reward' the more proactive ones, ABB top management utilized the more successful cases in their subsequent communication meetings. For example, global managers from 'developed' subsidiaries who had found practical ways to transfer best practices efficiently into transitional economies such as Poland or Ukraine, would take the stage and describe to their colleagues how they approached and resolved the main issues. In this way, self-examination, open communication and learning – rather than defensive behaviour in front of top management – were stimulated amongst the less proactive global managers, as well as a motivation to act and emulate their leading colleagues.

By implementing their approach across a wide range of situations, ABB top management sent a clear message of self-reliance and co-operative learning to its global management group, who were quickly galvanized into action. During the 1990–96 period, ABB successfully turned around over 160 acquisitions across Eastern Europe and other transitional economies – a rate of nearly two acquisitions per month – while maintaining a 200-strong headquarters in Switzerland. Virtually all of the massive technology transfer, internal benchmarking and other similar knowledge management initiatives that were required in order to achieve this were carried out through co-operation, open learning and continuous sharing of information amongst key global managers and ABB subsidiaries.

Gnostic rituals

The highly visible and action-oriented commitment to learning that open business values require from a company's leaders inevitably lead to the formation of gnostic rituals. These are regular communication and management development practices which crystallize a company's approach to social learning in a particularly visible, ubiquitous, intense and almost symbolic manner. Taken together, a set of gnostic rituals constitute the concrete manifestations of the spirit of a corporation, i.e. what it *really* values, stands for and believes in as a social entity. These rituals usually take time to develop, and are unique to a company's specific social context, the qualities of their leaders and corporate history. Therefore an organization's gnostic rituals are almost by definition difficult to replicate or transfer into other companies' social structures.

CASE STUDIES: GNOSTIC RITUALS AND THEIR INFLUENCE ON SOCIAL STRUCTURE AND SUCCESS – MCKINSEY & COMPANY AND DAEWOO

*In the cut-throat international management consulting sector, **McKinsey & Company** has commanded the league of leading firms during the past two decades, with over 20% premium in revenue per consultant over competitors such as BCG, A.T. Kearney and Gemini Consulting. During the same period, the company has also been recognized widely as the leading strategy consultancy, with a legendary reputation and* *illustrious alumni at the head of companies such as IBM, American Express and Westinghouse at one time or another. In order to maintain this remarkable performance, McKinsey aims at fostering a non-hierarchical meritocracy, where commitment to the highest standards of quality and open learning are expected to be commonplace across the company's 70 offices worldwide. One of the key ways in which the company maintains that meritocracy is the so called 'up or out' policy. In other words, McKinsey consultants are expected to be promoted to the next level within a specific time period, or they are invited to leave the company. The degree of rigour, intensity and commitment with which this company applies this policy all over the world has given birth to peculiar gnostic rituals, which explain much of the company's unique social structure and performance.*

McKinsey's 'up or out' policy represents the difference between individual success and failure for most of the firm's usually bright and over-achieving professionals. In order to implement this policy, all of the firm's offices utilize a standard evaluation document in English language called 'Evaluation Performance Review', or EPR. Each time a project team starts an engagement, a deeply ingrained ritual takes place involving the young McKinsey consultants. During the first week of the project, the team's engagement manager (EM) will spend a few hours with each team member to agree on what kind of performance they expect in the specific context of the client and the engagement that is about to start. A complementary document, available to everybody in the team, describes in detail what kind of behaviour corresponds to each performance level. Approximately halfway through an engagement (or after a couple of months of a long engagement), the EM will carry out an 'interim evaluation' of each McKinsey team member. The ritual will be as follows: the EM will complete a draft EPR for each member of the team, and will discuss it in face-to-face, private meetings that can last a few hours. Here, good areas and performance gaps are highlighted, and corrective actions or modifications are considered. The final part of the ritual takes place at the end of the engagement, when the final EPR is prepared by the EM, discussed and signed by the individual evaluated, as well as the EM and the partner or director of the engagement.

What is it that makes McKinsey's EPR a gnostic ritual of learning vis-à-vis other company's similar personnel performance evaluation activities? At McKinsey, EPR rituals enact key values that constitute the very essence of the company's social structure. To begin with, people do get promoted or leave on an everyday basis as a direct result of systematic EPR sessions. I estimated that about one-third of the company's graduate intake survive after the third year, to become senior EMs. Thereafter, one in three will make it to partner, and only one-third of partners would normally become directors. Overall, probably less than ten graduate hires out of one hundred will remain with the firm for more than one decade. Secondly, EPRs are normally a two-way ritual of learning. On the one hand, the EM does as much evaluation as coaching, explaining the kinds of behaviour, learning and quality standards that the firm expects from its members, what the existing performance gaps are, and how to close them.

McKinsey's EPR ritual is, of course, not free from errors. Occasionally people get promoted without the required calibre or are invited to leave as a result of other factors. But overall, the ritual more than fulfils its primary purpose, which is one of high-stakes coaching and learning as much as mere 'evaluation'. It is the consistency, fairness and competence of McKinsey professionals that has so far made EPR and other similar gnostic rituals effective tools of open and co-operative team learning. Indeed, despite the rigours and risks involved in McKinsey's 'up or out' policy, the firm has continued to attract exceedingly bright professionals and highly demanding clients.

***Daewoo**, the multibillion Korean industrial conglomerate each year sends young bright Koreans into long-term academic and working experiences abroad, internally referred to as* international missions. *These include not only Western locations, but especially transitional economies as far apart as Russia, Vietnam, Peru and Burma. Any manager who expects to make a leading career in Daewoo must pay their dues in these kinds of international missions, as exemplified by Kim-Woo Choong, the company's founder, as well as other top executives who spent their early years with the company doing business in remote geographic locations. As a result of these international missionary rituals, Daewoo continuously develops a global cohort of young managers capable of bridging barriers to cross-border learning, in order to transfer technological expertise and know-how across geographical, cultural and political divides.*

Following the collapse of Communism in Europe in 1989, Daewoo was a most unlikely first mover inside most of the former Soviet-dominated economies. The feat was made the more remarkable by the fact that Korea did not have diplomatic relations with these former Communist regimes until well after the mid-1990s. However, by 1995 Daewoo had already become a dominant foreign investor in countries such as Poland, Romania, Kazakhstan and Uzbekistan, with multibillion-dollar investments in sectors ranging from automotive to shipbuilding. Daewoo typically utilized few Korean co-ordinators, some of whom had spent their early international missions in each of these countries, in order to rapidly transfer technology, benchmarking and developing local managerial talent very early on.

Performance evaluation practices, personnel rotations, international assignment policies and regular communication meetings exemplify key areas where leading companies such as GE, McKinsey, ABB and Daewoo have implanted gnostic rituals that promote open values and learning across borders. What makes essentially simple events such as GE's *work-out*, ABB's *global manager meetings* or McKinsey's *EPR sessions* into gnostic rituals is the obsessive dedication of the top leaders to make them:

- consistent, transparent and ubiquitous happenings anywhere in the world;
- intimately ingrained into a company's career and performance developments; and
- continuously seeking to involve the behaviour of its key social players.

Guiding myths

Any company leader can move with sheer determination to instil open values amongst its key social players, and obsessively imprint gnostic rituals over time through skilful use of the company's social networks and other organizational mechanisms. However, such a social structure will not capture the *imagination* of a company's employees and other social players vividly enough to inspire consistent behaviour that transcends

> "Organizations that are continuously motivated to learn from its key social players often innovate more, and more single-mindedly, than their competitors. This is usually the case even when competition takes place across fairly standardized products and services"

the life-span of a strong leader or a specific managerial generation. Nevertheless, an organization's knowledge management strategy should stand the test of time, leading to a unique social structure that continuously devises new ways of creating market value through open learning between a company's employees, customers, suppliers, allies and other key social players. To achieve lasting success as a learning social structure a company often benefits from the existence and pervasive quality of its guiding myths.

Guiding myths are at the origin of every gnostic ritual of a great corporation. They are a collection of heroes, metaphors, events and expressions that express uniquely a company's historic *raison d'être*, the essential elements of its founding leaders' visions of the future, and its particular legacy of values and lasting contributions. As such, they constitute a truly inspirational dimension of the social structure of a corporation, as long as people can find plausible evidence of these guiding myths in their everyday experiences. Thus, a couple of youngsters inventing world-beating computer products in a garage are part of a company's guiding myths so long as its employees can find examples of informal learning, freedom to innovate, and small team-working approaches in their everyday corporate lives. By articulating a company's historically unique responses to difficult challenges such as learning and innovation, guiding myths constantly inspire people in an organization to act, either applying old company principles, or finding their own responses to new situations.

CASE STUDY: ANDERSEN CONSULTING

Andersen Consulting's (AC) approach to management consulting offers highly standard solutions to its clients' complex organizational problems – typically involving major process re-engineering and IT issues. In comparison with companies such as McKinsey, AC caters to a limited range of very large projects, which it addresses at a much lower average cost per consultant. AC has been able to carry out this strategy quite successfully by investing massively in IT and professional training that codifies specific approaches and solutions to be continuously learned and re-utilized at a minimum cost.

However, AC's unique approach involves much more than 'economics of re-use' or standardized solutions. For example, the offering of integrated management consultancy services which the firm pioneered during the early 1990s – combining strategic, process-based, change management and re-engineering services inside cross-functional *teams of consultants - was in itself highly innovative. Suddenly, firms offering differentiated consultancy services such as McKinsey & Company (strategy), CSC Index (process re-engineering) or IBM consulting (IT), had to compete against AC's 'integrated' approach. Based on this framework, AC enjoyed phenomenal growth, from less than US$1 billion during the early 1990s to nearly US$10 billion in 1999. However, a number of companies attempting to apply AC's approach, such as Gemini Consulting and CSC Index, failed to obtain the growth rates that AC's integrated approach achieved. What makes the astonishing differences in performance between AC and its competitors?*

One key difference is AC's unusually rich heritage of inspiring leaders and guiding events. From the company's inception earlier this century, Arthur Andersen, the Chicago-based accounting firm from which Andersen Consulting originated, reflected tightly its founder's uncompromising vision of high quality professional services. The US business accounting arena of the early twentieth century was plagued by differing and often contradictory views across states. Here, Arthur Andersen quickly made its mark based on its ability to pioneer innovative and high-quality solutions that were then adopted officially as common accounting standards across the US. The resulting obsession with devising and implanting high quality standards to complex problems became commonplace at Arthur Andersen - and later at Andersen Consulting. When applied to knowledge management approaches they led to AC's proverbial ability to reduce even the most complex learning challenges into standard pieces, which can be codified and shared openly amongst the company's professionals (numbering more than 50 000 professionals around the world). The intensity and cultural uniformity with which AC professionals learn quickly to learn and share key information through the firm's countless gnostic rituals, is often likened by its competitors - not without a hint of envy - to soulless but highly effective 'androids'.

A company's soul is not only about possessing guiding myths in the past, but is also in its ability to continuously generate new ones. Barnevik's leadership as ABB's first CEO attained mythical proportions in many ways, filling the company's employees minds with lasting stories, events and legacies that spell out the company's basic principles. Nevertheless, Göran Lindahl, who became the second ABB CEO in 1996, is presiding over the largest management restructuring in the company's history. Under Lindahl, ABB is rapidly transforming itself into a fast-growing high-technology services company in key areas such as industrial automation and power distribution. As it was during the company's expansion into Eastern Europe and Russia during the early 1990s, it is not ABB's 'possession' of 'knowledge' or specific technological competencies at any given time which necessarily explain the company's swift transformations. Rather, it is ABB's *inspiring leadership* as well as their global managers' *open business values* and *co-operative learning* that largely underpin its astonishing capacity to continuously transform itself.

SUMMARY

Transforming information into knowledge-based advantages

It is well known that the IT industry has become one of the fastest-growing business sectors in the world. Not only is the number of technological solutions to the same basic needs increasing at an exponential rate, but some of the underlying technologies are converging, creating an ever-increasing number of business and economic applications. This sheer growth and development easily misled companies into pursuing IT-based advantages single-handedly, overlooking central organizational aspects such as how to build effective social learning and innovation mechanisms.

In my view, a company's information infrastructure should follow, support and reinforce an already existing social structure of learning inside an organization – and not vice versa. However, by information infrastructure we do not mean only the IT supports – from data networking to Internet and intranet facilities – that are becoming increasingly commonplace and easy to imitate across firms. Instead, we mean the particular ways in which information is utilized inside a company by everyone, not just by IT professionals or specialists. The concept therefore encompasses the extent to which information is defined and managed by business demands, rather than being IT-driven, as well as the level of IT support for innovation and orientation for the future.

A central dimension in assessing a company's information infrastructure effectiveness concerns the quality of the inputs it provides routinely to management, and the existence of systematic processes to gather and analyse information across key managerial levels. Another key dimension, linked closely to the first, refers to the level of computer literacy across a company's employee base, particularly amongst the so-called 'knowledge workers', as well as the existence of systematic incentives to attain and continuously increase that literacy. Basic building blocks, such as common language and terminology inside a company, greatly facilitates the functionality of a company's specific information infrastructure. In a leading Italian bank I studied a few years ago, there were at least five valid definitions for what a customer was. Depending on which definition a manager decided to use, the number of new accounts over a six-month period would range from a negative number to 12 000 'new' customers!

There are a number of general principles around which a company can build a suitable information infrastructure, and it is useful to keep these guidelines in mind:

- Start by articulating your company's social structure of learning.
- Foster open business values as the core element of your company's knowledge management strategy.

- Focus on attracting open-minded individuals and developing their learning skills and computing literacy, as much as in acquiring state-of-the-art IT tools.
- Be involved – choosing a suitable information infrastructure is a leadership (not a 'specialist') decision.
- Inform your decision – have a clear framework to decide what information infrastructure better suits your company's social structure of learning

To conclude, the art is not in the concept. Indeed, it might be looked upon as somewhat paradoxical that the more our post-modern society seems to advance its information capabilities and technological competencies, the more sustainable business advantages seem to rely on raw human talent, as well as the so-called 'soft' cultural values.

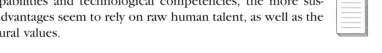

BEST PRACTICE

The five-stage process for developing an effective information infrastructure

Developing an information infrastructure that actively promotes and supports the company's strategies (the concept of open company values) requires the following elements:

1. Identify key social players

The company's social players (employees, customers and other stakeholders) provide the starting point when building an open and effective information structure. Furthermore the company's leaders provide the most effective and influential source of social players to promote openness, group learning and best practice.

2. Develop and build social networks

Social networks provide the necessary framework for leaders and other players to act and influence the values and direction of the organization. These may include meetings and gatherings from the corporate to the team level, across functions, geographic borders and businesses, both inside and outside a company's boundaries.

3. Encourage and support open business values

The next stage is for the company's key social players to share, communicate, encourage and implement the behaviour needed to learn and share information. This can include actions, for example, that mix talent and experience, as well as coaching, feedback mechanisms and communications that facilitate learning and mutual listening.

When encouraging open business values, the method used is as important as the content. The most appropriate methods can include living the message (or 'walking the talk'), as well as:

➡ ensuring that the message is simple and consistent;
➡ articulating the message around clear, specific actions that people can relate to and repeat; and
➡ emphasizing the message constantly.

4. Recognize and develop gnostic rituals

Gnostic rituals are those visible actions unique to a company that are difficult to replicate or transfer, but which formalize and continuously reinforce the values and social structure of an organization. These can include specific approaches to performance evaluation practices, personnel rotations, international assignments and regular communications mechanisms. Their value lies in the fact that they consistently enhance career and performance developments, and actively involve the behaviour of key social players.

5. Understand the importance of guiding myths

Guiding myths are linked closely to gnostic rituals, and encompass the company's vision of the future, the lasting values and inspiration behind the organisation. In essence, they are the *soul* of the company. Explicitly recognizing and understanding these guiding myths (which are often tacit or implicit within the minds of many people both inside and outside the organization) will help ensure that these values and sources of inspiration remain intact.

In addition, guiding myths can be created in the present – as well as the past. There are many examples everyday of events and legacies that serve to inspire and influence others, and it is these advantages of open business values and co-operative learning that lead to greater effectiveness and sustained success.

References

Morosini, P. (1998) *Managing Cultural Differences.* Pergamon Press, Oxford, UK.

Stewart, T.A. (1997) *Intellectual Capital, the New Wealth of Organisations.* Doubleday, New York.

15

The New Wave of Business Process Redesign and IT in Demand and Supply Chain Management

In this chapter, **Donald Marchand** focuses on the challenges that managers face in achieving the new wave of business process redesign (BPR) and IT systems needed to support their company's demand and supply chains. Five key questions are highlighted that senior managers need to address to ensure that their BPR and IT strategies maintain competitiveness.

CASE STUDY: THE CHALLENGES OF BUSINESS PROCESS REDESIGN AND IT

*Businesses dealing in products and services that move across borders electronically have faced two pressures in recent years: globalization and technological change. Nowhere is this situation more evident than in the **international banking and financial services industries**.*

At the time of writing, merger mania is sweeping the finance sector. In Germany, Dresdner and Deutsche banks are in talks about merging their retail operations. British banks Nat West and Lloyds-TSB are fighting a bidding war for Legal & General, a major British insurance and pensions group. French banks Paribas, Société Générale and BNP swapped bids, shares and meetings with French regulators at a startling pace during their 1999 merger shenanigans. America's First Union bank has acquired more than 100 businesses in 15 years, but the biggest consolidation of all was announced in 1999 when the Industrial Bank of Japan (IBJ), Dia-Ichi Kangyo Bank (DKB) and Fuji Bank decided that they would form the world's largest bank with assets worth $1270 billion.

The issues driving these changes are well-documented; they include:

- *Increasing competition and declining margins in the sector.*
- *The need for huge investments in IT systems.*
- *An undermining of the bank's traditional role as intermediary between borrower and saver (a process known as 'disintermediation').*

In these circumstances, business processes and IT systems need to be redesigned to enhance both the demand and supply chains, but the stakes in doing so are almost unbearably high. To remain competitive and to realize the benefits of mergers – and many other types of major investments and restructuring – requires business process redesign and heavy IT investment. Even in more mundane situations affecting service and particularly manufacturing businesses, the desire has returned to build competitive advantage using business process redesign and the burgeoning opportunities afforded by IT. The benefits may be considerable, but the risks and potential pitfalls easily match these. The key to success is therefore to look closely at the approaches that are being followed and to consider a number of vital questions before, during and after these changes are implemented.

Overview

Are you betting your company's demand/supply chain on business process redesign (BPR) and information technology (IT) again? The short answer for most large, international manufacturing and service companies today is a resounding *Yes!* The threat of Year 2000 system failures pushed many companies during the 1990s to replace their legacy systems supporting their demand/supply chains. Enterprise systems or Enterprise Resource Planning (ERP) systems promise seamless integration of a company's information flows from financial and human resource administration to order fulfilment, inventory management, logistics and even customer information. The transition to a single currency in Europe over the next few years is also motivating companies. Finally, the rapid evolution of Internet, intranet and extranet applications for business-to-business and business-to-consumer electronic commerce is driving firms towards BPR and ERP. In short, the rush to BPR and ERP is again vitally important for large North American and European companies.

What is interesting about this new wave of enthusiasm for BPR and IT is that it comes just a few years after the disillusionment with re-engineering associated with restructuring and cost-cutting in many of the same large companies. The new themes for BPR and ERP today are growth, product innovation and customer focus – very different from the downsizing and cost-cutting that distinguished re-engineering efforts.

> **"An essential challenge of the digital economy is how to integrate electronic commerce with established ways of doing business. At the same time, many senior managers will privately admit that they are concerned about the new business and IT forces converging on BPR and ERP"**

So why should senior managers be concerned about the evolution of this new wave of BPR and IT? First, most senior managers of large international manufacturing and service companies seem to be positive about these changes and new challenges. Those in manufacturing and service industries talk openly about growth, innovation and customer focus. These same managers have (or will have soon) invested millions more on enterprise systems from SAP, Baan, PeopleSoft and many other vendors of ERP software. Moreover, many managers are aware of, and supportive of, pilot projects and implementations of the Internet, intranets and extranets (business-to-business use of Internet technologies) inside and outside their company's with suppliers, distributors and customers.

To achieve the benefits of their commitment and to reduce the risks associated with BPR and IT projects simultaneously, senior managers must address five key issues related to implementing demand/supply chains using BPR and IT. Of course a company should address the five issues *before* it embarks on new BPR and IT projects. Even as BPR and IT projects evolve, managers should also keep these concerns in mind, in order to steer and evaluate their alignment with changes in business priorities and time frames. This chapter assesses the five key issues facing senior managers concerned with improving their demand and supply chain management using BPR and IT, and provides practical guidance for minimizing the risks.

What approach to demand/supply chain management is your company implementing?

If the mindsets of senior managers shape company strategies, project initiatives and investment priorities, then *their* views of how their company approaches demand/supply chain management are critical to appropriately targeting process redesign efforts and IT projects. This is more than a semantic concern. As Figure 15.1 suggests, there is no one view of demand or supply chain management in manufacturing and service companies today. Over the last ten years, there have been several phases of supply chain and demand chain management. Manufacturing companies have implemented these phases differently than service companies.

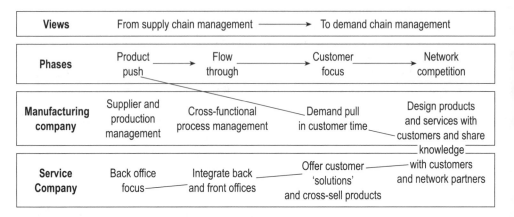

Figure 15.1: *Evolution of demand/supply chain management*

In manufacturing companies supply and, more recently, demand chain management has evolved through four major phases. In the mid-1980s, most large manufacturing companies were focused on implementing Manufacturing Resource Planning systems (Vollman et al., 1992), which were intended to rationalize sales forecasting with production planning and control in large companies. The first generation of these systems – *Material Requirements Planning* or MRP I – focused on the process of forecasting demand, developing a Master Production Schedule, detailed manufacturing capacity plans and material requirements plans for purchasing. The second generation – *Manufacturing Resource Planning* or MRP II – took advantage of developments in database management systems and faster, more powerful computers, and sought to integrate sales and forecasting, production planning, inventory control and purchasing activities. During this phase, supply chain management was internally focused and product-oriented.

During the late 1980s and early 1990s, manufacturing companies started looking at the entire supply chain, from external suppliers through manufacturing, distribution, marketing and sales as one continuous process, or 'flow through'. The main concern was making the cross-functional flows of products down the supply chain and sales and marketing forecasts up the supply chain as seamless as possible. This required a new generation of BPR and IT projects aimed at managing information in real-time across functional departments that, in the first phase, operated independently in most firms. During this third phase, manufacturing companies began to implement the first ERP systems, such as SAP's R/2 system which centralized information across the supply chain in large databases used by all the functions. Typically, in large companies these IT projects required five to seven years to implement due to the extensive re-engineering required in supply chain processes and information management, and because of the complexity of the databases and software being used.

In the mid-1990s, a significantly different view of supply chain management evolved as manufacturing companies moved from a 'product push' to a 'customer pull' view of the value chain; hence the change from supply to *demand* chain management. Senior managers began focusing on the growing need to respond to customer orders and sales in real time, to speed up order fulfilment, and to lower inventory costs along the whole supply chain. A new generation of software applications focused on integrating sales and order fulfilment with distribution and logistics, inventory management, production planning and control, and supplier management. The intent was clear: customize products to meet customer needs better, speed up order fulfilment and reduce inventory and working capital needs. This phase also coincided with a growing popularity of ERP vendors such as SAP, PeopleSoft, QED, J.D. Edwards and Oracle. These vendors provided application packages and integrated relational databases to automate the major administrative and operational functions running the demand/supply chain of a company.

Current developments driving demand chain management

Two developments have driven the fourth and most recent phase of demand chain management. First, most manufacturers today recognize that companies do not operate their supply chain in isolation but depend on networks of suppliers, distributors and partners for operations such as logistics and transport. Thus, manufacturing companies compete as members of a network of interdependent companies, against other networks of similarly organized firms (Poirier and Reiter, 1996). Thus, the term *network competition* has evolved to capture this facet of demand chain management.

The second development has been due primarily to the rise of the Internet in business-to-business e-commerce and, in particular, the use of Internet technology to link networks of interdependent firms together to serve customers. GE was one of the first firms to develop this capability in 1995 and 1996 through its 'trade processing network' which linked thousands of suppliers to its Lighting Division online for purchasing high-volume, lower-cost products. In the IT industry, GE ignited a subindustry of extranet software application providers, whose products can be used to share information from customers throughout networks of firms acting together to fulfil customer needs for products and services. In its most developed form, supply or demand chain management is being replaced with the integrated value chain or *integrated value network*. This is where a number of businesses using a specific channel manage the flow of goods, services and information along the entire value chain so as to increase customer value, enhance efficiency and develop competitive advantage for all stakeholders in the value chain. Thus, network-based competition using Internet technology provides an additional view of how companies can execute demand or supply management.

Similarly, over the last ten years the evolution of demand/supply chain management in service companies (banks and insurance companies, for example) has moved from automating back-office functions (cheque clearance, payment processing and policy administration) to front-office automation supporting services to customers (or through agents). In addition, as service companies focus on responding to customer demands and on cross-selling banking, insurance and other financial products at the point of sale, the need for integrating product information with services delivered to customers requires integrated databases and ERP-like systems. Finally, the use of Internet technology to interact directly with customers, agents and fund managers has also led to network-based competition in service companies. Each view of supply or demand chain management for service companies has required different BPR and IT projects aimed at the changing strategic priorities of service firms in various industries.

Understanding senior management views on integrated value chain management

Not surprisingly, the views of senior managers concerning supply, demand chain, or integrated value chain management vary considerably. The evolution of these views and the targeting of appropriate BPR and IT projects in support of these different perspectives requires careful evaluation within companies for three reasons.

First, it is not sufficient for senior managers to be committed to BPR and IT projects in support of demand/supply chain management. Senior managers must develop shared views and clear understandings of what approach to demand/supply chain management their company needs to pursue for competitive advantage. Many senior managers are committing their companies to BPR and IT projects with little or no competitive value.

Second, given the time to implement BPR and IT projects for operating effective demand/supply chains and the associated risks of failure, the choices today must not become constraints or block the choices that will need to be made tomorrow. Will today's ERP or IT projects become tomorrow's competitive burden? Will the opportunity costs of implementing such large-scale, complex projects grow too high? Will there be lock-in effects of automating today's way of doing business for the foreseeable future?

Finally, senior managers must avoid the herding or bandwagon effects that develop around the latest management concepts such as ERP and IT software products to support demand/supply chain management. The complexity of new ERP packages, coupled with the scale and high costs of such IT projects, can lead to a bandwagon effect. Like the previous wave of re-engineering for downsizing and cost-cutting, we are in the churning white water of the next major wave of change when senior managers regard ERP and Internet technologies as the answers to many unclear questions.

What is the competitive advantage for companies to redesign and automate similar aspects of their demand/supply chains in the same industry?

Many companies choose ERP applications and priorities in the same way that all the other firms in their industry do. While each of these companies individually claims to be seeking competitive advantage with these new BRP and IT projects, they are, nevertheless, investing in and implementing the same generic application priorities in their demand and supply chains. Over the last three years, I have asked hundreds of business executives in IMD executive programmes which application priorities they have chosen to implement. The vast majority name financial administration as the lead application, followed by manufacturing, inventory management and distribution. Other executives have also listed human resource applications and order fulfilment. Invariably, these managers have claimed to be pursuing competitive advantage in their industries by implementing the same applications as their leading competitors – in roughly the same order!

However, when challenged about the real pay-offs from this sequence of application priorities, these managers have acknowledged the apparent inconsistency. First, many claim that the Y2K transition required their companies to start with financial and manufacturing applications. Second, others claim a form of *competitive necessity* in their industries, since most of the major companies in the industry are adopting ERP applications in a similar manner and customers in their industry expect their company to operate this way as well. Third, some managers have admitted that internal debates about which applications would be automated first focused on financial, manufacturing and other *internally-oriented priorities*, steered their choices.

Assessing the competitive value of process redesign

Figure 15.2 provides a framework for assessing the competitive value of redesigning and implementing applications software in support of their demand/supply chain processes.

On the vertical axis is the return on information that most managers expect from better ERP software and databases, in terms of three types of business competencies

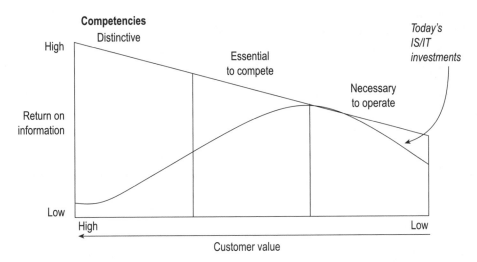

Figure 15.2: *Competitive value of today's IS/IT investments*

(Vollmann, 1996). I define 'return on information' as the business value that a company expects to receive through improving the quality, quantity, availability and use for decision-making of the information resources in its demand/supply chain. On the right side of the chart are the competencies that are necessary to operate a business, such as information systems in support of the general ledger, payroll, accounting and financial reporting. Applications in this category are required to run a business, but deliver no direct customer value.

In the middle of the chart are the competencies that are essential to compete, such as order fulfilment, manufacturing management, inventory management and distribution. In this category, customers expect that to be among the top players in an industry, companies need to have these capabilities. These applications provide some direct customer value not only if a company implements them well and uses them to promote better products and services, but also if they enhance customer value. At best, the top five to ten companies in the industry all receive comparable benefits from these applications. This is why these companies must execute these applications well just to stay in the running in their industry. For example, in the bulk chemicals industry today, all the leading chemical companies have implemented SAP ERP software for financial administration, process control, distribution and logistics. Managers in the chemicals industry believe that such systems are essential to control costs and manage information across the supply chain for on-time deliveries, and that industrial customers expect their suppliers to operate this way.

On the left side of the chart are the business competencies that can lead a company to be distinctive in providing customer value with information. In this category, managers mention information systems for customer profiling, product innovation, customer service and accounts management. Individual companies believe that these applications provide the highest return on information use since the information leads directly to higher perceived customer value.

On the question of where they allocate their IS/IT investments today, most managers reply that they invest in applications that are 'necessary to operate' and 'essential to compete'. Rarely do managers point out that significant portions of their current IS/IT investments are focused on applications that provide distinctive competencies with customers. The increasing slope of 'Today's IS/IT Investments' in Figure 15.2 occurs for two reasons. First, companies are investing much more money as noted earlier in ERP systems than they did in earlier years. Second, the cost for implementing complex BPR and IS/IT projects is increasing.

Yet on the question of where they would like to allocate their IS/IT investments in the future, most managers reply that they would like to spend more resources on information applications that make their companies distinctive in creating value with customers (see Figure 15.3). Thus, it appears that in many industries today, managers recognize that opportunities to compete with information along the demand/supply chain exist, but that their investments in ERP provide little or no distinctive advantage with customers. Thus, opportunities exist for firms to employ their IS/IT resources in 'zones' of information-based competition. They can lower the costs of installing and operating applications that are essential to compete and necessary to operate. They can also allocate IS/IT resources to applications that provide distinctive business competencies to use information to create customer value. Or they can do both.

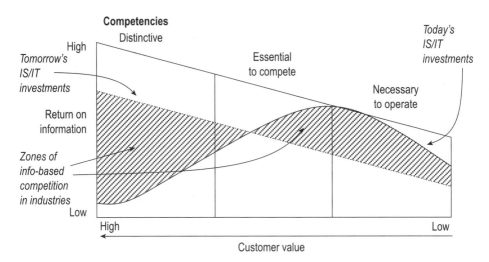

Figure 15.3: *Competitive value of tomorrow's IS/IT investments*

To compete in these zones of information-based competition, managers have three options:

- They can re-allocate their existing IS/IT budgets to spend less on the 'necessary to operate' and 'essential to compete' and more on distinctive competencies with information.
- They can allocate a larger proportion of new monies to the distinctive competencies that they must build.
- They can improve the relative distribution of IS/IT investments in order to spend incrementally more on distinctive competencies while reducing overall spending in the other two categories. In contrast to re-allocating existing monies in IS/IT, this option looks to future investment decisions.

Regardless of which investment option a company selects, smart firms have a significant opportunity in certain industries to invest over time in applications that provide their customers enhanced value and that differentiate their IS/IT portfolio from other companies in the same industry. Smart firms can also gain a cumulative competitive advantage by allocating their future information-based investments across all three types of competencies in the appropriate mix.

Should the software for a company's demand/supply chain be obtained as a package, or be custom-built?

The third issue related to BPR and IT projects in demand/supply chain management concerns the *decisions* that senior managers make. They can either purchase packages and configure them to business processes, or they can custom-build (or acquire) application systems that their competitors may not have. For many senior managers, the decision appears straightforward. Given the history of IS/IT project failures and delays in their companies or industries, most managers would rather buy packages from ERP vendors rather than build them internally or outsource development to an IS/IT consultant. Indeed, one clear barometer of this trend is the double-digit growth rates experienced by companies such as SAP, PeopleSoft, and Baan, which provide application packages to manufacturing and service companies in diverse industries. Therefore, at a glance the issue appears to be resolved: most companies should buy and install packages most of the time.

However, as with most situations, the reality is more interesting than it first appears. To address BPR and IS/IT projects in demand/supply chain today, managers have at least three options.

Option 1: outsource

The first option is to outsource key processes in the demand/supply chain to partner companies, who can manage the processes and the underlying information systems and technology more effectively than the company can do for itself. For example, as manufacturing companies have implemented just-in-time supplier delivery and just-in-time customer order fulfilment, they have increasingly *outsourced* their logistics and transport management to companies whose core competence supports these activities. Similarly, other companies such as leading clothes manufacturers and computer manufacturers have outsourced manufacturing functions to companies whose key competencies are managing these functions and the supporting IS/IT capabilities better than they can. In services industries, companies have used mergers and acquisitions to acquire the IS/IT competencies of their competitors (and divest those internal functions that have underperformed). In each of these cases, senior managers have evaluated which competencies should be retained internally and which could be developed externally using the distinctive competencies of other companies.

Option 2: acquire a package that enables management of the demand/supply chain to remain in-house

The same companies can also choose the second option: to tap the packages in support of demand/supply chain processes where managing these processes in-house is considered essential to compete. With this option, managers can choose either to acquire the 'best of breed' packages for demand/supply chain management from diverse IS/IT suppliers, or purchase 'integrated packages' from one supplier. To purchase the 'best of breed' companies must have the IS/IT capabilities to interface diverse packages and software from the vendors they believe offer the best application package that fits their needs. For the integrated packages, the company relies on one supplier, sacrificing dependence to gain the advantage of the integration of software and data that is possible only from the same supplier.

Option 3: use custom-built solutions

The third option is to custom-build or acquire software. This happens when the managers decide either that the application is so unique that it requires custom development, or when the uniqueness of the application provides distinctive advantage in the marketplace. Most companies no longer accept the rationale of building application software in-house just because the IS/IT function can do so. This is because with company histories of failed projects and underperformance fresh in their minds, senior managers may distrust the perceived capabilities of in-house IS/IT departments to deliver software systems on time and in budget with the required functionality. Thus, senior managers must examine carefully the reasons why application software should be custom-built or acquired.

For senior managers who have decided to retain control of the demand/supply chain processes inside their company, Figure 15.4 provides a framework for considering the options: acquiring packages or custom-building application systems for demand/supply chain management.

Managers should seek to employ packages in all administrative and demand/supply chain processes that are necessary to operate and add little or no customer value. In this case, some companies choose to use a version of the 80/20 rule. They adapt business processes to the functionality of the package so that 80–90% can be standardized on the software and only 10–20% configured to the unique needs of the business. Here managers seek to avoid BPR projects where customized software will be required, and to reduce both the overall costs and time of implementing packages where most of the functionality adds little or no direct value to the business (Davenport, 1998).

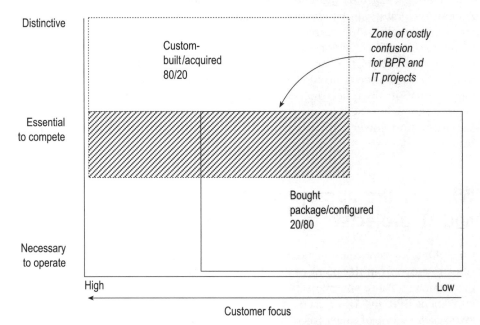

Figure 15.4: *Competitive value of custom-built and packaged software*

Where the applications software *can* support processes and information uses that provide distinctive competencies generating high customer perceived value, senior managers should look to custom-building these applications, or contract for their development on a proprietary basis. In companies where key customer-facing processes create unique customer value, there is a real risk of adopting packages for these processes and losing their distinctive advantage. In these cases, companies may be better off custom-building these applications and databases rather than standardizing processes, data and software on common industry packages.

Potential pitfalls

In the centre of these two options is the most difficult decision area: the *zone of costly confusion for BPR and IT projects*. In this decision zone, companies try to purchase packages and customize them extensively to the unique requirements of redesigned processes. Or they decide to custom-build an application that they need to compete, but which provides no distinctive competencies in their industry. In both cases, managers risk substantial time and resources undertaking complex BPR and IS/IT projects which may be essential to competing, but which actually *undermine* the drive for competitive advantage.

The trouble arises in these cases from two sides. For companies looking to implement ERP software packages, the problem involves excessively tailoring packaged software to the unique configuration of company processes – either existing or redesigned – with little or no competitive advantage in the industry. From the packaged software supplier side, the problem lies in the temptation to promote excessive tailoring of packaged software to generate implementation revenue for themselves or systems integrators. In either case, when these two difficulties converge, the results are costly, lengthy and complex BPR and IS/IT projects with very low probabilities for success. In effect, senior managers need to be clear about why they want to standardize applications that are essential to compete, in order to avoid costly customization since little or no competitive advantage comes from such projects. Without implementation discipline and clear purpose, companies that adopt packages and begin customizing them in major projects lose any advantages that might accrue to standardization, lower implementation costs, and shorter time to achieve expected results.

When is the appropriate time to implement BPR and IT projects?

I use the term 'time-to-implement' as an indicator of how long a BPR or IT project takes to move from the point of initial planning through its first phase of roll-out in the company. There are two sets of trade-offs associated with the time required to implement BPR and IT projects in demand/supply chain management. The first set involves the scope of each project in terms of complexity and scale versus the number of sites in the company where the project must be implemented. The second set of options focuses on the intensity of industry competition and how much time is available to a company to achieve the anticipated business results from such projects relative to its competitors in its industry.

Key issues when choosing the right time to implement major BPR and IT projects

There are no hard and fast rules for judging the time-to-implement for BPR and IT projects, but we can use the following time frames as guidelines:

short-term: 6 months–2 years
medium-term: 3–4 years
long-term: 5–7 years

Anticipated scope and complexity of the project

Managers must first address the anticipated scope and complexity of the BPR and IT projects for the company. In most companies, managers who wish to implement an integrated database across several functions in the supply chain, such as financial management, inventory management and manufacturing planning and control, are undertaking a project of higher complexity than, for example, implementing any one function on its own, such as financial management. The first project requires considerable cross-functional co-operation and co-ordination, but also agreement on data definitions and software functionality that the second project may not. Projects that require considerable BPR work in advance of, or concurrent with, the implementation of new software generally require more time to implement than projects where BPR is kept to a minimum for the sake of introducing the software more quickly. Thus, within the desired scope of BPR and IT projects, there are many trade-offs that require careful attention to the relationship between time-to-implement and the scope of the projects. Managers generally choose to implement projects on a modular basis rather than to go for grand, complex designs. However, the scope of what appears to be a moderately complex project may grow as companies seek to customize software packages to their processes, instead of adapting their processes to standard software packages.

Number and location of sites involved in the project

The second issue companies need to address is the number of locations or sites where the same software will need to be implemented within a company on a geographic basis. As Figure 15.5 suggests, the number of sites where the same project must be implemented, relative to its scope and complexity, will affect the time-to-implement BPR and IT projects. In this case, the variations among companies can be extreme.

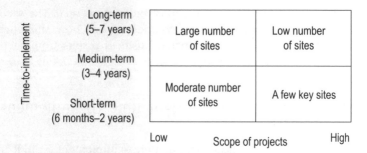

Figure 15.5: *Trade-offs for implementing BPR and IT projects*

CASE STUDY: THE IMPORTANCE OF THE NUMBER AND LOCATION OF SITES

An example of the effect of the number and location of sites is provided by a bulk chemical company in Western Europe that decided to implement SAP's ERP system on a regional basis rather than on a country-by-country basis. Although the project was complex, the fact that there was only one implementation of the software in the region shortened the time to implement from 5–7 years to 3–4 years. In contrast, an American pharmaceutical firm decided to implement SAP's ERP system in Western Europe on a country-by-country basis. The company estimated that it might take up to 5–7 years to complete the project unless all countries could be persuaded to adopt the same software, databases and process changes in the same way. For global implementation of demand/supply chain ERP software, the projects can vary from 5–7 years up to 8–10 years depending on the number of countries, regions or sites involved.

Thus, the trade-offs on time-to-implement, relative to the scope of projects and the number of sites involved, may affect the competitive value of such efforts. For projects that are necessary to compete, managers should aim to reduce the complexity of projects and the number of sites in which projects must be replicated. For example, if a company wants to implement a new payroll system, it may want to implement the system globally or regionally rather than on a country-by-country basis to reduce the time required. Similarly, the same company may want to implement a new distribution and logistics system that is essential to compete. In this case, it should consider putting the system in place on a regional basis to reduce the number of sites where the different project teams are implementing the same software.

Intensity of competition

The second set of time-to-implement trade-offs is associated with the intensity of competition in specific industries and the time it takes to capture the expected business benefits of BPR and IT projects related to demand/supply chain management. Figure 15.6 provides a framework for examining the options involved.

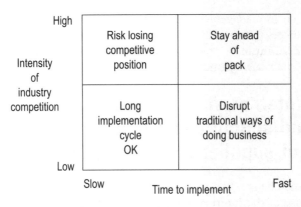

Figure 15.6: *Intensity of industry competition versus time to implement BPR and IT projects*

In companies facing 'moderate competition' (D'Aveni, 1994), managers can concern themselves with projects that improve the efficiency of the supply chain or the integrity of the information. This concern will move them from market forecasting, to production planning and control as well as financial management, inventory management and distribution. BPR and IT projects usually focus on achieving consistent data definitions among supply chain functions and removing unnecessary costs of paper handling, as well as old and inefficient software applications and labour. Firms facing moderate competition have the time to select and implement projects where defining common databases and definitions up front is critical to the level of process redesign and information integration that these firms seek to achieve for standardizing supply chain processes in multiple sites. Rarely do firms face moderate-to-low competition seeking to disrupt their industry through BPR and IT projects aimed at supply chain improvements.

In companies facing what D'Aveni calls 'hyper-competition', the intensity and speed

> **"In hyper-competition, managers must focus on BPR and IT projects whose business benefits can be achieved in the shortest time possible since the pace of competition does not permit their firms to implement long-term projects whose business benefits may not be captured in time"**

of competition requires them to focus on the demand side of the supply chain to create distinctive value with customers. How? Through improved customer information, order fulfilment and after-sales service. Such companies focus only secondarily on rationalizing those information management processes in manufacturing, inventory management and financial management that are essential to compete or necessary to operate. These companies must look for BPR and IT projects that can be implemented in the short-to-medium timeframes to either stay ahead of the competition or avoid losing their competitive position in their industry.

Time-to-implement represents a key dimension that senior managers can influence today to improve the competitive value of BPR and IT projects in support of demand/supply chain management. However, the scale of a company's business and its geographic diversity continue to have a significant impact on how companies can reap substantial business benefits from BPR and IT projects aimed at improving demand/supply chain management.

How will Internet, intranet and extranet use along the demand/supply chain influence customer, partner and supplier relationships?

The most dramatic change that occurred in demand/supply chain management in the 1990s was the use of the Internet and World Wide Web networks and technology to rethink customer, partner and supplier relationships and information management. Since 1995, senior managers in manufacturing and service companies have had to alter their perceptions of Internet use. It is no longer sufficient to simply have a corporate website. Neither is it sufficient to view Internet use as just an add-on to a company's current business approach – an alternative to providing information for customers and suppliers or another sales channel. For many senior managers, Internet technology is becoming a catalyst for rethinking the demand/supply chain of their industry and their positioning in networked-based competition with customers, partners and suppliers.

Increasingly, companies have begun to evaluate the pace and intensity of networked-based competition in their industry's demand/supply chain and the strategic value and capabilities of Net strategies, as Figure 15.7 illustrates.

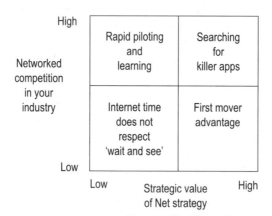

Figure 15.7: *Strategic value of net strategy in network-based competition*

In some industries, for example, companies have been able to achieve first mover advantages with direct, Internet-based models of selling their products. Dell, Cisco and Amazon are well-known companies that have achieved first-mover advantage with new direct models of doing business. They managed this at a time when the prevailing model in their respective industries was based on selling products through distributors and physical outlets.

In other cases, companies like GE have moved ahead of their competitors by identifying applications such as extranet use with suppliers. The GE Trade Processing Network today is not simply a successful example of using extranets with suppliers inside GE on a global scale. It has become a new line of business for GEIS and GE Capital to market to other networks of suppliers and manufacturers in diverse industries. Extranets for interacting online in secure, flexible network relationships with partners and suppliers are considered one of the 'killer applications' (Downes and Mui, 1998) capable of disrupting established ways of competing in demand/supply chains in many industries.

CASE STUDIES: DEVELOPING NET STRATEGIES FOR BUSINESSES WITHOUT *A KILLER APP*

For most companies who may not be in a position to develop a killer app in their industry or be a first mover, rapid piloting and learning from Internet experiments and trials seems to offer a viable path to developing Internet business capabilities and strategies. Companies can avoid the risk of being left behind by targeting initiatives that can derive both business benefits and valuable lessons. For example, the world's auto makers are now sponsoring many initiatives to learn how to sell cars and trucks over the Internet and how to integrate their dealer networks in direct selling and after-sales service. It was only three years ago that GM launched its first major website, developed by EDS; at the same time, it announced that its dealer network was sacrosanct. GM would never use its website to sell cars and trucks. During 1998, GM launched its second Internet site that now offered direct selling capabilities over the Internet. In between these two website launches, GM and every other major auto manufacturer witnessed the rapid build-up of direct selling of new and used cars through new start-ups such as Auto-by-Tel, AutoWeb and Microsoft's Carpoint. In just three short years, networked-based competition was redefined in the auto and truck retailing industry in North America. Today, auto manufacturers in Europe and Asia are seeing their markets for retailing transformed by similar direct marketing and selling start-ups.

Similarly, many other industries such as food and non-food retailing, banking, financial services, real estate, tourism, industrial machinery, special chemicals and freight delivery are experiencing the disruptive effects of innovative use of Internet technologies in networked-based competition more directly.

Internet time – rapid, real-time and continuous innovation – no longer respects 'wait and see' management attitudes even in traditional industries. Cemex, the very successful Mexican concrete company, is now applying the Burger King service model to the delivery of concrete – have it your way when you want it – to building sites in Mexico as well as other countries in which it operates. For established international concrete companies, disruptive Internet strategies are overturning decades of established practices between builders and concrete suppliers. Large numbers of cement trucks are no longer queued up at building sites in the morning to be poured during the day. Cemex dispatches trucks at customer request with the right grade and quantity of concrete at the right hour each day. Cemex's CEO believes that the use of Net strategies with customer and suppliers will catapult his company into global leadership in the concrete and building materials industry (Dolan, 1998).

SUMMARY

The new wave of BPR and IT in demand and supply chain management

New ways of managing relationships with suppliers, partners and customers in demand/supply chain networks are redefining how information and knowledge will create business value in manufacturing and service industries. While predictions about *where* Internet, extranet and intranet applications will most benefit demand/supply chain management are difficult to pin down, one trend is certain. *The substantial creative energies of new entrepreneurs and established companies in many industries are transforming demand/supply chains with Internet-based technologies and networks.*

BPR and IT will again undergo substantial change. Network-based competition will force firms to focus on rapid, flexible and agile business processes and IS/IT infrastructures to adapt in Internet time to networks of customers, partners and suppliers competing against other networks or clusters of companies.

BEST PRACTICE

Betting your company on 'hard' choices

Hard choices are decisions for which there are no clear successes or failures. Regardless of the decision taken, there are difficult risks, costs and unclear benefits associated with the outcome. For senior managers today, dealing with the new waves of BPR and IT in demand/supply chain management, the choices are difficult at best. There are no correct answers, best choices or optimum implementation paths.

In the previous era, re-engineering was associated with reducing costs and improving productivity through delayering, eliminating headcount, simplifying processes and automating what was left. The objectives were clear. A senior manager could judge and often count whether the company had succeeded or failed. Did we lower our costs, improve efficiency and become leaner? Choices were not easy during this period, but at least the expected outcomes were clearer.

Today, senior managers are confronting new waves of BPR and IT in demand/supply chain management as well as the use of the Internet in network-based competition locally, regionally and globally. In addition, in the run up to the Y2K problem, many senior managers invested in major and costly initiatives to redesign and automate demand/supply chain processes out of fear, uncertainty and doubt (FUDs in sales jargon). In all too many cases, they made their commitments with an unclear sense of the outcomes for their industry, their company or themselves. There has never been a time when BPR and IT are so closely associated with business performance and so risky in their potential to destroy shareholder value, profitability or market credibility.

In this environment, managers would do well to keep one decision rule for making hard choices in mind: try not to make decisions whose consequences cannot be undone or which will close off future options.

References

D'Aveni, R.A. (1994) *Hyper-Competition*. The Free Press, New York.

Davenport, T.H. (1998) Putting the Enterprise into the Enterprise System. *Harvard Business Review*, July–August, pp. 121-31.

Dolan, K.A. (1998) Cement Meets the Cyberworld. *Forbes Global Business and Finance*, June 15, pp. 1-9.

Downes, L. and Mui, C. (1998) *Unleashing the Killer App*. Harvard Business School Press, Boston, USA.

Poirier, C.C. and Reiter, S.E. (1996) *Supply Chain Optimization*. Berrett-Koehler, San Francisco, USA.

Vollmann, T.E. (1996) *The Transformation Imperative*. Harvard Business School Press, Boston, USA.

Vollmann, T.E., Berry, W.L. and Whybark, D.C. (1992) *Manufacturing Planning and Control Systems*. Irwin, Boston, USA.

Further reading

Clegg, C. et al. (1996) *The performance of Information Technology and the role of human and organizational factors*. Economic and Social Research Council UK.

Hoover, W.E., Tyreman, M., Westh, J. and Wollung, L. (1996) Order To Payment. *McKinsey Quarterly*, **1**, 38-49.

Slater, D. (1998) The Hidden Costs of Enterprise Software. *CIO Enterprise*, June 15, pp. 48–55.

White, J. (1996) Re-engineering Gurus Take Steps To Remodel Their Stalling Vehicles. *Wall Street Journal*, November 27, p. 1.

16

The IT Advantage: Competing Globally with Business Flexibility and Standardization

This chapter explores the challenge of developing the right balance between flexibility and standardization to enable companies to compete globally. In outlining the issues that senior managers must face in finding the right balance – and advantage – between flexibility and standardization over time, **Donald Marchand** also presents five approaches to going local, regional and global at the same time using IS/IT.

CASE STUDY: HEWLETT PACKARD'S IT ADVANTAGE

In the ten years from 1987 to 1997, Hewlett Packard (HP) significantly reduced the cost structure of their global business. Sales, General and Administrative (SG&A) expenses fell from 28% of turnover to 17%, whilst IT spending fell from 6% of turnover to under 3%. They achieved this with a corresponding increase in total revenues from $5 billion to $40 billion and maintaining a head count of about 100 000 personnel.

Such companies position themselves to operate high-capacity global networks, and achieve success through effective global management that is responsive to - and supportive of - business units. Worldwide networks and an IT infrastructure that is geared to effective information sharing, promoting best practice and allowing a rapid response to implementing vital changes has strengthened HP's position considerably. For example, Hewlett Packard bills all IT costs (including employees' e-mails) to the business unit managers, so as to encourage awareness of costs. Also, the culture of information-sharing across business units encourages the exchange of best practice expertise and knowledge between business units.

Global IT infrastructures unburden business units, allowing them to concentrate on value-creation and promoting growth. In an age when quality and value are needed across business units, companies like Hewlett Packard have found that combining business flexibility with IS and IT standardization is a key to success in coping with rapid industry and business change.

Overview

Companies that operate globally have a range of options for balancing business flexibility with standardization. Finding the right balance between business flexibility and standardization affects how a company is able to create business value with customers by being flexible in delivering its services and products to customers locally, regionally or globally. However, at the same time the company must manage its business processes and infrastructure to reduce demands on working capital, by adopting 'common' processes and IS or building capabilities to leverage the company's human knowledge and information across markets, time zones and geography.

In addition, implementing the right balance between business flexibility and standardization is not a one-time choice for most companies but a journey influenced by the product and service mix that a company delivers and the business processes and information required to deliver these products and services to customers and markets. Most companies begin their journey by establishing themselves in many local markets and focusing product and service delivery on local customers. Over time, companies establish relationships with customers or develop brands on a regional and global basis which require business processes and information to be managed regionally and globally, not just locally. In other cases, companies such as Procter & Gamble sell essentially the same products or services globally and require business processes and information sharing to be global as well.

On the one hand, business flexibility provides business unit or product managers in global companies with the freedom of choice to decide how to tailor their products and services, as well as their demand/supply chain processes, to the unique needs of local markets. As long as these managers can operate profitably by creating customer value in their business unit (BU) or country, they decide how their business processes, IS and IT infrastructures are configured and managed.

However, business standardization reflects the concurrent need to find ways of reducing the operating costs of the business or product units by seeking to 'share' best business practices or adopt 'common' business processes, IS and IT infrastructure wherever feasible. In addition, business standardization may be necessary for a company to leverage its human knowledge across the business and product units, or to share information and collaborate on projects for the benefit of the global company.

At the epicentre of senior management decisions about the appropriate business architecture for their global company are their perceptions about how information and knowledge should be employed in the company, and the appropriate role and investments in IS and IT infrastructure. Underinvest in IS and IT and the global company lacks the capabilities to compete in a networked business environment where speed, flexibility and quality of information sharing is critical; over-invest and the global company raises its operational costs and therefore its use of working capital.

> "Companies need to achieve *optimal investment* in IS and IT to compete in current business environments: speed, flexibility and quality of information-sharing are essential"

It also engages in frustrating efforts to implement business standardization which is resisted by the very business units that shared or common IS and IT systems are supposed to benefit.

This chapter will present five approaches to balancing business flexibility and standardization employed by global businesses, focusing on the criteria that general managers must consider in finding the right balance between business flexibility and IS/IT standardization.

Finding the right balance between business flexibility and IS/IT standardization

Approach 1: pursue flexibility and IS/IT standardization country-by-country, business-unit-by-business-unit

At some time in their history most global businesses operated with this approach. The business is organically grown country-by-country or BU-by-BU with a focus on local autonomy and flexibility. Since the company produces, delivers and sells products locally, the key processes of a company and its business information systems (BIS) such as manufacturing, distribution, marketing and sales, as well as its functional information systems (FIS), such as the general ledger, accounting, payroll and purchasing, are also developed and deployed locally.

Not surprisingly, the company configures its IT infrastructure for data, document, voice, video and mobile networking to support the local business with little need to achieve any synergies across country units or product lines.

Strengths of this approach

The strengths of this approach stem from the flexibility that country or BU managers have to configure their business architecture to the local market and customers. Either the country or BU management team perceives IS/IT as a 'support' function where costs can be minimized, or they treat IS/IT as a 'service' providing valued information services to the local company. Corporate management in such companies focuses on financial performance, management of brands internationally or perhaps centralized R&D, but rarely on IS/IT concerns since these are included in the management responsibilities of local managers.

Potential weaknesses

There are basically three weaknesses to this approach:

- The high costs of doing business globally since BIS and FIS are duplicated in each BU.
- Incompatible systems, IT infrastructure and information from BU to BU.
- Poor information-sharing and communications about customers across BUs.

These weaknesses surface in companies in three ways. Some companies need to reduce the costs of duplicate functional or business processes and IS/IT in local BUs, but are frustrated in their efforts by incompatible IT infrastructures and a melange of internally developed or externally tailored software. Each BU manager defends his BU's uniqueness even in functional areas such as payroll systems, general ledgers and accounting.

> **"Increasingly, companies need to deal with global customers and suppliers requiring co-ordination and information-sharing across business units. Companies can find themselves hampered by business units both unwilling to share information and with procedures that prove incompatible across business units"**

For companies that want to share standard financial reporting measures across all BUs, such efforts are stymied by inconsistent data definitions, incompatible databases or applications software, and local management practices. Finally, for companies that need to deal with global customers or suppliers requiring co-ordination and information-sharing across business units, a range of factors hampers these companies. These include local unwillingness to share customer information with other BUs, incompatible e-mail and messaging networks, and locally organized customer files whose quality varies with the customer relationships of the local company sales team.

Common complaints cited by managers in such companies include the following:

We have 156 of everything – general ledgers, payroll systems, data centres – regardless of value added to the company or of costs of doing business!

Our BU managers do not share best practices across BUs: we have lots of reinvention of BIS, FIS and IT in our company.

How many different spreadsheet packages, e-mail systems and operating systems does a global business need: when is 'flexibility' counter-productive?

To confront the weaknesses of the highly decentralized BU by BU approach, corporate managers in global companies have had to challenge the local authority and prerogatives of the country managers, or 'kings' as they are often called, without losing the benefits of a locally focused company. During the late 1980s and early 1990s, these concerns led companies to pursue the second approach to finding the right balance between business flexibility and IS/IT standardization.

Approach 2: realigning business and functional IS and IT infrastructure from the corporate centre

Recognizing that local BUs tend to concentrate on short-term business results and local operating concerns, corporate managers of global companies appointed senior IS/IT managers at the corporate centre with several important responsibilities. First, the chief information officer (CIO) was responsible for monitoring trends in the business and the IS/IT industry which could be opportunities for BUs to develop shared or common systems. Secondly, the CIO needed to develop and maintain standards across operating units for voice, video, data and mobile networking to enable regional and global communications and information sharing. Thirdly, the CIO was charged with lowering the costs of operating voice and data networks as well as consolidating data centres among each operating unit through 'shared services' initiatives.

While typically the corporate director of IS/IT reported to the chief financial officer, their operating authority was based on persuasion, not top-down mandate. They had to build coalitions among local BUs for setting companywide IS/IT directions and standards. Rarely could they compel a local BU managing director to adhere to a decision with which they disagreed since the BU manager could appeal, usually successfully, to their authority and prerogative to run their BU as they deemed appropriate as long as the BU's financial targets were met.

Strengths of this approach

There are three strengths to this approach:

- Companies that operate in a very decentralized business culture can maintain their dominance, but at the same time can also work towards shared BIS, FIS and IT synergies enabled, but not mandated, by the corporate centre.
- Some companies are successful at reducing the overall costs of IT operations by reducing the number of data centres and economizing on voice and data networks locally and globally.

- Awareness develops from the corporate centre about IS/IT best practices that can be used by local BUs.

Potential weaknesses

These strengths are often counterbalanced with three significant weaknesses in this approach. First, decisions take too long to make. A corporate director of IT complained that "it took us six years to reduce the number of general ledgers in the company from 160 to 30!"

Secondly, in most companies, IS/IT continues to be perceived as a 'cost centre' where there is continuous pressure from senior corporate managers to lower the cost of IT by reducing local BU service levels. In one company, the CEO was proud of saying that IS/IT costs were less than 1% of sales and would stay that way: "We are not in the IT business, but in manufacturing!"

Finally, the development of IS/IT standards is driven by committees of BU managers and corporate staff who require long decision cycles which often result in preventing rather than facilitating the adoption of IS/IT standards for networking, hardware, operating systems and common PC packages.

Approach 3: managing a global IT infrastructure in a decentralized business application environment

The third approach represents a hybrid between the other four approaches. The first two rely predominantly on managers of BUs deciding how IS/IT should be managed in a global company. The final two depend on strong top-down, regional or corporate leadership to implement. The third approach tries to balance two sets of needs.

Strengths of this approach

This approach first aims to meet the needs of a *bottom-up business culture*, where flexibility in deploying BU specific processes and systems is needed for growth and innovation. Secondly, it tries to satisfy the need for *company-wide synergies* for reducing costs of operating functional processes and systems as well as maintaining a transparent, interconnected global IT infrastructure that permits anyone in the company to communicate with anyone else, in any place, at any time.

With this third approach, decisions over BISs are specific to each BU, enabling BUs to tailor systems to their key business processes to maximize growth and profits. However, decisions about IT infrastructure and FISs are made on a global basis through a process known as *managed consensus*, where open debate is encouraged up to a point when a top-down decision is made and local BU managers are expected to implement the decision.

The underlying assumption is that FISs and IT infrastructure should be managed to help the company reduce its costs and working capital needs wherever possible. An example of this approach is the steps taken by Hewlett Packard, mentioned earlier. This approach has four strengths.

1. It provides the company with a transparent voice, data and video IT infrastructure on a pay-as-you-go basis. All IT costs are billed to the BU managers. The company's senior managers believe that every employee should be aware of the costs of doing business.
2. Although BU managers still make BIS decisions, the company's culture is marked by a strong spirit to beg, borrow and steal best practices from one BU to another. This culture promotes the transfer of best BIS practices from one unit to another without top-down decisions.
3. A global IT infrastructure provides a platform for the business units to use as they grow and change, without reinventing FIS and IT infrastructures each time. BUs can focus on creating value in the business rather than on maintaining functional systems and IT infrastructure.
4. This approach attempts, wherever possible, to maximize high levels of business flexibility with high levels of business and IT standardization, with the aim of promoting growth and value creation in the business and lower costs.

Potential weaknesses

The third approach to balancing business flexibility and standardization does have its weaknesses. It requires the development of a company culture of managed consensus, where global priorities are balanced with local business needs. In a company with a very decentralized, country-by-country culture, this may take many years. Secondly, the approach creates a powerful IT infrastructure function on a global basis which must balance IT standardization with the constantly changing needs of its local BUs. The dangers are twofold: either the IT people will fall behind the rapidly changing needs of the BUs, or the BUs will outsource the IT infrastructure to external providers and thus move back from the third to the first approach.

Approach 4: defining a regional approach to the business and IS/IT infrastructure

The fourth approach to finding the right balance between business flexibility and IS/IT standardization represents a clear move to a *top-down regional focus*. In companies that take this approach, the intent of senior managers in these companies is, for example, to treat Europe as one country (thus moving away from the country-based model).

These global companies primarily perceive their customer supply chain as regional, rather than country-specific, and want to align their key processes, information management, IS and IT infrastructures to reflect regional leadership, direction and operations, rather than more fragmented and costly local operations. These companies may be in business-to-business industries such as bulk chemicals, where the markets are more regional than global, or in fast-moving consumer goods industries, such as consumer electronics, where retail chains expect their suppliers to operate on a regional rather than purely local basis.

Strengths of this approach

The strengths of this approach are twofold. First, regional operations allow these companies to reduce costs by adopting standard BIS and FIS across regions, rather than within each country. To the extent that these companies adopt common

> **"Where regional management of information-sharing and communication are advantageous in order to respond to regional market diversity, a company should align its people, culture and processes to mirror their markets and customers"**

processes and systems, they save on the time implementing BIS and FIS since they have to install only one system in each region. Secondly, these companies align their people, cultures and processes to operate in a regional mode, closely mirroring their markets and customers. Treating Europe as one country accommodates specific regional concerns and business climates that are different from the North American or Asian regions. Thus, the company can manage information sharing and communication on a regional basis to respond to local market diversity.

Potential weaknesses

To work successfully, this approach needs considerable top-down management. Managers in such companies speak about 'breaking' the country dominance and displacing the 'country kings'. Clearly, considerable changes in company culture and power distribution among managers are required. But this is only one of the weaknesses; another is that the regional focus takes a long time to implement – in some companies up to ten years. These companies must align their whole business system to reflect the regional focus, which requires a consolidation of organization, authority and culture in one consistent direction. If markets change quickly, such commitments to business regionalism may be difficult to change rapidly.

Approach 5: globalization of the business and IS/IT infrastructure

The fifth approach simply extends the fourth from the regional to the global level. In this case, a global company has moved from perhaps approach 1 or 2 in the 1980s to approach 4 in the late 1980s and 1990s. It is now moving again from approach 4 to the globalization of its business processes and systems.

Companies in this category possess very strong top-down cultures. They operate in global markets where, for example, selling their products in France is basically the same as selling their products in South-East Asia. Such companies want to roll out a product in the US market and three months later in the Chinese market. To do so requires consistent and accurate information for global decision-making, common processes, information and systems to reduce costs, eliminate time delays and minimize complexity. In addition, new business and functional information systems have to be implemented only once worldwide, rather than in every region and country. This approach saves money in FIS and BIS implementations as well as in the deployment of one standard, global IT infrastructure.

Strengths of this approach

What are the strengths of this approach? The first is the complete alignment of the company's business strategy, culture, processes, information, systems and IT infrastructure worldwide. Assuming common markets, products and brands worldwide, such a company is in an excellent position to maximize profitability and business opportunity globally. Business flexibility, in the sense mentioned here, is not important, since business value is created with global brands. Cost economies and productivity are critical, especially in low-margin and highly competitive industries such as fast-moving consumer goods. In these cases, the speed and effectiveness of doing business globally are facilitated by worldwide IT infrastructure as well as common business and functional systems.

Potential weakness

There is, however, a weakness in this approach: the necessary business uniformity and consistency require a strong company culture with top-down leadership. Again, the good news is that the whole company has a consistent way of doing business, which is also a potential vulnerability if business conditions or markets change to require a more flexible model of global business operations.

GLOBALIZATION DECISIONS — SEVEN KEY PRINCIPLES

"How can our group of 20 diversified companies provide flexibility for each operating company to grow and innovate and, at the same time, reduce administrative overheads and employ information technology effectively across the group?"
  - *Chairman of one of the largest industrial groups in the Asia–Pacific region*

"Our business focuses on providing local services to customers in 22 countries. Will our biggest foreign competitor enter our region with a business infrastructure that relies on 22 country operations? No way!"
  - *President of the largest division of one of the world's leading elevator companies*

"We must provide our country markets with high flexibility to operate effectively on a local basis. Yet, to compete with global brands against regional and global competitors, we must adopt common processes in our supply chains and leverage IT on a global, regional and local basis. The challenge is not if, but how to do so."
  - *CFO of one of the world's largest food product companies*

  How is it that some companies have been able to achieve the benefits of local flexibility to promote market responsiveness and global standardization to achieve lower costs simultaneously? Consider the following seven principles which have guided the decisions of senior executives of global companies in North America, Western Europe and the Asia–Pacific Region.

1. *Differentiate between business and functional uses of IT* - *the intent here is to distinguish between business information systems, which create direct business value in sales and services, from functional information systems (FIS) which serve accounting, HR and purchasing functions.*

2. *Globalization of IS/IT does not mean blanket centralization* - *rather than deciding whether to centralize or decentralize, the goal should be to determine the right balance between systems needed to operate locally, regionally and globally.*

3. *Globalizing the IT infrastructure and functional information systems make the company more rather than less flexible* - *within the context of 'managed consensus', managers need to define which business issues demand flexibility and which are support or non-value-adding operations.*

4. *Optimize the overall cost structure; don't simply lower the operating costs of each business unit* - *many BU managers are extremely possessive about their resources. This situation is fuelled by the fact that in some companies years of fighting for services from central data centres has instilled a strong resistance among local BU managers to consideration of the 'global picture'.*

5. *Implementing the virtual corporation requires more rather than less IS/IT standardization* - *however the virtual corporation is defined, one theme dominates: that knowledge and information are shared in many forms within the company and between customers, suppliers and partners. This growing need for human networking and partnership requires carefully constructed IS/IT standards. A worldwide approach to IT infrastructure provides a platform for competing in a more virtual and networked world. Better IT infrastructure is the glue that holds the company together when decentralized BUs co-operate to serve customers better.*

6. *Maintaining the right balance between business flexibility and standardization requires corporate discipline and empowerment of business units* - *business and functional managers will sometimes disagree, as will local BU managers, corporate/global managers, and IS managers working in BUs and IT managers supporting a global IT infrastructure. Successful companies manage these inevitable creative tensions, and managers must know that once decisions are reached they must be implemented swiftly and effectively.*

7. *Balancing business flexibility and standardization is a journey, not a destination* - *successful companies realize that setting the right balance is a long-term journey of continuous learning and improvement rather than short-term reactions to corporate crises.*

BENCHMARKING

Which is the best approach to business flexibility and IS/IT standardization?

Managers of global businesses should use three criteria to determine which of the five approaches to balancing business flexibility and standardization is right for their company.

1. Which approach allows our company to create business value and lower overall costs at the same time?

Does your approach to managing business flexibility on a local, regional or global basis permit you to lower operating and working capital costs and simultaneously create business value in markets? Sadly, the answer to these questions in many companies is 'We don't know!' This is particularly the case in companies operating with approaches 1 or 2. These companies assume that local flexibility leads to value creation, but often do not know at what price in Sales, General and Administrative (SG&A) expenses, working capital use across the value chain, or their IS/IT investments.

2. Does IT infrastructure permit your company to be more rather than less flexible in responding rapidly to business change?

In many companies today, business changes require rapid shifts in strategies, processes, products, markets and customers. To what extent do these business changes also require the reinvention of FIS and IT infrastructure at the same time?

Companies using approaches 1 and 2 have no standards to rely on when business process and system changes are required. Companies using approaches 4 and 5 have IT infrastructure standards, but are less flexible in their ability to change business processes and systems, since their business cultures are uniform and consistent across regions and globally. Companies employing approach 3 stabilize FIS and IT infrastructures over time so that BU managers and corporate leaders can focus their attention on implementing changes in business processes and systems. Changes in and across the BUs can be made more rapidly than companies using approaches 1 and 2, since the BUs can rely on global functional information systems and worldwide voice, video and data networks to support the new ways of doing business.

3. Does your company's IS/IT infrastructure enable your employees and managers to share information and communicate instantaneously worldwide?

This criterion addresses an increasingly vital concern in the global, knowledge-based economy. Even the most localized of BUs today have to use and share information globally. Most global companies are beginning to use World Wide Web technology to manage information internally (intranets), to communicate externally with customers and shareholders (Internet) and to exchange information with suppliers, dealers and partners (extranets). As these new business applications of networking technology and information management evolve, managers of global companies are challenged to think of their company as an extended business network that includes customers, suppliers, employees, partners and even competitors. These issues are explored in greater detail in Chapter 17.

SUMMARY

The IT advantage: competing globally with business flexibility and standardization

Finding the right balance between business flexibility and IT standardization is essential. If achieved, it can provide a significant *business advantage* on which to build a dynamic, information-sharing organization; if it is not achieved, costs, flexibility, synergies, knowledge and ultimately competitiveness can all suffer. However, achieving this balance is made much harder when the need to compete locally, regionally and globally is overlaid on to the range of other business considerations.

Table 16.1 provides an overview of the five approaches outlined in this chapter, which are aimed at achieving the right balance to support global competition with flexibility and standardization.

Table 16.1: *Overview of the five approaches aimed at achieving the right balance to support global standardization*

Possible approach	Strengths	Weaknesses
1. **Pursue flexibility and IS/IT standardization country-by-country, BU-by-BU**	• Country and BU managers are able to configure their organization according to the local market and customers. • Corporate (central) managers are able to focus on issues other than IT as these are the responsibility of local managers.	• Global business costs are much higher as costs of BIS and FIS can be duplicated many times over. • IT systems and infrastructure are incompatible, again leading to higher costs, reduced communication, or both. • Poor information-sharing across BUs.
2. **Realigning business and functional IS and IT infrastructure from the corporate centre**	• The corporate centre can *enable* business units to exploit synergies and share business and functional information systems. • Some costs can be reduced as economies are achieved. • The corporate centre develops an awareness of IS/IT best practice, which is then more widely disseminated.	• Greater bureaucracy can result and consequently decisions take too long, reducing flexibility. • If IS/IT is perceived as a cost centre, there can be pressure from the centre to reduce service levels to local BUs (sometimes quite arbitrarily).

Table 16.1: *Continued*

Possible approach	Strengths	Weaknesses
3. **Managing a global IT infrastructure in a decentralized business environment**	• The IT infrastructure is provided on a pay-as-you-go basis. IT costs are billed to BU managers and there is an increased awareness of costs at the point where they are incurred. • The managers of BUs make decisions relating to information systems, but the company's decentralized culture promotes the spread of best practice. • A global IT infrastructure provides a platform for business units to use as they grow: therefore businesses can focus on creating value rather than maintaining systems. • Business flexibility is maintained with high levels of IT standardization; as a result value creation and growth benefit and costs are lowered.	• A company culture of 'managed consensus' is required, with the ability to balance global priorities with local business needs. • The time needed to establish this delicate balance and company culture can be years. • The central IT infrastructure needs to be standardized on a global basis whilst also meeting the constantly evolving needs of local BUs.

4. **Defining a regional approach to the business and IS/IT infrastructure**

   - Costs are reduced as the regional focus allows companies to reduce costs by adopting standard BIS and FIS across regions (rather than countries).
   - Time is saved and information is standardized as one system in one region needs to be implemented, rather than several (or many) across a number of countries.
   - People, cultures and processes are aligned to operate in regional mode, often mirroring closely the markets and customers that they are serving.

   - Considerable top-down management is needed to make this system work effectively.
   - Changes in company culture and management authority are needed.
   - A regional focus can take a long time to implement (often because of resistance from entrenched country managers).
   - Because of the time required to change to a regional focus, it can be difficult to adapt quickly to market changes at the same time.

5. **Globalization of the business and IS/IT infrastructure**

   - The business's strategy, culture, processes, information, systems and IT infrastructure worldwide are completely aligned. This matters where markets, products and brands are global and business flexibility is largely unimportant.
   - Cost economies and productivity – often crucial in these types of business (such as fast-moving consumer goods) – are greatly enhanced.
   - The worldwide business infrastructure facilitates speed and effectiveness.

   - Business uniformity and consistency are emphasized; this requires a strong company culture and top-down leadership.
   - The system is less suited to changes in business conditions and markets, where a more flexible approach to local operations may be needed.

BEST PRACTICE

Competing globally with business flexibility and standardization

What approach to a global IS/IT infrastructure will maximize digital business relationships across time zones and regions, while still providing flexibility to adapt to local markets and BUs and respond to rapid business changes?

When considering which approach will prepare companies to operate in the global networked environment, it is useful to consider that:

- Companies using approaches 1 and 2 (pursue flexibility and IS/IT standardization country-by-country, BU-by-BU, and realigning business and functional IS and IT infrastructure from the corporate centre) will find it difficult to operate IT infrastructures that require global management and co-ordination.
- Companies adopting approaches 4 and 5 (defining a regional approach to the business and IS/IT infrastructure and globalization of the business and IS/IT infrastructure) will find it easier to adapt to new networking changes.
- Companies using the third approach of managing a global IT infrastructure in a decentralized business application environment may be best positioned to operate high-capacity global networks, and still respond to BU needs for internal and external information sharing. These companies can leverage their experiences with operating worldwide networks and IT infrastructure as well as a company culture focused on sharing best practices and implementing business changes rapidly.

Which approach is the best? The answer is the approach that helps you manage a global company with maximum customer focus and business flexibility, while at the same time optimizing the costs of working capital and standardizing administrative functions and IS/IT infrastructures that do not create direct business value.

17

Building E-Commerce Capabilities: the Four-Net Challenge

Applying the right mix of information and knowledge is an essential prerequisite for an effective e-commerce strategy. In this concluding chapter, **Donald Marchand** outlines the business and information management challenges faced by managers. The seven principles affecting the success of e-commerce are analysed, together with the four key business uses of e-commerce. The chapter concludes with a practical guide to developing effective e-commerce strategies.

CASE STUDIES: BUILDING COMPETITIVE ADVANTAGE WITH E-COMMERCE

*The power of the Internet to build competitive advantage is matched only by its power to threaten and erode profitability if rivals use it against you first. For example, the online bookstore **Amazon.com** is redefining their industry in terms of what is sold, how it is sold and the level of support and service that accompanies it. Amazon enables you to download and keep entire chapters, they provide detailed reviews, and they will keep you informed of new titles in your preferred areas of interest. In terms of their own internal operations, they carry five times as many books as a conventional book-store, with greatly reduced inventory costs. As a result, many other booksellers are establishing their own operations to exploit the potential of e-commerce, but they inevitably encounter the problems (and benefits) of being follower rather than a first-mover. Critics claim that despite their phenomenal growth and reputation Amazon.com is not as profitable as smaller bookselling operations, but this misses a key point. E-commerce offers promise and provides a threat in equal measure, and this reason is so significant that large booksellers, tiny ones and even entirely new ones, are now using the Internet to compete.*

Although the Internet often has the highest profile, the impact of e-commerce is not limited to what can be done on the Internet and Web. Extranets, intranets and industrynets are also elements of e-commerce that are continuing to gain in significance: their commercial potential is being exploited now, often in ways that are almost surreptitious. An example is the 1996 European Football Championship held in England, where an intranet established by the organizers helped to provide 6000 journalists with 2500 pages of information. This provided details of 368 players from 16 countries as well as information about matches. Selected pages were also downloaded on to the Euro 96 Internet site, and the overall effect was to stimulate and sustain enormous interest in the tournament resulting in success for the organizers. Not only were football supporters happy, but commercial partners such as broadcasting companies and sponsors were also pleased with a system that set new standards for international sporting events.

Overview

'To Dell or Be Delled', 'To Amazon or Be Amazoned' – these are the challenging, almost menacing, watchwords of business change that general managers must address in the new era of the Internet and e-commerce. On one side are the new entrants – the Net billionaires – taking aim at the successful business models of the pre-Internet era. In order to disrupt established ways of business in traditional industries, they move fast, stay flexible and use leverage in Internet time. The stories of Internet success and rivalries have achieved almost mythical proportions: Amazon versus Barnes and Noble, Microsoft's Encarta versus Encyclopedia Britannica, Dell versus Compaq, Charles Schwab versus Merrill Lynch, and AutoWeb, Carpoint and Auto-by-Tel versus established car companies such as GM, Ford and DaimlerChrysler.

On the other side are the successful, established companies of the pre-Internet era.

Their managers must learn a new vocabulary of business: *infomediaries*, *intranets*, *extranets* and *virtual communities*. More importantly, they must learn the new ways of doing business in their industries that have been outlined in previous chapters: engage in one-to-one Internet selling, exploit virtual value chains, build customer loyalty, employ 'direct' models of doing business with customers, and search for 'killer applications' to achieve competitive advantage. For these managers the challenge is to build their e-commerce capabilities fast enough to exploit the opportunities presented by the new business era. They must exploit their established positions before new entrants claim either first mover advantage in their industry, as Amazon did to Barnes and Noble, or position themselves between the customers and suppliers as new and threatening intermediaries in their industry, which is what AutoWeb and Auto By Tel did to the established car manufacturers and their dealers in the US.

While the era of e-commerce may not totally change the conventional ways of doing business, managers in established companies must recognize that there is a new game with different, if not entirely new, principles of doing business. In this Chapter we will:

- Focus on the seven key principles of e-commerce business that managers must consider as essential to learning and business strategy in the new era.
- Outline the four main ways to exploit Internet technology inside and between companies and consumers, developing the right mix of approaches. (I call these approaches the four nets: Internet, intranets, extranets and industrynets.)
- Explain the key questions and concerns that managers should address as they develop four-net strategies in their companies.

The seven principles of e-commerce

The Internet and e-commerce challenge managers to think in different ways about their businesses. Each day, managers are bombarded with spectacular and abundant news about success stories, new Initial Public Offerings (IPOs) with meteoric stock values, young entrepreneurs in their twenties and thirties who have made their mark almost overnight in the world of e-commerce. A new world is emerging and the message is clear: either get on board or you will be left at the station.

However, behind these exhortations to managerial action is a curious lack of practical, working principles for making sense of e-commerce. What key ideas drive

> **"Seven fundamental principles determine the way that business is carried out on the Internet – and the results that are achieved"**

e-commerce? How does a manager get started? To address these key questions, I have identified seven principles of e-commerce. They come not only from the experience of managers who work in e-commerce, but also from the growing managerial literature on the implications of e-commerce for established businesses and industries. I believe that when managers try to understand what e-commerce will mean to their companies, these seven principles influence both the context in which to look for clarity, and their mindsets.

Principle 1: the Internet adds a new perception of business time

In business, people experience time in many ways. Some global shifts in business occur over decades. A good example is the evolution of the Internet itself and the impact of IT on industries. Other industry shifts in products and services evolve over five to ten years – key products appear and dominate an industry for years or decades. Company-specific planning and budgeting cycles range from one to three years.

Why are people obsessed with time? If for no other reason than because time signifies mortality. We need to get things done or make things happen in time. A curious feature of Internet time is that it is basically perceptual, rather than objective.

First, while Internet time signifies many things to different people, one leading feature is this: the Internet is experienced in the present. Everyday. Real time, any time, now, $24 \times 7 \times 365$, local and global at the same time. Across time zones, geography and business activities, Internet time is always *now*. The Internet is always 'on' somewhere in the world; like foreign exchange rates and stock valuations, business activity on the Internet is always happening. Opportunities are won and lost minute-to-minute, globally.

Second, the Internet compresses time and action into shorter and shorter intervals. Since change occurs simultaneously with actions taken on the World Wide Web, everything is urgent on the Internet. Feedback on actions taken or comments made on the Web comes immediately, from anyone logged on to the Internet. Once a company is on the Web, it participates in a world of unrelenting urgency where business strategy and action are compressed into today's activities – but each today is 24 hours, and the urgency to participate is always high.

Third, Internet time requires managers to respond rapidly to both the important and the trivial simultaneously. If business activities are always in real time and urgent, then distinguishing between what is important on the Web and what is trivial is hazardous at best. Dissatisfied customers on the Web do not complain to neighbours about your company; they complain to hundreds and thousands of consumers through chat rooms, bulletin boards and their own websites. Similarly, competition on the Web is fast and observable. One company's innovation on the Web is it's competitors' chance to copy it or counter quickly. The strategies of companies on the Web are transparent to their customers and competitors alike. The result of all this? Today's competitive advantage is tomorrow's competitive necessity.

So Internet time introduces a new perception of business time as always 'on', urgent, and demanding a rapid response. The challenge for managers is to reconcile their industry, company and personal perceptions of time with the perceived reality of Internet time.

Principle 2: Internet business learning is continuous, evolutionary and rapid

The metaphor for learning and innovation on the Internet is the process of designing, releasing and improving software in the IT industry. Software products like Microsoft Windows are never developed once with 100% of the features and quality required by customers, launched into the market until the product cycle matures, and either withdrawn or redesigned from the bottom up to be launched again or replaced some years in the future. The standard product design, release and improvement cycle applicable to cars, insurance, banking, consumer goods and industrial products does not apply to software.

Software features are tested continuously in the marketplace with groups of customers, and are never considered complete or correct. Software products are released with known quality defects or 'bugs', since companies want to be first in the market with their products. They assume that bugs will be corrected with later versions. Software companies aim for modular releases of their products rather than for grand designs, since customer acceptance of the product is always uncertain until the product is used. Thus, learning and doing in the software industry are compressed into single acts that evolve continuously with customer interactions and the responses of competitors. From a quality perspective, products are never perfect. With new products and new versions of established products, being first to market is critical.

For managers in established companies in many service and manufacturing industries, the cycle of Internet learning with products and services is foreign to the way they normally consider designing, releasing and improving their products. In their minds, being first to market is always good – but not with defective products. Version management is fine, but versions must be well-planned and tested thoroughly before release. Product strategies must be formulated clearly before products are designed and released to the market. Companies should design products right the first time.

These accepted principles of product innovation in established companies are now being actively violated, not only in the IT industry with PCs, printers and cell phones, but also in more traditional industries such as automobiles, insurance, banking and retailing. It is in these established industries where Internet learning is influencing the cycle of product design, release and testing – try it, revise it and, most of all, do it rapidly!

Principle 3: e-commerce requires creative destruction and construction

In the traditional marketplace, the *content* of the business (what it sells), the *context* of a business (the place where it does business with customers), and the *infrastructure* of the business (the physical, people, information and technological resources required to do the business) are highly integrated and difficult to separate. In the market space, the world of e-commerce, it is possible to reconfigure the content, context and infrastructure of the business so that the accepted business model of the company and the industry is fundamentally redefined (Rayport and Sviokla, 1996).

CASE STUDY: THE POWER OF THE INTERNET TO REDEFINE ENTIRE INDUSTRIES

An example of an industry being fundamentally redefined is the retail banking industry today. Here, the evolution of an integrated business model dependent on a mix of branch offices that promote products, and direct channels of ATM, phone and Internet banking, is about to be threatened by a new model that fundamentally reconfigures the content, context and infrastructure of banking and financial services. Over the last decade, most progressive bank managers were pleased if their banks redefined the branch as a sales office rather than as a transaction processing office. Bankers worked hard to develop alternative direct channels through ATMs, phone and now Internet banking, that would give their customers access to bank services at lower transaction costs to the bank. The progressive bank managers focused on lowering the costs of doing banking, increasing direct services and developing their branches into sales and services offices. They considered themselves highly successful if they could profitably execute these changes over several years.

Today, however, the content, context and infrastructure of banking is under threat from companies like Intuit. Intuit offers millions of higher-income households the possibility of linking directly to banks, insurance companies and asset management firms over the Internet and selecting their financial service providers on an as-needed basis. Instead of being locked into the products and delivery channels of a particular bank, customers can choose from a broad array of financial services providers from their home or office PC. All they have to do is use the Quicken software as the window to the world of financial services.

This emerging model of retail banking threatens the integrated model in three ways. First, it is clear that Intuit, through its Quicken software, becomes the new intermediary with customers rather than the banks directly. The banks become product suppliers. Second, the new model will appeal to higher-income segments of customers, leaving lower margin customers to traditional banks. Third, as banking deregulation goes forward in many countries, Internet access to banking, insurance and many other forms of financial services will be available to customers with a point and a click, through programmes such as Quicken and through partnering arrangements between firms like Intuit and financial services providers.

Therefore, as new business models based on the Internet and Web develop around the world in the market space, the process of creative destruction and construction will continue in industries. The challenge for managers in established companies is to anticipate the forms of creative destruction that are likely to occur in their industries. Then they have to begin reconfiguring their value chains to take advantage of these changes before new entrants displace them.

Principle 4: e-commerce offers information richness and reach to customers at the same time

The fourth principle of e-commerce goes to the heart of a classic business trade-off between reaching large segments of customers with limited amounts of information, or reaching small segments of customers with rich amounts of information (Evans and Wurster, 1997). Until the advent of the Internet and the Web, this trade-off was clear. It was manifested in the ways companies advertised their products and services. For companies wanting to reach millions of customers, a 60-second commercial on television provided opportunities to communicate information content, brand identity and emotion in a concise but shallow message. TV and print advertising was truly mass-produced, and offered reach but very limited richness. If a company wanted to share lots of value-adding information with customers, it had to target them rather carefully to limit the numbers to be reached and to make sure that these customers were in fact the high-margin individuals or group.

On the Internet, a company has the possibility to get around the classic trade-off between customer reach and information richness. It can access millions or thousands of customers one-to-one, and provide them with rich information content about its products and services. How a company segments its customers into low- and high-value segments is not constrained by the capability to deliver either limited amounts of information to many, or great amounts of information to a few. Companies can efficiently personalize their information richness to as broad or narrow a segment of customers as they wish.

Thus, classic marketing, advertising and sales strategies can be redefined to take advantage of the unique properties of the Internet to have every customer only a point and click away from the company. For example, many companies have used agents for insurance, department stores for retailing, and branches of banks as primary but expensive channels to reach customers with rich information about products and services. In the context of using the Internet as a vehicle for customizing information delivery and use one-to-one, the purposes of these channels must now be redefined. Insurance agents, branches in banks, dealers for cars, and stores for retailing may not disappear as some futurists have argued. But, there will be fewer of them than in the past. And they will have very different value-adding roles in terms of customer contacts, personalization and intimacy than they did when they just distributed information and processed transactions with customers.

Principle 5: Networks increase interactivity exponentially among people, companies and industries

Interactions – the searching, co-ordinating and monitoring that people and firms do when they exchange goods, services and ideas – pervades all business activities globally. Robert Metcalf, the founder of 3COM Corporation, observed some years ago that new technologies are valuable only to the extent that many people use them. He characterized this relationship between technologies and use by people as follows (Downes and Mui, 1998):

For any communications network, the number of nodes (N) on a network yields that number squared in potential value (N^2) to users.

This principle, which came to be known as Metcalf's Law, suggests that more people using phone and e-mail networks is better than few. Similarly, millions of people using the Internet create the conditions for massive increases in human and business value of the Internet to people and firms.

The Internet, like all new technologies, such as cellular phones in the 1990s and fax machines in the 1980s, has reached a critical threshold of use. Beyond this point (the inflection point on the curve), the value of using the Internet increases exponentially. Thus, the Internet with hundreds of millions of worldwide users has moved beyond the inflection point in the curve of technology usage. Through the interactions that it enables, it is now creating human and business value of exponential proportions.

Moreover, as McKinsey research has noted, the levels of interactions in industries, firms and workers are already at very high levels (Butler et al., 1997). At the industry level, interactions account for over 50% of all labour in service industries, and even in mining, agriculture and manufacturing, they amount to 35%. At the firm level, interactions constitute a large part of even an industrial company's activities. According to McKinsey, in one US electric utility, 58% of all employee activity could be attributed to interactions. Finally, at the individual level, interaction activities do vary with different types of workers 'peaking at nearly 80% for managers and supervisors, and troughing at 15% for workers primarily engaged in physical labour.' However, as the labour mix shifts toward predominantly information and knowledge workers, interactions will dominate work activities.

Into this context of growing interactions within industries, firms and among workers comes the Internet – the ultimate network of networks – with the potential to increase the business and human value of interactions exponentially. The challenge for managers, especially in established companies, is not only to perceive or imagine the huge potential value of the Internet and e-commerce. This step alone may require many managers to make a significant leap of faith that Internet entrepreneurs have already made. They must also move beyond 'discounted cash flow' justifications to engage in Internet learning and business opportunities. 'Just do it' may be an exciting reason for Internet entrepreneurs to exploit business opportunities, but it still represents a major leap of faith for managers in established companies where return on investment justifications of new projects are the rule, not the exception.

Principle 6: Turning data into information and usable knowledge for people and companies will redefine the role of intermediaries in e-commerce

There are four characteristics of information on the Internet that are critical to the discovery of new business opportunities.

1. All information on the Internet is digital – it can be disseminated to a few or many people at the click of the mouse.
2. Information is costly to produce, but cheap to *reproduce* – economists note that the production of an information product such as a book or recording involves 'high fixed costs but low marginal costs' (Shapiro and Varian, 1999). This characteristic of information means that information products must be priced according to what people will pay for them, rather than their cost of production. In addition, since reproducing information products is cheap,

they can be made available to people and companies at very low marginal costs, creating a condition for information overload.

3. Information needs to be sampled for people to fully appreciate its value and benefit – this characteristic of information is what economists call an *experience good* (Shapiro and Varian, 1999). You do not know that you will find an information product useful until you try it. Again, the tendency in experience goods is to make samples of the good widely available. The aim is to get as many people as possible to try the product before they buy it. On the Internet, many companies have used push technologies to try to get prospects to sample their information goods and services. This has led to a proliferation of aggressive tactics to move information to your desktop to get you to try a new service or buy a new product.

4. People that are using information benefit from intermediaries – this characteristic concerns the need for economizing on accessing, collecting and using information by people and companies. All humans and groups of people have a limited attention span and time to search for and use information. In a world of digital information abundance, the need for focusing one's attention and time on the use of the right information at the right time creates an enormous business opportunity for *infomediaries* (Hagel and Singer, 1999). Infomediaries are people or companies who help other people and companies to focus on just the right information for their needs, saving customers both attention and time.

Fiduciaries, retailers, brokers and investment managers have played the infomediary role in the past. On the Internet many significant opportunities exist to help people and companies navigate for critical information that saves time, attention and money. To succeed, infomediaries must establish trust with customers to understand their information needs and how they can be met. Infomediaries must thus establish a brand reputation that, in turn, builds trust and permits them to negotiate with customers to access and manage information about them.

There are basically two types of infomediaries on the Web today (Hagel and Singer, 1999). The first type are *vendor-oriented* infomediaries who aggregate customer information and transactions on behalf of companies wanting to sell their products and services. The companies act either as lead generators or as audience brokers. Companies such as Auto-by-Tel and Carpoint provide useful information to prospective car buyers and generate leads for dealers who wish to sell cars. In return for targeted leads on new or used car buyers, the dealers pay the lead generator commission on sales and subscription fees to join the service. On the other hand, audience brokers such as DoubleClick sign up networks of commercial Web sites and co-ordinate advertising campaigns across them. Audiences brokers track the click streams of prospective customers as they view ads, browse and shop at member sites. While vendor-oriented infomediaries generate value for vendors and customers alike, their primary focus is to represent the business interests of supporting companies.

The second type of infomediary is *customer-oriented*. It acts on behalf of customers, seeking out information or completing transactions on the Web. The customer-oriented infomediary comes in several forms: the filter, the agent and the proxy. What is important about these infomediaries is the trust that they must generate with customers. In essence, customers must be willing to share information about themselves, their interests and their behaviours. In addition, these companies are challenged to attract enough customers on the one side to build critical mass for their own business. On the other side, they must generate enough transactions across diverse products and services to develop rich profiles of customer behaviours of interest to potential vendors who might wish to transact through the customer-oriented infomediary.

Filters, for example, are customer-oriented infomediaries who filter unwanted marketing messages from reaching customers. Customers can specify in advance any category of unwanted messages they want screened from view. *Agents* act on behalf of the customer to locate information of interest to them or carry out transactions on their behalf. Agents like the online stock traders E-Trade and Quote.com are the most prevalent forms of customer-oriented infomediaries on the Web. Agent services can be found in many retailing sites such as Amazon.com and Buy.com, as well as in consumer service sites of travel agents and real estate brokers. Finally, *proxy services* act on behalf of customers on the Web without revealing the identity of their customers. These services set up vendor relationships and offer their customers the opportunity to decide what they will or will not reveal about themselves. Cybergold.com is a form of proxy service, since the company represents thousands of consumers who receive cyber dollars to browse and shop at Web sites in the Cybergold community. Cybergold provides incentives for customers to shop, but leaves the decision to the customer whether to engage in direct browsing and shopping.

The business opportunities surrounding the infomediary role on the Web extend to consumers and business customers alike. For established companies, the challenge is to think of their customers and product information in a new way that will allow them to serve their customers better by representing their interests better than competitors. There is a danger here. Established companies may be too slow to act on the Web as infomediaries. This lag will provide new entrants with the chance to intervene with customers by providing better information about the established companies' products and services (and those of their competitors) than they can.

Principle 7: List pricing will give way to spot or fluid pricing in e-commerce

On the Web, two contending forces affect pricing for information goods and services. The first has to do with the impact of the Internet and Web on *transaction costs*. Transaction costs are the 'inefficiencies' between buyers and sellers in a marketplace. These are related to *searching costs* for business opportunities, *information costs* associated with communicating about products and services, *decision and negotiating costs* related to completing trades or deals, and the *policing and enforcement costs* of terms and conditions and payments settlement (Downes and Mui, 1998). First articulated by the economist Ronald Coase in the 1930s, the transaction costs view of business suggests that companies are created because the costs of organizing and maintaining them are lower than the costs involved when individuals conduct business with each other using the market. However, companies must organize (incur *co-ordination costs*, according to Coase) to manage these transaction costs, and this organization adds to the price of goods and services for customers.

With the Internet and the Web, the costs of transactions can be lowered significantly. To transact business, individuals and companies can get in touch with each other directly. Thus, established companies that incur significant co-ordination costs on top of transaction costs for their goods and services must not only include these added costs in the prices of their goods and services, but must vary them by the co-ordination costs of doing business in various countries. As a result, established companies seek to differentiate their prices according to where they do business and by identifying the price points where they can make the most profit. With the Internet and Web, customers can instantly determine the variable pricing by established companies in various countries and demand the cheapest price. The consequences for competitiveness of this levelling effect of prices, also known as price transparency, is explored by Jacques Horovitz in Chapter 4, but the main point to note here is that it increases price competition and in turn makes list pricing by companies meaningless. Why should a customer pay the list price for a car in one country when in the neighbouring country the list price for the car from the same manufacturer is 10–20% lower?

Thus, implicit in this view of transaction costs is what Downes and Mui (1998) have called the *Law of Diminishing Firms*. "As transaction costs in the open market approach zero, so does the size of the firm. The concept of the firm as a fixed entity, defined by permanent employees and fixed assets, is giving way to the *virtual organisation* where employees may be part-time and the assets of the firm largely variable rather than fixed." This change pressures established companies to lower prices or move to variable pricing in the face of more demanding and knowledgeable customers.

The second force impacting fluid or spot pricing on the Web is the reality that almost any service or good that can be described or shown on the Web can be bought and sold online, either through auctioning or trading mechanisms. As customers seek relevant information about products and services and compare prices, and as suppliers monitor customer behaviour and purchasing patterns to offer the best deals, interaction costs are so low on the Web that competitive bidding and trading are encouraged. Websites such as Ebay.com represent this wave of online trading and auctioning of goods and services. In addition, new entrants such as industry-to-industry.com and Asiansources.com offer business-to-business customers the same opportunities to engage in online trading and auctions of new and used industrial goods and services. For example, in the southwestern US, Energymarket.com offers manufacturers the opportunity to spot price electrical energy off the Southern California Edison grid. Manufacturers can download the energy to their factory sites day-to-day.

The dual impact of declining transaction costs on the Web for exchanging goods and services in online markets coupled with the shift from fixed to fluid pricing, means that the traditional pricing strategies of established companies in many industries will not be sustainable. The challenge will be to adapt their pricing strategies to the realities of fluid pricing and to manage their own organizations to lower their costs of co-ordination internally and with customers so that they can still be profitable.

Four-net strategies: evolving business practices

The seven principles of e-commerce challenge managers in established companies to rethink their basic business capabilities and strategies. However, if this challenge were

> "To achieve success, businesses must not only understand the general principles of e-commerce, but must find the specific mix of strategies that best meets their needs"

not enough, managers must also find the right mix of Internet-based strategies among four ways of using Internet-based technology and networking inside and outside their firms. In short, I call these the four-net strategies:

1. *Internet strategy* – involving business-to-customer relations.
2. *Intranet strategy* – involving the use of Internet capabilities inside a company to manage information and knowledge.
3. *Extranet strategy* – involving business-to-business interactions for suppliers, partners and even competitors.
4. *Industrynet strategy* – involving new types of intermediation in industries, especially around the building of *virtual communities*.

The challenge for managers is not just to assess the best business case for investing in the four-net strategies individually; they must also determine the right *mix* of these strategies to position their companies in the world of e-commerce.

Internet strategy – business-to-customer relationships

Internet strategy is all about improving customer perceived value in the customer-supplier relationship, as Table 17.1 suggests. Companies must establish seamless relationships with consumers or business customers that cover the whole of the customer–supplier lifecycle (notably using those techniques outlined earlier in Chapters 3, 4 and 5). Over the last five years, companies have developed a range of Internet practices that can impact each phase of developing customer perceived value, from improving the customers' buying process and decisions, to enhancing the quality of customer service, and to rewarding and retaining loyal customers. Table 17.1 also provides a range of these Internet practices across each phase of customer acquisition, service and retention.

Table 17.1: *Customer-perceived value on the Internet – emerging practices*

Emerging practice	Example
Improve quality of service and satisfaction	
• Speeding delivery	First Union three-minute credit approval
• Improving value by exposing customers to all price alternatives and best buys	Fidelity Investments Commission Calculator

Table 17.1: *Continued*

Emerging practice	Example

Improve quality of service and satisfaction

• Adding value by theming 'packaging' or giving more for the same price	Wells Fargo data can be loaded on to popular money management software, Quicken
• Confirming orders and/or knowing where you stand	Dell, Federal Express
• Opening channels of communication for complaints handling	QVC feedback desk
• Zooming on individual customer needs over time	Peapod.com creates personal shopping list

Improving customers' buying processes and decisions

• Reaching new targets for a retailer that would not be reached by a small retail outlet	Over 50% of Sharper Image's Web customers are new customers
• Providing information and education online – in real time – about products/services/sites	AutoWeb is selling thousands of cars each month on the Web
• Targeting one-on-one offers that suit particular needs	CNN newsclips adapt to specific needs
• Improving convenience and reducing customer effort by remote purchasing	Groceries delivered direct to the home
• Adding to the customers' choice while not having to carry the inventory for display	Amazon offering 2.5 million books (versus 500 000 books in a conventional bookstore)
• Reducing customers' FUDs (fears, uncertainties and doubts) by showing products and allowing trial of downloads	30-day trial for downloaded software
• Helping customers to decide	At Amazon.com you can read a sample chapter

Reward customer loyalty

• Making special offers to specially targeted customers	Wal-Mart.com
• Creating exchange opportunities for customers	Ebay.com
• Creating new business opportunities for customers	Asiansources.com

What is surprising about these Internet practices is how fast they have developed and moved from being competitive advantages for companies that first employed them to being *competitive necessities* for companies using these capabilities today on the Internet and Web.

CASE STUDIES: FROM COMPETITIVE ADVANTAGES TO COMPETITIVE NECESSITIES

Federal Express was the first express delivery company in the 1980s to offer end-to-end tracking of the status of a package from pick-up to delivery, making that information available to customers online. Today, every Internet retailer must provide positive tracking of customer orders and deliveries online using the information services of their express delivery partners.

*Similarly, on the Internet most customers expect companies to provide one-to-one service and to customize their offers to different segments of customers. For **Wal-Mart**, this means offering goods on its website that are not sold in its stores (at everyday low prices) and trying to attract to its site customers who would not necessarily shop in its stores. For **Ebay.com**, one-to-one service means assisting customers to locate easily the specific goods they would like to purchase at auction and letting their customers know when auction opportunities for specific categories of goods arise. For **Asiansources.com**, the one-to-one focus extends to helping Asian business customers create business opportunities online and linking them with trading partners all over the world.*

In just a few years, Internet strategy for businesses has moved rapidly from the information broadcasting stage of Web presence, to the next stage of adapting goods and services and acquiring, interacting with and retaining customers – all of which require a range of sophisticated practices that have quickly become competitive necessities for doing business with customers on the Web.

Intranet strategy – Web capabilities inside your company

Intranet strategy is about moving Web capabilities inside your company to manage information and people's knowledge more effectively. A company intranet offers the possibility of developing internal websites where all the information about a key subject is updated from one site to be available on a point-and-click basis throughout the company.

Many companies have moved rapidly in recent years to add Internet technology to their corporate data communications network and to permit people in various departments, business units and geographic regions to build websites for disseminating information about their activities to others in the company. While these developments sound positive, several important business issues have emerged.

Cost implications of intranets

First, managers in many companies have realized quickly that adding Internet capabilities on to their existing corporate data network and IT infrastructure can be quite costly. It turns out that intranets require heavy IT infrastructure investments in desktop and server hardware and software, communications capacity on existing e-mail networks, browsers, and authoring software and online services. Finally, managers must consider the time and effort of business and IT people to build, update and enhance websites throughout the company. All of these additional investments or costs usually appear *before* the business value of using intranet information and online services becomes apparent. Thus, managers are asked to 'bet on the future' and upgrade their IT infrastructures company-wide before they can realize the business gains from their intranet sites. To address this gap between incurred costs and unrealized benefits, the IT industry has been quick to flood the business markets with investment pay-back claims of widely varying credibility: 'Typical Intranet pay back is over 1000%!' '$1 spent on the intranet yields $10 in combined savings and productivity!' 'Intranet pay-back periods range from 6 to 12 weeks!' While intranet developments inside companies have led to a boom in IT sales, the challenge for managers in most companies has been to differentiate between intranet sites that add value and those that do not.

The downside of enthusiasm

The second issue managers have to confront arises from the enthusiasm of people inside their companies to build and offer sites of widely varying content and usefulness on the internal network intranet. I call this phase of intranet development inside companies the 'let a thousand flowers bloom' phase. In this phase, which may last for several years inside large companies, hundreds of websites providing information of dubious or little value to the business proliferate on the internal network. In this phase, people in functional departments like HR, legal, public relations and accounting, and folks in corporate and staff offices, develop websites for broadcasting their information across the company. While all of this bottom-up creativity sounds good, it often leads to chaotic proliferation of incompatible website standards, as well as presentation styles and databases of uneven or poor content. In addition, to correct these problems, various departments start requesting additional support budgets to 'improve' their intranet sites.

In one global company, in only one budget cycle, the CEO received 50 requests of over $1million *each* for improving the intranet sites of the staff and units inside the corporate office alone! These requests from the corporate office did not include hundreds of additional requests from the company's 200 country business units and multiple brand organizations. The CFO of this company estimated that approving even half of these requests across the global company would have consumed all of the discretionary money available for IT improvements during the next year.

The need to use intranets to best effect and enhance competitiveness

The third issue that intranets raise among company managers concerns the justifications for what information should be the target of internal website developments. Managers must come to terms with the criteria that will influence decisions about investing in a range of Intranet sites inside their companies. Figure 17.1 provides a guide to distinguishing between which types of information inside a company create the most business value and which types of information are simply necessary to have or essential to use to run the key processes in the business. While websites can be developed for managing information in each category to either create business value or reduce costs, managers need to decide which investments in intranet websites will lead to the highest 'return on information' use for their business.

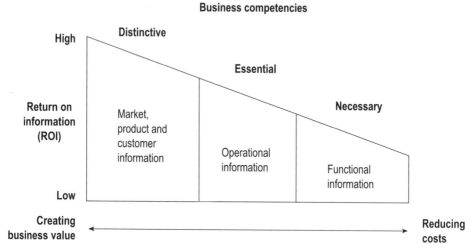

Figure 17.1: *Intranet strategy requires a company to examine how it wants to manage information*

For example, many HR intranet sites inside companies let employees search their own records to determine vacation or sick leave or assess retirement benefits. These sites are usually the most heavily used. The information on these sites is functional and necessary to have. Similarly, operational information like production plans is

> "When developing intranets, it is vital to distinguish between those activities that directly and significantly improve competitiveness, and those that simply enhance internal communication and support activities"

essential. However, neither of these types of information actually help a company to *compete* by using information to create business value with customers. Thus, in developing intranet strategies, managers must distinguish between intranet sites that are necessary to have or essential to compete from those that create business value by permitting their people to use information to better sell or serve customers or design new products. For example, Hewlett-Packard has developed an intranet site called the 'Electronic Sales Partner' that makes thousands of product-related documents available to its sales force online. H-P estimates that sales people gain one to three hours of selling time each day as a result, and that translates into millions of dollars in increased productivity and sales each year.

Intranet strategy requires managers in a company to manage their website investments and information resources in a focused and deliberate manner. If better information management of internal information is to be achieved through intranets, then managers will have to move from the phase of letting a thousand intranet sites bloom to the phase of developing a balanced portfolio of sites. This will require managers to invest in intranet sites that are not only essential and necessary to operate, but that increase the company's return on information by creating new business value or serving customers better.

Extranets – Web capabilities for business-to-business interactions

Extranet strategy is all about digital business-to-business relationships and commerce. In the past, companies have been restrained from developing rich, business-to-business digital relationships since electronic data interchange (EDI) required extensive standardization of hardware, software, networks and data for exchanges between manufacturers and suppliers, for example. Invariably the relationships between companies were limited mostly to transaction processing of purchase orders, invoices and payments. Due to the cost of setting the IT up between two companies, these relationships tended to be narrow and confined to large companies.

CASE STUDIES: USING EXTRANETS TO DEVELOP
BUSINESS-TO-BUSINESS RELATIONSHIPS

In 1996, General Electric was one of the first global companies to employ Internet and Web technologies between its Lighting Division and suppliers worldwide. GE Lighting wanted to execute a full array of purchasing transactions, including the ability of suppliers to download GE product specifications and to communicate with GE through a secure, encrypted software link over the Internet. The GE extranet, known as the trade processing network (TPN), brought immediate business benefits to the Lighting Division by reducing the cycle time in the purchasing process and by providing global reach to its supplier community. With the help of GEIS, the IT arm of GE, and GE Capital, which launched an extranet consulting group, TPN was deployed in seven other GE business divisions during 1997 as well as licensed to other manufacturers to use with their suppliers.

*The success of GE's TPN has led many other companies to deploy extranets not only with their suppliers, but also with their distributors, dealers and customers. For example, **Heineken** in the US was one of the first companies to deploy an extranet with its 450 beer distributors to speed up order processing and delivery. The Heineken project, called HOPS (Heineken Operational Planning System), began in late 1995 and was implemented fully by 1997. At about the same time, **Harley-Davidson** began implementing an extranet so its small dealers in the US, and later internationally, could file warranty claims for customers 24 hours a day, seven days a week. The extranet also permitted H-D to share information and communicate with its small dealers online, rather than through phone, fax and postal mail. Harley-Davidson estimated that* *the extranet for dealers saved them over $4 million in development costs over a more traditional IT development approach. Finally, companies such as **CISCO** and **Dell Computer Corporation** have also implemented direct extranet links with their business customers. Dell calls these dedicated Extranet links 'Premier Pages' and has implemented over 22 000 Premier Pages with companies worldwide for direct ordering though Dell and sharing of product and servicing information.*

Business-to-business e-commerce is often referred to as the 'killer application' of the Internet. Forecasters in the IT industry have noted that business-to-business e-commerce is growing at a much faster rate than business-to-consumer e-commerce. In the period 2000–2010, they estimate that business-to-business e-commerce will transform the way all players in manufacturing and service industries not only execute transactions among each other, but also share information and collaborate on projects of mutual benefit. Extranet strategy will involve not just changes in the ways businesses share information, collaborate and execute transactions, but will be a disruptive force in industries where existing middle men add little or no value to business relationships.

Industrynets – new forms of intermediation in industries

Industrynet strategy involves thinking of new ways to eliminate, redefine or create new roles for digital intermediaries in specific industries. For example, over the last five years, new Internet intermediaries such as Auto-by-Tel, Carpoint and Autoweb have redefined the selling of new and used cars by auto dealers in the US and now in Europe and Asia. These new players have threatened the dealer networks of leading auto manufacturers such as Ford, GM and DaimlerChrysler. Similarly, in the stock trading industry, companies such as E-Trade, Schwab and Quote.com have brought discounted equity trading over the Internet to millions of small investors and threatened the established agent-based trading approaches of Merrill Lynch and Morgan Stanley Dean Witter. Finally, in retailing the rise of Amazon.com and Buy.com have threatened not only established booksellers like Barnes and Noble, but are also challenging dominant retailers such as Wal-Mart. In fact, Buy.com has a website called Buytenpercentlessthanwalmart.com.

In each of these examples, two key business questions arise: first, will the new players disrupt the dominant position of established players? And second, do these new players have a long-term business strategy to win Internet and industry dominance?

The answer to the first question is undoubtedly yes. In industry after industry, established players are now responding to the dual threats of new, disruptive intermediaries in the value chains of their industry and of seeing their traditional forms of intermediation threatened or collapse. A case in point is Merrill Lynch. During 1998, the CEO of Merrill Lynch said that the company would continue to sell stocks through its army of well-paid brokers and not engage in discounted brokering on the Web. In June 1999, the same CEO announced that not only would Merrill sell stocks on a discounted basis, but the company would also set up an Internet site to do so by December 1999. Thus, in many industries today, established companies are carefully eyeing the emergence of new and potentially threatening new Web businesses in their industries. No wonder 'To Dell or Be Delled' or 'To Amazon or Be Amazoned' are the key phrases on the opening slides of many senior manager strategy briefings today.

In the case of the second question, the answer is also yes, but with some caveats. The long-term business strategy for companies such as Amazon.com, Buy.com and Ebay.com is not simply to become the leading transaction processor in their industry for consumers and business customers. Rather, the long-term strategy of these Internet companies is to become the leading organizer of a major *virtual community* in their industry that can attract not only millions of customers, but also vendors who will pay to transact business with their customers. The dual focus on aggregating a critical mass of customers and customer profiles with a critical mass of third-party companies willing to pay the aggregating company for access to its customers and its knowledge of customers is the dominant, long-term strategic play of such companies. The main intent is to build virtual communities of millions of loyal customers over time and to leverage the knowledge gained from these customers with other vendors who are willing to pay for access to these companies. Known as *portals*, these companies exploit first-mover advantage to establish brand image and customer recognition to build virtual communities for commercial gain.

The caveats involved in successfully building virtual communities are twofold. First, as Figure 17.2 suggests, virtual communities require a company to create a 'dynamic of increasing returns' among loyal customers and vendors. Creating this dynamic requires very skilful development of sustainable value for customers who will become members of the ongoing virtual community. In addition, the company must also gain the trust of customers to use information about customer buying patterns, profiles and communications to attract vendors. This balancing of customer and vendor interests is critical to sustaining the four cycles of increasing returns in Figure 17.2.

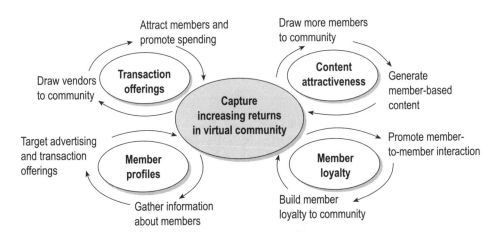

Figure 17.2: *Virtual communities are driven by the dynamics of increasing returns*

Source: Hagel III, J. and Armstrong, A.G. (1997) *Net Gain*. Harvard Business School Press.

The second caveat is that the process, as illustrated in Figure 17.3, of starting and building a virtual community requires a five-to-seven-year effort, since a number of critical thresholds must be achieved. In this process, three elements are important:

1. The company must seize first-mover advantage to gain scale. Being a follower is not an acceptable position for other new entrants or established companies.
2. The company must manage costs and cash flow carefully. Profitability must be sacrificed to continuous re-investment. Therefore, managing the perception, as Amazon does, that the company is making money but re-investing to reach critical mass, is vital to sustaining the virtual community strategy.
3. The company must continue to create value for new members and sustain value for existing members. Prospective members must move from 'browser' to 'user' to 'member' quickly, and existing members must find ongoing value in the communications and information-sharing of the virtual community.

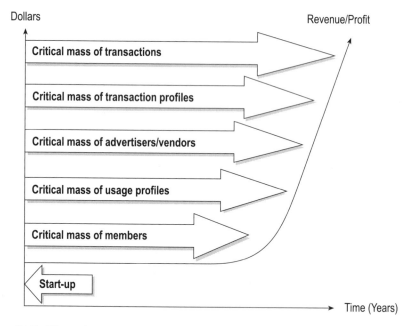

Figure 17.3: *Virtual communities must reach critical mass over time to succeed*
Source: Hagel III, J. and Armstrong, A.G. (1997) *Net Gain*. Harvard Business School Press.

Thus, the long-term success of the industrynet company intent on moving from transactions alone to building a virtual community of millions of people is no small challenge. While we are seeing clear examples of new and disruptive industrynet companies in industry after industry, it remains to be seen how many of these ventures will build sustainable and profitable virtual communities over time. These caveats should not, however, lead established company managers to believe that time is on their company's side, since in many industries the long-term play among new entrants to establish virtual communities is already well underway.

The e-commerce future has just begun

The Internet has been around commercially since the 1980s, e-commerce since the 1990s. For two decades, some managers have been tempted to think that the era of e-commerce will pass without the radical transformation of business worldwide. They think, 'Like other management trends and buzzwords, e-commerce will come and go and business life will continue pretty much as usual'. For several important reasons, however, this time business life will be in for a real shock.

First, as more and more manufacturing and service companies move from pushing products to pushing services, they are exposing themselves to more, not less, information-based competition. If we assume that all companies in the near future will have more or less the same access to global networks and Internet technology, then the shift to information-based competition will intensify as the playing field of the Internet expands globally to include millions of consumers and businesses.

Second, in industry after industry, small new entrants that are well financed through venture capital and Internet stock valuations are focused on 'pirating' the value chains of established companies. Whether the competition is for the 'eyeballs' of consumers or a share of the 'executive mind' in business-to-business interactions, there is one target of entrepreneurial energies: the inefficiencies of traditional industry value chains and the margins of established players in those industries. New entrants are seeking to disrupt the established companies by launching new industrynet ventures that redefine the roles of industry players in business-to-business and business-to-consumer relationships.

Third, for established companies, having an Internet presence does not equate to implementing four-net business strategies. Established companies must quickly move from Level 1 and 2 (*see* Figure 17.5) to the breakout level of e-commerce thinking. E-commerce is about transforming business and industries today, not about continuous improvement. It is the reason that CEOs like Jack Welch have sought to anticipate this change in their businesses and have begun to disrupt their industries and their companies before competitors and new entrants disrupt *them*.

Finally, compressed Internet time is obliterating the distinctions between learning and doing, strategy and action. Business learning is as much affected by Internet time as business action. The urgency of Internet time is attacking the timeframes of established industries and companies. Business is always 'on' with the Internet somewhere on the globe. The demands for rapid, effective responses are growing. Like new entrants, established company managers will have to learn by doing and to invent strategy through action.

The Internet and e-commerce are bringing a new reality to business just as they have to human interactions around the world. One thing is for sure: as e-commerce and four-net capabilities transform industry after industry and business after business in our new era, it is better to be on, than watching, the journey.

SUMMARY

Building e-commerce capabilities

E-commerce challenges managers to think differently about their industries: not only questioning why things are the way they are but *how* the new technology can be leveraged to create competitive advantage. Seven principles of e-commerce provide a practical starting point for addressing this challenge:

1. The Internet adds a new perception of business time

The three effects of this are that the Internet is always available and working; that time and action are compressed, there is a culture of urgency and the ability for feedback to be swift, if not immediate; and that managers need to respond to important and 'trivial' issues quickly, as something trivial on the Internet can be amplified and distorted rapidly into something much larger.

2. Internet business learning is continuous, evolutionary and rapid

Because the nature of the Internet is one of continuous, sustained and fast evolution, it makes little sense to wait and perfect ideas. The opportunity – and expectation – exists to launch, test and perfect products and services using the Internet, and this can be a powerful method of building customer loyalty, innovation and advantage.

3. E-commerce requires creative destruction and construction

The content (what is sold), the context (where and when it is sold) and the infrastructure of the business can be fundamentally redefined using e-commerce, with massive repercussions for the strategy of the business and its operations. The example of Amazon.com highlights the changes that can blast through an industry like book-selling, but other industries normally regarded as conservative and traditional – such as retail banking – are also being redefined. A valuable place to start is therefore with the fundamentals of the business: identifying and creating new opportunities, as well as removing and destroying old practices that existed only because the Internet was not there yet.

4. E-commerce offers information richness and reach to customers at the same time

E-commerce blurs the traditional business trade-offs between reaching large sections of customers with limited information, or small segments of customers with rich amounts of information. The Internet can often provide both, and this allows marketing and sales strategies to be redefined, taking advantage of the unique closeness of many current and potential customers through a one-to-one medium.

5. Networks increase interactivity exponentially among people, companies and industries

Interactions, defined as the searching, co-ordinating and monitoring that people do when they exchange goods, services and ideas, increase when the number of users passes a critical mass. Clearly this has been exceeded with the Internet, and the resulting potential value of the Internet has reached exceptional proportions. Often all that is required is the faith to believe that the opportunity to innovate using the Internet exists and commit to it – for many managers, particularly in traditional businesses, this is difficult to achieve.

6. Turning data into information and usable knowledge for people and companies will redefine the role of intermediaries in e-commerce

Four characteristics of information are critical to the development of new business opportunities:

- Information must be in digital form.
- Information is costly to produce but cheap to reproduce, and this can lead to information overload.
- Information is an 'experience good': information products often need to be sampled to appreciate their value.
- People and companies need to economize on information: they need the right information at the right time, and have only a limited amount of time to spend on accessing, collecting and using information.

As a result of these factors, two types of intermediary (or infomediary) have emerged: *vendor-oriented* ones who represent potential purchasers (e.g. Auto-by-Tel and Carpoint), and customer-oriented ones acting on behalf of customers seeking to trade on the Web. The business opportunities associated with infomediaries – and their value and expertise – is continuing to grow.

7. List pricing will give way to spot or fluid pricing in e-commerce

Two forces impact on pricing on the Web: *transactions costs*, which can be significantly lower than for other channels, and *price transparency* where price differentials (usually between different territories) for the same product or service are exposed. The dual impact of these two factors means that traditional pricing strategies will become undermined by e-commerce. The situation therefore becomes one of innovating using price – or risk being undermined by it.

Understanding the seven principles of e-commerce clearly helps to outline the challenges in developing a successful e-commerce strategy, but responding to these seven principles and developing an effective e-commerce strategy can involve taking action on the four nets – Internet, intranet, extranet and industrynet.

BEST PRACTICE

Developing strategies for successful e-commerce

E-commerce for most companies does not come in only one flavour, but requires a mix of four-net strategies designed to add new capabilities to today's ways of doing business, and to rethink and transform the capabilities of business for future success. To achieve the benefits of e-commerce and develop the right mix of strategies, managers in established companies must ask four key questions.

What is the mindset of your company toward e-commerce in your industry?

While many managers in established companies are beginning to perceive the urgency of responding to e-commerce initiatives that have evolved in their industry, fewer are willing to significantly change their ways of justifying business initiatives to accommodate the seven principles of e-commerce noted earlier in this chapter. The journey for most established company managers is to move from being laggards and slow followers in their industry with e-commerce to being fast followers and even early adapters and innovators, as Table 17.2 suggests.

Table 17.2: *Understanding the mindset of your company toward e-commerce and digital business*

Mindset to e-commerce and digital business	Business justification	Strategic priority
Early adapter	Missionary	Innovation
Fast follower	Experimenter	Add value
Slow follower	ROI oriented	Minimize risks
Laggard	Wait and see	Reduce costs

These shifts in managerial mindset toward e-commerce require corresponding changes in the ways that business projects are justified in most companies, from traditional return on investment calculations to 'learn by doing' and being the innovator for early adapter advantage. In addition, the strategic priorities of managers towards e-commerce must also shift from reducing costs and minimizing risks to adding value with customers and being innovative in reaching new customers with new products and services.

One thing is certain. It is not enough for managers to say that they have Internet or intranet strategies and initiatives. They must anticipate the inevitable disruptions that extranet and industrynet initiatives will bring to their industry. Jack Welch mandated that in 1999 every GE business division should establish an e-commerce business unit whose key purpose is to figure out ways for GE to disrupt the industries in which GE's divisions do business – before new entrants or other established companies disrupt them. To date, relatively few senior managers of established companies have committed themselves and their managerial resources as Welch has to disrupt or be disrupted with e-commerce in their industry.

What levels of E-Commerce should your company exploit?

As Figure 17.4 suggests, companies can exploit e-commerce capabilities at three levels. The first level is *experimentation*. Here, a company has no clear e-commerce business strategy linked to its business strategy. Its initiatives are *ad hoc* and bottom-up. Typically, at this level, e-commerce initiatives focus on technology issues rather than on the quality and appropriateness of information and services. While this phase is an important learning experience for managers and people, it is nevertheless important for a company to move from this level quickly.

At the second level, *integration*, a company uses its e-commerce to support its existing business strategy and approach. Many companies deploy Internet and intranet capabilities at this level, focusing on serving existing customers or enhancing existing processes and ways of using information. At this level, company managers view e-commerce as a way of improving productivity or operational effectiveness.

At the third level of *transformation*, managers view e-commerce as a driver of their future business. In this case, the company seeks to use extranets to redefine its relationships with customers, dealers, distributors, and suppliers. The managers at level three also seek to disrupt their industry by launching new business units or transforming existing business units. At this level, they aim to use information to create business opportunities and to establish asymmetries in the exploitation of customer, competitive and operational information against other companies in their industry.

In short, at level three, a company tries to break out of its existing business mindset about e-commerce and consciously disrupt its industry with new business models before it is itself disrupted and loses.

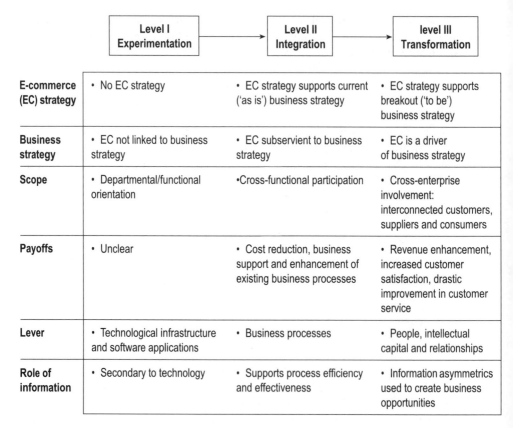

Figure 17.4: *Strategies for doing digital business*

Source: Kettinger, W.J. and Hackbarth, G. (1999) Reaching the Next Level in E-Commerce. *Financial Times Mastering Information Management Series*, 7, pp. 14–15.

What combination of four-net initiatives is appropriate for your company?

There is a clear tendency among managers in established companies to consider four-net initiatives as independent strategies. Either these managers seek to optimize individual strategies in the company, such as their intranet focus, or they fail to perceive the need for optimizing a mix of four-net strategies and capabilities to transform their business. In the first instance, they see only their part of the elephant and, in the second instance, they overlook the competitive potential of integrating four-net strategies over time.

In one global consumer goods company, the focus of senior managers has been on Internet strategy to reach consumers and on intranet strategy to automate existing information. The senior managers of the company have chosen to defer focusing on extranet approaches with its suppliers and supermarket chains and on industrynet strategies to disrupt their industry. On the other hand, their biggest competitor is actively exploiting extranets with supermarket chains and forming strategic alliances with new entrants for industrynet learning and future exploitation. While the company has developed its Internet and intranet capabilities at level 2, senior managers have targeted extranet and industrynet strategies at level 3. The second company is clearly positioning itself with a portfolio of four-net strategies to improve its current ways of doing business and learning new ways of e-commerce *before* its chief competitor does.

It is important that companies develop the right portfolio of four-net strategies, which exploits today's ways of doing business *and* prepares for tomorrow's. With the pace of business developments across the four-nets as rapid as it is, companies that approach these capabilities in a fragmented manner or fail to build competencies on all four critical aspects of their e-commerce business are – and will be – at a competitive disadvantage.

Who should be involved in developing and implementing e-commerce strategies in our company?

Like most change initiatives, top management must encourage and vigorously support four-net strategies, developing and implementing them at the bottom of the company. It is dangerous for senior managers to think that outside consultants can package the answer. It is equally dangerous for them to view their own roles as passive, supporting what is happening in their company but remaining, at heart, uninvolved. As we noted earlier in this chapter, managers and companies must learn four-net strategies by *doing* and not just planning. Thus, to fully realize the potential of e-commerce strategies, companies must utilize a broad range of people and constituencies across the enterprise.

For large companies, tapping the energy and enthusiasm of managers and people is critical to fostering a climate where 'breakouts' in mindset and action are possible. Unless people, information and IT are leveraged effectively for future industry leadership in e-commerce, very few companies will reach level 3.

Perhaps it is most fitting that the CEO, Jack Welch, who invented the breakout concept as a way of getting his managers to think creatively about their businesses, should also be among the first CEOs of large, global companies to use e-commerce as a vehicle to break out of its current ways of doing business and seek future industry leadership in competing with e-commerce.

References

Butler, P., Hall, T.W., Hanna, A.M., Mendonca, L., Angust, B., Manyika, J. and Sahay, A. (1997) A Revolution in Interaction. *McKinsey Quarterly*, **1**, pp. 5-23.

Downes, L. and Mui, C. (1998) *Unleashing the Killer App*. Harvard Business School Press, Boston, USA.

Evans, P.B. and Wurster, T.S. (1997) Strategy and the New Economics of Information. *Harvard Business Review*, September–October, pp. 71–82.

Hagel III, J. and Singer, M. (1999) *Net Worth*. Harvard Business School Press, Boston, USA.

Rayport, J.F. and Sviokla, J.J. (1996) Exploiting the virtual value chain. *McKinsey Quarterly*, **1**, pp. 21–36.

Shapiro, C. and Varian, H.R. (1999) *Information Rules*. Harvard Business School Press, Boston, USA.

Contributors

DONALD A. MARCHAND
Professor of Information Management and Strategy
E-mail: marchand@imd.ch

Donald A. Marchand is Professor of Information Management and Strategy at IMD. His special interests include information and knowledge management as competitive competencies, electronic commerce and demand/supply chain management, and the strategic roles of information, people and IT in global businesses.

Professor Marchand was Director for the IMD/Andersen Consulting Partnership Research Project entitled **Navigating Business Success**. This two-year study examined the perspectives of senior executives on the management of information, people, and information technology in achieving superior business performance. The study includes surveys of over 1300 senior managers representing 103 international companies in 22 countries and 25 industries as well as over 25 case studies. The Project was completed in December 1999.

Professor Marchand is a well-known speaker and advisor to senior executives of leading service and manufacturing companies in Europe, North America and the Asia Pacific.

Professor Marchand is the author/co-author of six books and over 140 articles, book chapters, cases, and reports. He is the co-editor of *Mastering Information Management* published by Financial Times Prentice-Hall, London, 2000. He is also the co-author of *Information Orientation: The Link to Business Performance*, a forthcoming book published by Oxford University Press, 2000.

From July 1987 to June 1994, Prof. Marchand was Dean and professor of information management at the School of Information Studies at Syracuse University.

He received his PhD and MA at UCLA and his BA at the University of California at Berkeley. He has also served as Vice President of Worldwide Chapter and Alliance Development for the Society for Information Management – SIM International.

ANDREW BOYNTON
Professor of Management
E-mail: boynton@imd.ch

Andy Boynton is a Professor of Management and the Director of IMD's new Executive MBA Program. He has previously held faculty positions at IMD, the Darden School at the University of Virginia, and the Kenan-Flagler Business School at the University of North Carolina Chapel Hill.

Professor Boynton has written numerous articles on strategy organization transformation, and the competitive use of information for leading journals such as *Harvard Business Review*, *Sloan Management Review*, and the *California Management Review*.

He is the co-author *of Invented Here: Maximizing Your Organization's Internal Growth and Profitability*, which was published by the Harvard Business School Press in the spring of 1998. He is actively conducting research and consulting with firms in North America, Europe, Asia and Australia.

Professor Boynton has an MBA and a Ph.D in Strategic Management from the Kenan-Flagler Business School, University of North Carolina Chapel Hill.

JEAN-PHILIPPE DESCHAMPS
Professor of Technology and Innovation
Management
E-mail: deschamps@imd.ch

Jean-Philippe Deschamps is Professor of Technology and Innovation Management at IMD.

Prior to joining IMD in November 1996, he was based in Brussels as a Corporate Vice-President with Arthur D. Little, and Chairman of the firm's Technology and Innovation Management practice, which he created in 1981. He has thirty years of international management consulting experience throughout Europe, North America, Asia and the Middle East. He has lectured in several business schools throughout Europe and is a frequent speaker at Management Center Europe. He has been invited twice as a speaker to the World Economic Forum.

He is the co-author of a book, *Product Juggernauts – How Companies Mobilize to generate a Stream of Market Winners*, (Harvard Business School Press, 1995) which has been translated into several languages and features on the list of Harvard Business School best-selling teaching materials.

He focuses his research, teaching and consulting activities on product-based competition, with a particular interest in product creation and the management of innovation as a seamless cross-functional process.

He graduated from Ecole des Hautes Etudes Commerciales in Paris and received his MBA from INSEAD and from the Harvard Business School.

XAVIER GILBERT
Professor of Industry Analysis and Strategy
E-mail: gilbert@imd.ch

Xavier Gilbert is Professor of Industry Analysis and Strategy and holds the LEGO Chair in International Business Dynamics. He was Acting Director General of IMD from early 1992 until June 1993. His areas of special interest are competitive analysis, strategy implementations with specific attention to management development implications.

He has considerable experience in executive education having been Professor of Business Administration at IMEDE – one of the two founding Institutes of IMD – from 1971. During that time he directed several programs including the Program for Executive Development and the one-year MBA program.

Professor Gilbert is a consultant, chiefly on strategy formulation and implementation, to several leading companies in the fields of consumer and industrial manufacturing, and retailing.

He is a graduate of ESSEC (Ecole Supérieure des Sciences Economiques et Commerciales) Paris, and has a Doctorate in Busines Administration (DBA) from Harvard University.

STEWART HAMILTON
Professor of Accounting and Finance
E-mail: hamilton@imd.ch

Stewart Hamilton is Professor of Accounting and Finance at IMD. He has been teaching at IMD since 1981.

He combined a twenty-year career in public accounting practice with teaching at the Universities of British Columbia, Calgary and Windsor in Canada, and for more than ten years, in the Law Faculty at the University of Edinburgh. He appears regularly as an expert witness in a wide range of civil litigation cases, including share valuation disputes, professional negligence claims, loss of profits disputes.

His consulting activities have covered a wide range of UK and European companies in banking, pharmaceuticals, heavy engineering and most recently international venture capital. His current research interests are in corporate failure, risk management and investor protection.

He has co-authored books on Company Law and taxation and written many articles for the professional and financial press. In 1999 he co-authored the winning European Case Awards (Finance Case), The Barings Collapse (A): Breakdowns in Organizational Culture & Management.

JACQUES HOROVITZ
Professor of Service Marketing and Management
E-mail: horovitz@imd.ch

Jacques Horovitz is Professor of Service Marketing and Management at IMD. He focuses on how to compete through service and improve customer satisfaction with heavy emphasis on service as a strategy for differentiation, customer loyalty programs and creating a service culture.

He has a wide range of experience. He has practised service marketing and management as Executive Vice President marketing and sales for Club Med North America as well as Managing Director, Marketing and International of the GrandVision group, a retail speciality store chain; and as coach to the Executive Committee of Disneyland Paris. Second, he has advised the CEOs of over 100 companies throughout Europe on service, having founded, developed and managed a pan-European Consulting company with offices in seven countries and 50 consultants. Finally, he has extensively researched and published in the areas of service strategies and service quality, relationship marketing, customer bonding.

His book, *Quality of Service*, published by InterEditions in 1987 became a worldwide success: translated into ten languages. He recently published a new book called *The Seven Secrets of Service Strategy*, FT/Prentice-Hall, London, 1999.

Professor Horovitz graduated from the Ecole Supérieure de Commerce de Paris, France, and has a M. Phil and a Ph.D (Doctorate) from the Graduate School of Business, Columbia University, New York.

Robert A. HOWELL
Professor of Strategy, Accounting, and Finance
Email: howell@imd.ch

Robert A. Howell is American and Professor of Strategy, Accounting, and Finance at IMD. For more than 30 years Professor Howell has combined a career of teaching at leading business schools with a consulting practice serving major global corporations.

Prior to joining IMD in January 1999, he had been a Professor of Management Accounting at Thunderbird – The American Graduate School of International Management (1995-1998); Professor of Management and Accounting at the Stern School of Business, New York University (1977-1999); and Assistant Professor of Business Administration, Harvard Business School (1967-1972).

Professor Howell also managed his own consulting firm, The Howell Group, LLC for more than twenty years. His clients have included GE, Applied Materials, Cummins Engine, Hallmark, Motorola, Johnson & Johnson, Boeing, Northrup Grummans, Nestlé, Siemens, and many others.

He was the lead author for two major research studies: *Management Accounting in the New Manufacturing Environment* (1987) and *Cost Management for Tomorrow-Seeking the Competitive Edge* (1992). His writings have appeared in *Harvard Business Review, Business Horizons, Management Accounting, Emerging Practices in Cost Management, The Handbook of Cost Management*, and other leading publications.

He holds a DBA in Management Controls from Harvard University, and MBA in Industrial Management from The Wharton School, University of Pennsylvania, and a BS in Electrical Engineering from Bucknell University.

SEAN A. MEEHAN
Professor of Marketing Management and Strategy
E-mail: meehan@imd.ch

Sean Meehan is Professor of Marketing Management and Strategy at IMD. His teaching encompasses marketing and corporate strategy. He has designed and/or delivered management development programs for Coopers & Lybrand Corporate Finance, COSA, Hilti A.G., Swiss Re and the Institute of Management Consultants.

Professor Meehan has received awards for his research on market orientation including the Marketing Science Institute's Alden G. Clayton award, the Academy of Marketing's Houghton Mifflin award and scholarships from the Economic & Social Research Council and London Business School.

He is currently managing an international research program examining the nature and effectiveness of market orientation and customer value creation processes. His other research interests include convergence in the financial services sector and the marketing of professional services firms.

He graduated with an honours degree in business studies from Trinity College Dublin, a masters degree in marketing from the University of Manchester Institute of Science and Technology, and a doctorate in marketing from London Business School. He is also a Certified Public Accountant (Massachusetts).

PIERO MOROSINI
Professor of Strategy and Execution
E-mail: morosini@imd.ch

Piero Morosini is Professor of Strategy and Execution at IMD. He has, since 1988, besides his academic interests in mergers, acquisitions and alliances, pursued an international career in strategy consulting, as well as change management in the financial/banking industries.

Prior to joining IMD, he was a Managing Consultant at Andersen Consulting Strategic Services Group in Milan Italy, having formerly worked at McKinsey & Company (1989-92), JP Morgan (1992-94), Robert Fleming (1994-95) and the Andean Community (1984-86), in several locations across Europe, the US and Latin America.

He is a Thought Leadership award winner worldwide at Andersen Consulting Strategic Services Group (1997-98), and has been a Research Fellow at the Wharton Risk Management Center, Philadelphia (1995-98), as well as at the Strategy Department of the Bocconi University, Milan (1993-94).

He has authored a book entitled, *Managing Cultural Differences: Effective Strategy and Execution Across Cultures in Global Corporate Alliances* (Pergamon, Oxford, U.K., 1998).

He has attended graduate studies at The Wharton School, University of Pennsylvania, Philadelphia (1986-88), where he obtained a Ph.D. in management, an MA in Decision Sciences and an MBA, and has graduated in Economics at Universidad del Pacifico, Lima (1984).

BART VICTOR
Cal Professor of Moral Leadership
Email: Bart.Victor@Owen.Vanderbilt.edu

Bart Victor is the Cal Turner Professor of Moral Leadership at the Owen Graduate School of Management, Vanderbilt University. His research interests include the social and moral consequences of new organizational forms, the process of strategy making, and the development and application of organizational knowledge for strategic advantage.

He has published work on ethical climates, organization design, and business ethics. He is also co-author with Andrew Boynton of *Invented Here: Maximizing Your Organization's Internal Growth and Profitability*, Harvard Business School Press, 1998.

JOHN W. WALSH
Professor of Marketing
E-mail: walsh@imd.ch

John W. Walsh is Professor of Marketing at IMD. His research interests include the application of economic and econometric models to marketing issues, managerial and consumer decision-making, and marketing and competitive strategy.

Prior to joining IMD, Professor Walsh was the Abraham A. Mitchell Term Assistant Professor of Marketing at the Wharton School, University of Pennsylvania. He has also worked as a consultant with Monitor Company, Cambridge, USA.

Professor Walsh has extensive consulting experience in the telecommunications, health care, soft drinks, computing and consumer electronic industries.

He has Ph.D and MS degrees from Cornell University, New York, and a B.Sc. degree from Trinity College Dublin, Ireland.

Professor Walsh has written numerous articles for practitioner and academic journals including the *Financial Times, European Management Journal, Marketing Science and Oxford Economic Papers*.

Index